D1617300

Christianity and Society in the Modern World

Series editors
HUGH McLEOD AND BOB SCRIBNER

Social Discipline in the Reformation: Central Europe 1550–1750

In the same series

The Social History of Religion in Scotland since 1730
Callum Brown

The Jews in Christian Europe 1400–1700
John Edwards

A Social History of French Catholicism 1789–1914
Ralph Gibson

Forthcoming

Calvinism and Society
The reformed tradition in Europe to 1700
Philip Benedict

Popular Evangelical Movements in Britain and North America
1730–1870
Louis Billington

Women and Religion in Early Modern England 1500–1750
Patricia Crawford

The Clergy in Europe
A comparative social history
Gregory Freeze

Religion and Social Change in Industrial Britain 1770–1870
David Hempton

The Western Church and Sexuality in Europe 1400–1700
Lyndal Roper

Social Discipline in the Reformation:
Central Europe 1550–1750

R. PO-CHIA HSIA

Routledge

LONDON AND NEW YORK

First published 1989
by Routledge
11 New Fetter Lane, London EC4P 4EE
29 West 35th Street, New York, NY 10001

Set in 11 on 12½ Garamond by Columns of Reading
Printed in Great Britain by T. J. Press (Padstow) Ltd
Padstow, Cornwall

British Library Cataloguing in Publication Data

Hsia, R. Po-chia
Social discipline in the Reformation: central Europe 1550–1750
1. Europe. Christian Church, history
I. Title   II. Series
274

Library of Congress Cataloging in Publication Data

Hsia, R. Po-chia, 1955–
Social discipline in the Reformation: 1550–1750/R. Po-chia Hsia
p.   cm. – (Christianity and society in the modern world)
Bibliography: p.
Includes index.
ISBN 0-415-01148-5
1. Reformation – Europe, German-speaking. 2. Counter-Reformation – Europe,
German-speaking. 3. Church and state – Europe, German speaking – History. 4. Europe,
German-speaking – Church history. 5. Holy Roman Empire – Church history.
I. Title. II. Series.
BR307.H78 1989
274.3′06 – dc19

89-3538

Contents

Acknowledgments   vi

Introduction   1

1   Lutheran Germany   10

2   Calvinist Germany   26

3   Catholic Germany   39

4   The confessional state   53

5   Cities and confessionalization   73

6   Culture and confessionalism   89

7   The moral police   122

8   Confessionalism and the people   143

Conclusion   174

Notes   186

Further reading   188

Index   213

Acknowledgments

As with any synthesis, the work of many colleagues is indispensible. Instead of burdening the reader with numerous footnotes, I have listed my indebtedness in the suggestions for further reading. In addition to the collective multitude of scholars, I would like to thank Professor Heinz Schilling, Professor Hans-Christoph Rublack, Dr Georg Schmidt, and Dr Luise Schorn-Schütte of West Germany for sharing with me their ongoing researches. I wrote this book between moves and places; some semblance of continuity was created by the kindness of Marianne Hraibi and Patsy Carter – the interlibrary loan staff at Dartmouth College – who met my incessant requests with unfailing good cheer. Robert Scribner invited me to write for the series and carefully went over the manuscript. It is a special pleasure to acknowledge my appreciation of his cunning as editor and historian.

Introduction

In historical writing, the Reformation has long captured the imagination of scholars and students: the struggle for conscience, the clash of faiths, the disintegration of Christian unity, the rise of liberty and toleration have become commonplaces in history texts. Research tends to concentrate on late medieval conflicts leading up to Luther, and ends with the Religious Peace of Augsburg in 1555. This agenda characterizes also much of the current emphasis on social history. Historical interest, it seems, wanes with the passing of the Peasants' War of 1524/5, the Anabaptist revolution at Münster in 1534/5, and the general retreat of the common people from the stage of religious drama.

Until quite recently, the period after 1550 was an orphan of German historiography: Cultural and literary historians eagerly await the birth of Goethe; military and political historians hail the rise of Prussia; and for many modern historians, who cherish the twins "Reformation" and "German unification," the complicated and confusing intervening centuries of confessionalism seem almost an illegitimate child of German history.

All this has changed in the past decade. German historians have reassessed the significance of the "confessional age" for their own history, detecting central themes in subsequent developments of state and society. Above all, historians of religion and society have argued that the Reformation and Counter-Reformation were not so much distinct, opposing historical phenomena, as structurally similar developments in the long-term transformation of the society of early modern Central Europe. The period from 1550 to

1750, then, calls into question the nature of German history; it offers complex historical patterns for comparison with developments in Western Europe, particularly in regard to the relationship between state and religion; and lastly, the history of Christianity cannot be adequately understood without studying the consolidation of official religions and their relationship with popular religion.

Among German historians, the challenge to the traditional view has come from four directions. In the 1960s, Gerhard Oestreich introduced the concept of "social disciplining" to describe changes in early modern German society. The enforcement of church discipline, the consolidation of confessional identity, and the demand for religious conformity complemented developments in political and philosophical thought. Neo-stoicism, eloquently argued by the great humanist scholar, Justus Lipsius, served to elevate the authority of the prince; in Calvinist territories, military reform, state building, and neo-stoic philosophy went hand-in-hand. According to Oestreich, the rise of absolutism in the late seventeenth and eighteenth centuries, the creation of powerful military states, such as Prussia, rest upon this foundation of "social disciplining," by which the people became obedient, pious, and diligent subjects of their German princes.

A second impetus has come from the research of historians interested in the Catholic Reformation. Eager to correct the "bad press" of the Counter-Reformation in Rankean historiography, which tended to equate Protestantism with the development of the German nation, Ernst Walter Zeeden and his students advanced the concept of "the formation of confessions" (*Konfessionsbildung*) to denote the coequal developments of the Lutheran, Calvinist, and Catholic reformations. Their research emphasizes the structural similarity in the major confessions: Lutheranism, Calvinism, and Tridentine Catholicism all developed coherent systems of doctrines, rituals, personnel, and institutions in the intense competition for souls. A major achievement of Zeeden and his students is the opening up of new archival sources, the copious visitation records, for the comparative study of confessional formations. To enforce confessional conformity, the three major confessions instituted periodic "visitations" at the diocesan and parochial levels (in Calvinist areas, the synodal, classes, and communal records):

teams of officials from the central government, both ecclesiastical and lay, questioned local clerics, bailiffs, jurors, townsmen, and villagers on their religious life. They documented church finances, conditions of church buildings, the conduct of the clergy, figures on church attendance, baptism, weddings, communion, and burials, the presence of nonconformists and "heretics," and a host of popular religious beliefs and practices. The systematic publication of inventories of these visitation records, although cut short by the lack of funds, has opened up vast resources for the historian of popular religion and confessionalism. Based on the study of visitation records, the cumulative effect of the many local case studies is to give us an accurate and profound picture of the impact of confessionalism in rural society.

More recently, Heinz Schilling and Wolfgang Reinhard have advanced the concepts of "social disciplining" and "confession formation" to new theoretical sophistication. They speak of the concept of "confessionalization" (*Konfessionalisierung*), thus underlining the process of changes that involved the religious, political, cultural, and social structures of early modern Germany. In an influential essay, Reinhard formulated three theses of confessionalization:

1 that the Reformation and Counter-Reformation were structurally parallel, with the Counter-Reformation expressing many "modern" traits, such as individualism and rationality;
2 that confessionalization created social groups, "the three confessions," by a variety of means, including the formulation of dogma, confessional propaganda, education, discipline, rituals, and language;
3 that confessionalization strengthened political centralization when the early modern state used religion to consolidate its territorial boundary, to incorporate the church into the state bureaucracy, and to impose social control on its subjects.

Schilling's own research focuses on the interplay between politics in the empire and confessional conflicts. In a study on the city of Emden, he shows that in the 1590s Calvinism could mobilize citizens in defense of civic republicanism against the centralizing policies of a Lutheran prince, the Count of Friesland. The opposite pattern, however, characterized the struggle in Lemgo, a territorial town in Westphalia, as Schilling demonstrates in a second study. When the Count of Lippe adopted Calvinism in 1605 and declared a "Second Reformation" for his land, the Lutheran citizens of Lemgo defied the will of their lord and defended their traditional religion and civic privileges all the way to the imperial courts. In his current research, Schilling systematically analyzes Calvinist church records to study the process of "social disciplining" in Calvinist north Germany, thus logically pursuing the avenues opened up by Oestreich and Zeeden. He has formulated a four-phase periodization of confessionalization between the 1540s and the late seventeenth century that will undoubtedly stimulate future discussions.

Scholars of literature and folklore are responsible for the fourth, and last, direction of research. The vast repertoire of Baroque sermons, plays, paintings, and poetry, together with numerous Baroque and Rococo churches, express the cultural wealth and productivity of Catholic Germany. Similarly, Lutheran Germany created the forerunner of a national vernacular literature, in addition to a sophisticated musical tradition. Most importantly, we have to understand this cultural production as part of the structure of confessional society. Created out of a specific confessional milieu for a particular purpose, printing, pilgrimage, and artistic objects acquired historic meaning only in the context of their reception. Far from the "cultural desert" depicted by some historians, the confessional age in Germany experienced a boom in cultural expression.

Little of this research is available to non-specialists. The aim of my book is to offer a synthesis in English; an introduction to recent German scholarship. I have based my work on monographs, published primary sources, and many case studies, buried in scattered German local historical journals. The scope of this study covers the years 1550 – 1750, although the dates should be understood as approximate signposts of a fluid historical landscape rather than as fixed boundaries. Geographically, the book draws examples from all German-speaking areas of Central Europe, including Austria and Switzerland, although the main focus is on the heartland of the Holy Roman Empire. Several concepts employed in the book require explication. By "confessionalism," I mean the formation of religious ideologies and institutions in Lutheranism, Calvinism, and Catholicism. The concept denotes the articulation of belief systems (in "confessional texts"), the recruitment and character of various professional clerical bodies, the constitution and operations of church institutions, and systems of rituals. "Confessionalization" refers to the interrelated *processes* by which the consolidation of the early modern state, the imposition of social discipline, and the formation of confessional churches transformed society. By using the terms "the people," or "popular religion," I try to distinguish the majority in society – the lower classes in cities, the vast majority of rural dwellers – from those active in confessionalizing German society. I do not imply that the people were powerless, merely passive spectators in this theater of confessional politics, quite the contrary. I suggest rather, that confessionalization, by definition, involved the common people as both object and subject: they were both the objects of discipline and confessional indoctrination, and subjects in this drama, to the extent that they supported, opposed, or ignored state and church, or appropriated official religion for their own socio-religious practices.

The three main divisions of this book correspond to the aforementioned tripartite concept. In the first section, chapters 1 to 3, I discuss "confessionalism." I describe internal developments in Lutheranism, Calvinism, and Catholicism between the Interim of 1548 and the expulsion of Protestants from Salzburg in 1731. In sketching the historical development of the three confessions in separate chapters, I hope to stress the distinctiveness of each, without losing sight of the significant structural similarities between them. Such structural similarities, such as the social origins of the clergy, the function of clerical institutions, and confessional propaganda, are analyzed in depth. A chronological and geographical framework is set out in these initial chapters, before the exposition of common themes in the following sections.

"Confessionalization" is the first theme. Chapter 4 analyzes the relationship between state building and confessionalism. It argues that the process of political centralization, discernible in the fifteenth century – the adoption of Roman Law, the rise of an academic jurist class, the growth of bureaucracies, and the reduction of local, particularist privileges – received a tremendous boost after 1550. Conformity required coercion. Church and state formed an inextricable matrix of power for enforcing discipline and confessionalism. The history of confessionalization in early modern Germany is, in many ways, the history of the territorial state. However, confessionalization could also mobilize resistance to the consolidation of princely power: the struggles between princes and cities, central government and estates, and different political factions, were often played out in confessional confrontations. The language of confessional polemics threatened to subvert the language of political discourse. I have chosen four instances to illustrate the many actual examples of the dialectic between politics and confession: first, the Austrian Habsburgs consciously promoting an imperial Catholic cult to bolster their legitimacy; next, in Brandenburg–Prussia (Austria's rival for leadership in the Empire in the eighteenth and nineteenth centuries), Calvinism and Pietism serving the reason of state; thirdly, Salzburg, an ecclesiastical principality, adopting a rigorous policy to root out Protestantism and extend state control to remote mountain communities; and finally, the example of the Wetterau counties proves that confessionalization and state building also affected the smaller territories, as they strove to imitate their powerful neighbors.

Confessionalization had a different history in the cities of the Holy Roman Empire. Excluded from the right of "reformation," the famous provision of *"cuius regio, eius religio"* of the Peace of Augsburg, magistrates of imperial cities usually governed over confessionally mixed urban populations. Many imperial cities evolved into biconfessional cities, with Catholics and Lutherans living and working together peacefully, sometimes even sharing church buildings. Other cities tried to preserve a distinct confessional identity, but tolerated religious minorities for the sake of economic gain. A few cities evolved into multiconfessional cities: the territorial city of Oppenheim had Calvinist, Catholic, and Lutheran communities, while Frankfurt counted among her population members of the three major confessions, as well as Jews and Anabaptists. Confessionalization and mercantilism created a new type of early modern city, when princes encouraged religious refugees to establish new urban communities for the promotion of trade and manufacture. The history of cities and confessionalization is analyzed in chapter 5.

In chapter 6 I discuss "acculturation," embracing confessional propaganda in the larger context of cultural production and consumption. The emphasis is on Catholic Baroque culture and the legacy of Lutheranism. Catholic Germany did not regain lost territory merely by force of arms. After 1648, the Catholic advance in the empire relied mostly on a highly sophisticated culture that appealed both to the elites and to the people. The major weapons were the production of Catholic devotional literature, book censorship, the influence of Spanish culture, Jesuit drama, catechism, hymns, and Latinity. Catholic Germany evolved its own distinctive culture, one that was only eclipsed by the rise of a vernacular national literature in Protestant Germany during the eighteenth century. The figure of Luther bequeathed to Lutheran Germany much of its cultural heritage. By this I mean more than Luther's German Bible, hymns, catechisms, and writings; legends of the great reformer, "hagiographic," literary, dramatic, and visual depictions of Luther helped to consolidate a bourgeois confessional identity. Literacy and music, so dear to the message of the evangelical movement, also inspired a rich cultural creativity in Lutheran Germany. Education, the last theme in this chapter, served confessionalization in two important aspects: schools tried to mold the young into pious Christians and obedient subjects, and universities, thoroughly confessionalized, trained reliable officials and clerics for the confessional territorial states.

"Confessionalization and the people" is the theme of the third section. The first part, chapter 7, examines the effort by the state to impose religious and social discipline. The moral police intruded into the private lives of the people, regulating their sexual behavior, family life, and church attendance. While the structure of the moral regimes may have been similar, the confessions set different priorities in controlling the people. Records of the Calvinist church, analyzed to identify areas where social disciplining occurred, show that the regulation of sexuality was a major preoccupation. In Catholic territories, the imposition of confessional uniformity seemed to be the overriding goal, whether in a relatively centralized territorial state such as Bavaria, or in the confessionally mixed ecclesiastical principality of Osnabrück. The records of control generated by the confessional moral regimes tell more than one story. Evidence points to widespread and common resistance to confessionalization in Lutheran, Catholic, and Calvinist territories. Resistance could take the form of opposition to the Calvinist reformation or recatholicization; more often, it represented popular and local resentment of external interference in communal life. Villagers perceived clerics and officials as bearers of an alien culture; and official confessions often appeared intrusive in folk traditions and religion.

The interaction between popular and official religions, as I argue in the final chapter, is crucial to understanding the historical significance of confessionalization. In responding to confessionalization, a wide spectrum of nuanced responses was open to the people, ranging from resistance, indifference, acquiescence, cooperation, or appropriation to active participation. Only by remembering this complexity of popular response can historians ask meaningful questions as to the "when," "how," and "why" of confessionalization. One such question would deal with the consolidation of patriarchy. All confessional regimes, particularly the Protestant confessions, supported the authority of the "house father," someone who was to represent godly and magisterial authority to others in his household. Correspondingly, princes, magistrates, pastors, and schoolmasters all invoked patriarchal authority to justify their power. The problems of class, gender, family, and childhood are clearly related to the redistribution of social power brought about by confessionalization, the success of which, in turn, cannot be understood without a social analysis. Another question concerns popular magic: though it was an avowed goal of all three confessions, the suppression of popular magic met with uneven success, particularly, it seems, in Protestant villages. Catholicism, however, managed to ingest a part of popular magic in the revival of pilgrimage, while eliminating other aspects in savage witch hunts. A third question affects the relationship between confessionalization and popular magic in the witchcraze that afflicted much of Central Europe. It appeared that in both Catholic and Lutheran territories, popular pressure could assume a role equally important to confessionalization in triggering witch hunts. The fourth and final problem is the relationship between confessionalization and psychohistory. The relationship between mental illness and religious culture, the impact of confessionalization on suicide, the dialogue between medical, legal, and theological discourses are some of the probing questions posed by scholars in a yet largely unexplored territory. Finally, marginal religious and social groups must be considered. By studying nonconformists, Anabaptists, and Jews in Central Europe, we can gain an outsider's perspective and look into the confessional blocs from the edge of society, a reminder that historical processes, however powerful, always leave room for social alternatives.

1
Lutheran Germany

When Martin Luther died in 1546, the Protestants in the empire were about to face their first major crisis. Protestant theologians and the papal legate having failed to reach a doctrinal compromise, Emperor Charles V declared himself an implacable foe of the new evangelical Christians and vowed to enforce religious conformity in the Empire with the help of his Spanish and Italian troops. The military defeat of the Protestant Schmalkaldic League at the Battle of Mühlberg in 1547, the conquest of imperial cities in the south by the emperor's troops, and the imposition of a Catholic restoration and religious compromise, the so-called Interim, threatened to undo the work of the Reformation.

But instead of restoring the Catholic faith in the empire, the military and political solutions forced upon reluctant Protestant Germans by their emperor became the issues that eventually consolidated a militant Lutheran confessional identity. Resistance sprang up everywhere. In Strasbourg, where the patrician ruling families sacrificed their religious conscience for a political compromise that saved the Alsatian city from direct imperial occupation, the pastors, led by Martin Bucer, went into exile. After the adoption of the Interim, with the tacit toleration of the magistrates, Lutheran burghers kept harassing the Catholic clerics who were legally allowed to celebrate mass, adding to the political pressure that ultimately led to a renewed suppression of Catholic services in 1560.

In Saxony, Hesse, and other Protestant territories, preachers urged their rulers and congregations to resist the implementation of the Interim. In Regensburg, where the Reformation was introduced only as late as 1542, the magistrates expressed their evangelical loyalty and resistance under the very nose of the imperial regime, by binding the city's books in covers marked with emblems of Protestant resistance. The figures of John Hus (the proto-reformer burnt in Constance in spite of an imperial safeconduct in 1415), Martin Luther (whose own recent death seemed to have prefigured the martyrdom of Protestants), the Elector of Saxony (captured and imprisoned by Charles V), and Lucretia (whose rape and suicide provoked the ancient Romans to overthrow the tyrannical yoke of their king) appeared as emblems of religious liberty and of Lutheran political resistance to an unjust Catholic emperor.[1]

The fragility of the Interim, imposed by force of arms, became manifest in 1552. Moritz of Saxony, a Protestant ally of Charles V in 1547, turned against the emperor, and led a renewed Protestant alliance to a swift military victory over the totally unprepared imperial forces. Peace was restored three years later, on September 25, 1555 at Augsburg. The Religious Peace of Augsburg was the most important constitutional agreement of the Old Reich: first, it recognized the legality of the Lutheran Augsburg confession and established a constitutional parity between Lutherans and Catholics in the Empire; and secondly, it established the principle of secular sovereignty in the governance of the Church within the confines of the territorial state, as expressed in the famous expression *"cuius regio, eius religio."* Modified and confirmed in the peace treaties of Westphalia that ended the Thirty Years' War, these principles remained in effect for the duration of the Old Reich.

For Lutheran Germany the second half of the sixteenth century was a watershed in the formation of a confessional identity. The debate over Luther's legacy and the intensifying struggle against Calvinism sharpened divisions within Lutheran ranks. Deeply influenced by humanism and the idea of Christian unity, Philip Melanchthon and his followers represented a direction that distrusted theological polemics and clerical power. Counting many jurists and physicians among their ranks, the Philippists, as they came to be called, were blamed by their opponents, the self-styled orthodox or Gnesiolutherans, for accepting the Interim. Militant in their confessional consciousness, orthodox Lutherans believed they were living in the last age of history and interpreted their struggle against Rome as the final battle between the forces of Christ and Antichrist. In particular, orthodox Lutherans were eager to root out "cryptocalvinists" and purify their confession. These struggles often took on the form of factional court politics and social conflicts, as we will see in chapter 2.

In 1580, confessional consolidation in Lutheran Germany reached its culmination in the adoption of the Book of Concord, a systematic formulation of doctrines and rituals subscribed by most, though not all, of the imperial estates and cities that claimed allegiance to the Augsburg Confession of Faith. In the empire, North Germany formed an almost solid Lutheran bloc – Saxony, Hesse, Brunswick, and Brandenburg being the major territories. Southwest Germany constituted another center of gravity, focused on the Duchy of Württemberg. The many dynastic divisions between 1555 and 1618, however, weakened the political strength of Lutheran Germany: For example, Hesse, a leading Lutheran state under Philip until 1547, was divided repeatedly into fraternal territories in fierce competition with one another.

With the spread of Calvinism in the empire, Lutheranism faced a vigorous rival for leadership in the Protestant cause. It would be a mistake, however, to dismiss Lutheranism as old and weakened, forced off center stage by the more dramatic confrontation between Calvinism and the Counter-Reformation. Lutheranism still commanded a broad and loyal following, and had struck deep roots into large parts of the empire. One of the foci of this confessional identity was the legacy of Luther, a point discussed at greater length in chapter 6. For now, let us examine some of the structures that constituted this confessional identity.

Reformation centennial 1617

In April 1617 the Protestant Union of princes and imperial cities met in Heilbronn. Frederick V of the Palatinate proposed organizing a jubilee of the Reformation to promote Calvinist–Lutheran rapprochement and express Protestant solidarity against the Catholic Habsburgs. Almost simultaneously, theologians at the University of Wittenberg asked their prince, Johann Georg of Saxony, to organize a jubilee. In October, numerous ecclesiastical and academic festivals celebrated the centennial of the Reformation. Sermons, solemn processions, school plays, fireworks, woodcuts, commemorative medals, and printed works strengthened the self-image of the evangelical Church as the true repository of the pure Gospel, liberated by Luther, God's elected servant, from the yoke of the antichristian Roman Church, and standing under God's special protection. The Reformation was commemorated in the Protestant territories and in the imperial cities of Nuremberg, Strasbourg, Ulm, Augsburg, and Frankfurt.

One of the central motifs in the Reformation Jubilee was the persistence of the Antichrist. Rome had not yet fallen. In 1617 the Lutherans faced a formidable foe, with the Habsburgs and the Catholic League in the Empire poised to roll back the confessional frontier. On the eve of a major conflict of arms that was to last thirty years, the intense eschatological mood of the jubilee was unmistakable. Sermons, hymns, religious drama, prognosticas, pamphlets, and theological exegeses all documented this intense Lutheran eschatology, a tradition unbroken from the mid-sixteenth to the end of the seventeenth century. Contrary to Luther's advice, some theologians even tried to calculate the exact timing of Christ's Second Coming. During the first decade of the Thirty Years' War, when the initial triumph of Catholic arms led to the Edict of Restitution of 1629, desperation turned to millenarian prophecy in Lutheran Germany, when young children dreamed dreams of divine revelation, and pastors cried out for repentance in anticipation of the temporary yoke of the Counter-Reformation Antichrist. Paul Gerhardt, whose hymns inspired many generations of Lutherans, composed a poem during the war to console the faithful by reminding them of the imminent return of Christ in Judgment:

> The Time is now near,
> Thou art here, Jesus Dear;
> The Wonders that should tell
> All people thy Coming,
> They are, as we have felt,
> In multitude happening.

Die Zeit is nunmehr nah,
Herr Jesu, du bist da;
Die Wunder, die den Leuten
Dein Ankunft sollen deuten,
Die sind, wie wir gesehen,
In grosser Zahl geschehen.

The figure of Luther, quite naturally, provided Protestant Germany with another celebratory motif. The Reformation centennial consolidated the legacies of Luther into a coherent tradition and reshaped his life into the secular focus of a church in need of symbols of identity. History itself thus became a principle of legitimation; commemorations of the years 1517, 1530, and 1555 in subsequent centuries served as historical rituals confirming the identity of Lutheran Germany.

The new clergy

Who kept alive Luther's legacy? Like him, Luther's heirs were pastors. The Reformation created a new social category in Lutheran Germany: the self-replenishing clerical estate (*der Pfarrstand*), recruited primarily from the middling burgher ranks, a fact that stood in sharp contrast to the social origins of the Counter-Reformation Catholic clergy.

The first Lutheran clerics were by necessity ex-Catholic priests, many of whom "became" Protestant by virtue of a proclamation by territorial princes. In Württemberg, of the 2,700 evangelical pastors of the sixteenth century, 297 were former priests and monks, most of them belonging, naturally, to the first generation of Protestant clergy. In Ernestine Saxony, at least one-third of the first generation of evangelical pastors had been Catholic clerics. The first two generations of Lutheran pastors came overwhelmingly from the middle to lower echelons in the cities. Of the 75 Lutheran pastors in sixteenth-century Nuremberg, over 80 per cent came from artisan–burgher families; another 6.6 per cent were from merchant families; 5.3 per cent were of peasant origins; and 4 per cent were recruited from families of jurists.[2]

Soon rapid self-recruitment aided by the endowments of scholarships by princes turned the Lutheran pastorate into a largely self-perpetuating social group. In sixteenth-century Württemberg, the social origins of 511 of the 2,716 pastors are known; the great majority (63 per cent) were sons of pastors:

Table 1.1   Social Origins of Lutheran clerics in 16th-century Württemberg

Occupation of father	Number	Percentage
pastor	323	63
artisan	50	9
teacher	17	3
peasant	4	0.8
others	117	24.2
Total	511	100

Source: Martin Brecht, "Herkunft und Ausbildung der protestantischen Geistlichen des Herzogtum Württembergs im 16. Jahrhunderts,"*Zeitschrift für Kirchengeschichte* 80 (1969), 163 – 75.

This seems to have been a general pattern. In sixteenth-century Oldenburg, of the 95 pastors whose fathers' occupations are known, 55 were clerics, 16 peasants, 7 merchants, 6 sextons, 6 magistrates, 2 noblemen, and 1 a schoolteacher.[3] Again in Württemberg, in Tübingen District, up to 77 per cent of pastors who served between 1581 and 1621 followed their father's vocation.[4]

Compared to the pre-Reformation clergy, Lutheran pastors were well educated. The great majority had attended university, thanks in part to the scholarship endowments of the princes who needed to train clerical bureaucrats to staff their territorial churches. Thus the university in Tübingen became the training institution for the vast majority of pastors in Württemberg, a function fulfilled by the University of Jena for Ernestine Saxony, the universities at Leipzig and Wittenberg for Albertine Saxony, and the University of Heidelberg for the Palatinate.

As we have mentioned above, the social origins of the Lutheran clergy tended to become more homogeneous, or at least restricted to fewer social groups. Another salient difference between the Lutheran pastorate and the Catholic clergy regarding their origins was regional concentration versus geographical dispersion. In other words, while the Counter-Reformation called forth Lux-embourgers, Netherlanders, and Italians to save German souls, Lutheran pastors tended to be native sons, with Saxons, Hessians, Württembergers, and others administering their fellow country-men, except for those in higher positions of teaching and admin-istration. As a case study, let us examine the social and economic position of the Lutheran clergy of Württemberg in greater detail.

By 1621 almost all Württemberg pastors were recruited from within the duchy and trained at Tübingen. While the rank-and-file hailed from households of pastors and artisans, the higher ranking clerics appeared to be closely connected with the urban govern-ment, in particular with the political elite – the honorable civic classes (*die Ehrbarkeit*) and officials – that dominated the provincial estates, the *Landtag*. Similar to "dynasties" of officials who served successive dukes, "dynasties" comprising three generations of pastors were not uncommon among the more prominent clerics. Intermarriages between "pastor dynasties" further reinforced social inbreeding among the Lutheran clergy. Johann Maier of Din-kelsbühl, ordained pastor in 1542, was the progenitor of a three-generation pastor dynasty in Württemberg. Three sons followed their father's vocation. One of the sons, Jakob, had five more sons who answered their clerical calling. Altogether, nine Maier men in three generations served in the Lutheran pastorate between 1542 and 1658. Or take the example of Schwäbisch Hall, an imperial city close to the Duchy of Württemberg. During the Old Reich, 97 of the 124 city pastors were native sons; in the 21 rural parishes within Hall territory, 50 per cent of all pastors were natives. Altogether, 247 out of 439 pastors were natives; one-quarter of urban pastors and one-third of rural pastors followed their father's profession. Generational succession seems to have been one way for a father to ensure an adequate retirement pension. Except for a few choice posts, the pastorate was not a well-paid profession. The average pastor lived on a state stipend that was equivalent to the income of an artisan; in poorer rural parishes, pastors and their wives had to farm on the side to make an adequate living. Peasants did not like to send their sons for years of study; and merchants considered the vocation unattractive because of the genteel poverty of the pastors.

After completing elementary education, boys inclined to study went on to Latin schools or one of the Protestant cloister schools in the duchy, where strict discipline, obedience, and a "monastic" way of life was characteristic. Competitive examinations ensured that the gifted and pious could attend the university at Tübingen on scholarship, thus providing limited social mobility for sons from poor families. After the completion of theological studies and ordination, the young pastors were assigned to their parishes, where they would marry and bring up a family, if they had not already done so. Their whole life long, pastors were under the watchful eye of the consistory in Stuttgart. From examination, school attendance, university study, to appointment, transfer, promotion, retirement, and death, the pastor lived and worked as a saver of souls in the territorial Church and as a functionary in the territorial state.

In Württemberg, a stipend from the state made up the major portion of a pastor's income. In urban parishes such as Tübingen, cash income was much higher than in rural parishes such as Tuttlingen near the southern frontier of the duchy. In rural parishes, the pastors themselves collected the tithe and engaged in agriculture, either by leasing out arable lands, or by farming the land and raising livestock themselves. Thomas Wirsing, a rural pastor in Dinkelsbühl territory, kept a diary. He hired a servant and seasonal laborers to farm his land, while he himself took on administrative and supervisory work. In rural Württemberg, as in the Lutheran Southwest in general, the pastor was an important, but by no means the most powerful figure in village life.

During the course of the seventeenth century, the bureaucratic character of the Lutheran pastorate became even more obvious. The Protestant clergy constituted, in essence, a branch of the civil bureaucracy. Again, taking Württemberg as an example, the social origins of Lutheran pastors in the eighteenth century illustrates the interpenetration of the clerical and official castes. Four facts stand out, if we compare the social compositions of the Lutheran pastorate in sixteenth- and eighteenth-century Württemberg. First, the proportion of artisans remained little changed. Secondly, for peasant families, a career in the Lutheran Church was just as unattractive in the eighteenth century as it was in the sixteenth. Thirdly, the single largest contingent of pastors came from clerical families, between 63 per cent of all sixteenth-century pastors and more than 44 per cent of all eighteenth-century pastors. And

Table 1.2 Social Origins of Lutheran clerics in 18th-century Württemberg

Occupation of father	Number	Percentage
high official	183	6.0
low official	535	17.4
high clergy	246	8.0
pastor/deacon	1,106	36.1
merchant	136	4.5
Bürgermeister	126	4.1
artisan	305	9.9
peasant	6	0.2
others	424	13.8
Total	3,067	100

Note: Out of a total of 3,208 pastors in 18th-century Württemberg, the social origins of 3,067 are known. Source: Martin Hasselhorn, *Der altwürttembergische Pfarrstand im 18. Jahrhundert* (Stuttgart, 1958).

lastly, the civil bureaucracy furnished up to 23.4 per cent of all pastors in the eighteenth century, whereas in the sixteenth century, officials tended to consider clerics their social inferiors.

Research into other Lutheran territories has not been as thorough as for Württemberg. But if Württemberg's experience was at all representative of the social development of the Lutheran pastorate, the patterns of social recruitment had clear implications for the restructuring of social relations in early modern Lutheran Germany. The significance is twofold.

The integration of the territorial Church into the territorial state was a continuous development between the Reformation and the end of the Old Reich. The Lutheran Church became a de facto department of the state bureaucracy; and the pastor was molded into a loyal official of the prince. Through the consistory, the Lutheran clergy regulated itself: by recruiting and training newcomers, by disciplining and punishing dissenters within its ranks, and by promoting and rewarding orthodoxy and loyalty. The individual Lutheran pastor served as an outpost of state authority in remote rural parishes, supplementing and helping local officials, the *Amtmann* and *Schultheiss*. The bureaucratization of the Lutheran clergy guaranteed its loyalty to the Lutheran state because this development separated the confessional allegiance between the state and the ruling house. Thus, in the early eighteenth century, when Lutheran pastors criticized the Württemberg dukes for conversion to Catholicism, they were, in fact, defending their loyalty to the vision of a bureaucratized state and a well-ordered confessional society. The degree of social interpenetration between the official caste and the Lutheran pastorate in the eighteenth century is an eloquent testimony to this process.

In parallel development to the first trend, in its social character Lutheranism became an urban religion, in stark contrast to Catholicism. As a rule, the peasants did not get one of their own as pastor. The rural pastor was a man who had lived and studied in cities. His visions were never completely molded by the world of the villages. His status ensured his ambiguous role as insider/outsider, a mediator between peasant beliefs and an urban culture and religion, between local village affairs and the central state.

The state church

How was the Lutheran Church organized? In what ways did the Lutheran clergy become servants of the state? There were two mechanisms of control. Structurally, the Lutheran pastorate was organized into a strict hierarchy, ultimately subject to the authority of the prince. Furthermore, the periodic church visitations by teams of secular and clerical officials probed into the conduct of both the parish pastors and their flock.

Once again, Württemberg represents a case study. The reformer Johannes Brenz first laid out the mechanisms for control in the 1536 Württemberg Church Ordinance. The first church visitation took place in the same year under Brenz's direction. Quickly institutionalized, the visitations functioned as an instrument of the state for controlling the pastorate and the laity. Charged to question ministers, deacons, and schoolmasters about their teachings, daily life, and exercise of office, the officials conducting the 1544 visitation also enjoined pastors and local officials to inform on one another, in addition to denouncing dissidents. The 1547

Visitation Ordinance specified that the commission was to consist of a nobleman, a burgher, and a theologian; the Augsburg Confession, Melanchthon's *Loci Communes*, and princely ordinances served as texts for examinations; minutes of the interviews were to be kept and sent back to Stuttgart; several chancery officials were to consult periodically with the commissioners; and the land was divided into 23 deaconries, subject to superintendents of the Church in Stuttgart, the capital.

In the so-called Great Church Ordinance of 1559, the principle of territorial administration was even more clearly applied to the control of the Württemberg Lutheran Church. It formalized the office of Special Superintendents, created by Duke Christoph in 1551 to visit the deaconries quarterly. Appointed by the Church Council (Kirchenrat), a department of the central government, the Special Superintendents represented the creation of a central Church administration with the specific function of supervising and visiting the local churches. The 1559 Ordinance also institutionalized the office of the General Superintendents, established in 1553 by Duke Christoph. The four General Superintendents, sat in session with ducal councillors appointed to the Church Council; together, the clerical and secular officials constituted the Synod:

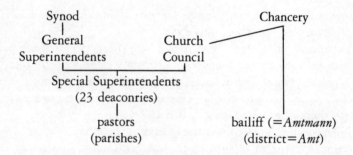

The parish or the community had few rights over clerical appointments. The Church Council recommended a candidate, who would preach to the congregation; and when there was no objection, he became pastor.

As an agent of the state, an embodiment of civic values, and a curate of "true" religion, the Lutheran pastor stood at the frontier of the confessional territorial state, expanding the boundary of discipline, morality, piety, obedience, and sobriety. His obstacles were the culture and behavior of the common people: their beliefs in magic, rooted in an agrarian way of life; their sexuality, vulgarity, and merrymaking.

Anchored in the middling ranks of respectable bourgeois society, the Lutheran pastor often expressed undisguised contempt for his social and moral inferiors. Such a man was Johann Balthasar Schupp, Lutheran pastor in Hamburg, and a self-appointed reformer of the common people. In 1649, the thirty-nine year old Schupp became the first pastor of St Jakob's in Hamburg, a new parish created to minister to the urban poor. Before his appointment, Schupp had lectured for eleven years on history and rhetoric at the University of Marburg and had served for three years as court preacher in Hessian and Swedish service. Schupp directed his sermons more against the "godless people" within the Lutheran Church than against the small Catholic and Jewish communities in Hamburg. In his excoriating sermons, Schupp criticized the "immoral" behavior of the lower classes in the harbor city; he singled out servants, maids, beggars, soldiers, and journeymen as targets of moral censure. He found that "the common riffraff (*der gemeine Pöbel*) has become only a repository of all scandals, blasphemy, and filth."

Schupp was representative of the type of Lutheran pastor who saw the need to reform the Church in the first half of the seventeenth century. The consolidation of Lutheran orthodoxy during these decades was predicated upon two premises: the failure of the state churches to instil morality in the common people; and the need for the ministers to maintain moral autonomy in admonishing the godly magistrates to fulfill their office. Thus the reform strove to mold Protestant Germany according to Christian social precepts, and voiced a limited critique of princes and magistrates where their policies undermined the vision of a Protestant Christian society. The leading spokesmen for the reform movement included Polycarp Leyser, Johann Benedikt Carpzov, and Johann Gerhard in Thuringia and Electoral Saxony, and Johann Valentin Andreae in Württemberg. Andreae expressed his vision of a perfectly well-ordered Christian society in the utopian work, Christianopolis (1619), where architectural perfection, articulated in the uniformity and regularity of city planning, corresponded to order and discipline in society and perfect harmony in the individual soul.

An expression of a limited critique of the magistrates was represented by pamphlets decrying the policy of inflation during the so-called *Kipper-* and *Wipperzeit* of 1620 – 3. In order to finance the cost of the Bohemian campaign, the Habsburg Emperor Ferdinand II gave permission to a private consortium to mint coins and systematic debasement of coinage led to uncontrollable inflation in the Empire. Numerous pamphlets decried this irresponsible monetary policy. Many of these were published by Lutheran ministers in Thuringia, Electoral Saxony, and in the larger imperial cities. The Lutheran theologians compared themselves to Old Testament prophets, attacked minters of false coins as avaricious and devilish, and admonished the magistrates to protect the poor. There was, however, a self-imposed limit to their social critique: it was tempered with a call for social peace. They explicitly condemned rebellion. Indeed, the equation of divine and secular authority in the state remained unchallenged within the Lutheran tradition until the end of the seventeenth century. The idea was unequivocally expressed by the Lutheran jurist Veit Ludwig von Seckendorff (1622 – 92). In his influential work *The Christian State/ In which Christendom asserts itself against the Atheists and such people* published in 1685, the state, whatever its shortcomings, was presented as the only bulwark against the greatest enemies of orthodoxy and disorder, namely, atheism and anarchy. Seckendorff argued that secular authorities should rule according to the Decalogue and the Lutheran clergy was clearly secondary to the godly magistrates in Seckendorff's Christian State:

> The Authorities (*Obrigkeit*) should be more than the executors of spiritual power, but must also take upon themselves the furtherance of Christian teachings and the creation of good church laws. The authorities have the might to reform the inadequacies of the Church and the clerical estate.

The call for reform in the early seventeenth century ascribed a leading role to the godly magistrates. As the century progressed, religious energies unchannelled by the official state churches found other avenues of expression. The rise of pietism at the end of the century echoed the call for reform voiced by earlier generations of pastors.

Pietism

The consolidation of orthodoxy in Lutheranism, sealed by the acceptance of the Book of Concord in 1580, signaled the emphasis of doctrinal purity over personal piety. The call for a "reformation of life," to follow upon Luther's "reformation of teachings," echoed across the entire spectrum of German Protestantism in the later decades of the sixteenth century. Many felt that the emotional, moral, and individualist elements in the early Reformation movement had been replaced by the dogmatic scholasticism of institutionalized, Lutheran state churches. Within the ranks of the Lutheran ministry, there were those who decried doctrinal intolerance and polemics, and pleaded instead for an experiential and biblical religiosity.

These forerunners of pietism were strongly influenced by the devotional literature of the English Puritans, widely translated and read in Protestant Germany. They came from within the ranks of the Lutheran ministry: Valentin Weigel (1533 – 88), son of a Lutheran pastor at Hayn in Meissen, and himself pastor in Zschopau, whose writings manifested the influence of the nonconformists and spiritualists Paracelsus, Sebastian Franck, and Caspar Schwenckfeld; Stefan Praetorius (1536 – 1603), whose works were published by Johann Arndt; Philipp Nicolai (1556 – 1608), son of a pastor in Waldeck, who himself entered the Lutheran ministry, initially as pastor at Herdecke in Westphalia, then as court preacher to the Countess of Waldeck, and later as pastor in Hamburg; Johann Gerhard (1582 – 1637); and the great mystic, Jakob Böhme (1575 – 1624).

The most important of these early "pietists" was Johann Arndt (1555 – 1621). Born in Saxony-Anhalt, the son of a village pastor, Arndt entered the ministry in 1583, worked in Quedlinburg, Brunswick, Eisleben, before becoming in 1611 superintendent at Celle. His devotional treatise, *Of True Christendom* (*Vom Wahren Christentum*), was an edifying, intensely personal testimony to an emotional Christocentrism.

Like the other forerunners of the pietistic movement, Arndt thought of himself as a true Lutheran, but both he and they came under attack from orthodox Lutheran theologians. Criticized by Lucas Osiander of Tübingen, Arndt was nonetheless defended by another Tübingen professor of Lutheran orthodoxy, Johann

Andreae. Others were not as fortunate. Weigel, for example, could not publish his writings during his lifetime. His followers were labeled "separatists" and "radical enthusiasts" (Schwärmer) by orthodox Lutherans.

The real beginning of pietism came after the Thirty Years' War. By tradition, Philipp Jakob Spener (1635 – 1705) is considered to be the founder of the pietist movement. Born in Rappoltsweiler in Alsace, Spener studied in Strasbourg and Basel. In 1666, at the age of thirty-one, he accepted an appointment as senior preacher of the ministry in Frankfurt, an appointment sponsored by the magistrates but strongly opposed by the local pastors. His earlier work aroused no controversy: he preached against Catholics, Calvinists, and Jews; he urged the magistrates to establish a work house for the poor and orphans, a model for similar institutions in Berlin, Kassel, and Stuttgart. In 1670, Spener organized a *collegium pietatis*. Informal at first, members met once or twice a week; Spener led the group in prayers and readings, followed by common discussions of a particular devotional tract; the conversations avoided dogmatic disputes and focused on piety and the love of Jesus. The initial members of the *collegium* were drawn from the academic–patrician elite. Later, women and men from all walks of life began to attend the discussions, until the *collegium* became in 1675 a sort of public institution. In 1675 Spener published a devotional treatise, *Pia Desideria*, in which he wrote of his fervent eschatological visions of the fall of Rome and the conversion of Jews. Shortly after the organization of the *collegium pietatis*, orthodox Lutherans accused Spener of separatism and radical spiritualism. But the practice of pietistic conventicles spread to other Lutheran cities. Spener himself left Frankfurt in 1686 to accept the post of first court chaplain in Dresden, a position he left later to become the pastor of St Nicolas in Berlin.

Under Spener's influence, pietism as a movement rapidly gained strength between 1690 and 1740. It was especially strong in Brandenburg–Prussia where the Hohenzollerns promoted pietism as a political counter-weight against Lutheran orthodoxy and as a bourgeois ideology for an absolutist–militarist state (see chapter 4). In 1692, Elector Frederick III appointed August Hermann Francke, a follower of Spener, to the new Prussian university at Halle, elevating him to the Professorship of Theology in 1698.

The Elector extended protection to other prominent pietists attacked by orthodox Lutherans, including Gottfried Arnold (1666 – 1714), the author of *Unpartheyische Kirchen- und Ketzerhistorie* (1700), a massive four-part work of church history highly critical of Lutheran orthodoxy. Another center of pietism was Württemberg. The years 1694 to 1743 also represented the critical period of Swabian pietism when conventicles (*Stunden*) sprang up as part of a grass-roots movement. But this spontaneous beginning of pietism did not shield it from confessional politics, as the movement became an instrument of the Prussian state in the early eighteenth century.

2
Calvinist Germany

The Calvinist movement in the empire achieved its greatest success between 1560 and 1620. In the 1550s refugees from Marian England and the Low Countries formed the first exile communities in northwest Germany: Emden in East Friesland, Wesel on the Lower Rhine, and Frankfurt. Another impulse for Calvinism in the empire came from the Huguenot churches in France. Not surprisingly, the movement initially affected German cities on the western border. In 1559 Calvinists agitated for reform in worship in Metz, Trier, and Aachen, but were quickly suppressed.

Calvinism succeeded in Germany when it joined forces with the Reformation of the princes. The breakthrough came in 1563 when Frederick III (1559 – 76), Palatinate Elector, proclaimed the Heidelberg Catechism for his territory. The de facto toleration of the Calvinist Palatinate was achieved at the 1566 Imperial Diet of Worms, but Frederick's political isolation inside the empire remained until 1578. In that year, the counts of Sayn–Wittgenstein and Nassau–Dillenburg professed the Reformed religion, to be followed by a wave of conversions until the outbreak of the Thirty Years' War: the imperial city of Bremen (1581), Neuenahr (1581), Solms–Braunfels (1582), Gebhard Truchsess, the deposed Archbishop of Cologne (1583), East Friesland (1583), Isenburg–Ronneburg (1588), Bentheim–Tecklenburg (1588), the Palatinate–Zweibrücken (1588), Hanau–Münzenberg (1595), Isenburg–Büdingen (1596), Anhalt (1596), Baden–Durlach (1599), Hesse–Kassel (1605), Lippe–Detmold (1605), Wöhlau (1609), Liegnitz (1609), Brieg (1609), Holstein–Gottorf (1610),

Brandenburg (1613), Beuthen (1616), Jägerndorf (1616), and Mecklenburg–Güstrow (1618).

Geographically, the Rhineland formed the heartland of Calvinist Germany, with the Palatinate bestriding the middle Rhine as the most powerful reformed territory and with the communities of the Lower Rhine in the Duchy of Jülich–Cleve and in the Counties of Berg and Mark enjoying the broadest social basis. The cluster of small territories in the Wetterau (Nassau–Dillenburg, Solms–Braunfels, Wied, Sayn–Wittgenstein, Isenburg–Büdingen, Hanau–Münzenberg) and Hesse–Kassel formed another region. Yet a third geographical region was Westphalia (Lippe, Bentheim–Tecklenburg). A number of duchies in Silesia and Moravia, at the extreme eastern frontier of the Empire, officially adopted Calvinism between 1609 and 1616. In Brandenburg, conversion was limited to the ruling Hohenzollerns, while the subjects remained Lutheran.

What were the reasons for the rapid rise of Calvinism in Germany, a development described by some historians as "the Second Reformation"? The immediate reason, one expressed by all reformed theologians and princes, was to further the work of the Protestant Reformation. According to them, Lutheranism had not gone far enough in eradicating all vestiges of "papist superstitions." Where Calvinist worship was proclaimed, the churches were "purified": the High Altar, clerical vestments, paintings, and sculptures disappeared; bread replaced wafers at communion, to be broken and not consecrated; exorcism vanished from infant baptism; and all Catholic vestiges in Lutheran ceremonies were rooted out. A rational, learned, and "true" religion was to replace the "magical" beliefs and rituals of the ignorant people. The reformation of living had to follow upon the reformation of teachings. Wilhelm Zepper, Professor at the Calvinist Academy of Herborn and reformer at Nassau–Dillenburg, expressed it forcefully in his 1596 treatise *On Christian Discipline*. In the Foreword, Zepper described "the doctrine of faith" and "the doctrine of living" as the twin pillars of the spiritual church. The first reformers had their hands full, according to Zepper, in fighting the corrupted teachings of Rome so that they neglected the doctrine of living. Moreover, people at the time were weary of "the papal yoke," with its tyrannical discipline of auricular confession, indulgences, and excommunication, and hence turned away altogether from Christian discipline. Those who clung to the principle of *"sola fide"* became indifferent to good works, criticized Zepper,

> so that it is highly necessary, just as in God's praise a reformation of one main part of Christianity had taken place, we must also have the pure teaching of the Holy gospels, together with the correct usage of the Holy Sacraments and the uncorrupted external worship of God, in accordance with their institution by our Lord Jesus Christ: that is, also in the other main part of Christian living and behavior . . . so that public sins, blasphemies, and transgressions among us Christians . . . may be turned and done away with . . . either by separation from the Lord's Table until visible betterment, or in extreme, special, and unrepentant cases . . . by excommunication . . .

Instituting a Christian life through church discipline provided the internal impetus for the Calvinist movement. Other external factors accounted for its rapid rise. First, the growth of Calvinism was directly related to the suppression of the humanist–Philippist tradition within the Lutheran Church in the 1570s. In other words, the consolidation of Lutheran orthodoxy drove many to Calvinism, those who could not accept the doctrinal definitions of the Book of Concord. Secondly, the formation of an alliance of Calvinist princes has to be understood in the context of imperial and European confessional politics. The rise of German Calvinism represented both a natural growth of the international Calvinist movement and a reaction against a more aggressive Catholic Counter-Reformation. The last factor behind the rise of Calvinism was common to both Catholic and Lutheran confessionalization: the enforcement of church discipline functioned as an instrument of social control in the emerging territorial states of all three confessions.

From "cryptocalvinism" to the "Second Reformation"

"Cryptocalvinism" was a pejorative term applied by the Lutheran clergy to those who opposed Lutheran orthodoxy. Let us recall the relatively fluid situation within the Protestant ranks in the middle decades of the sixteenth century: defined by a common front against Catholics on one side and Anabaptists and Zwinglians on the other, Protestantism in the empire, at least until the mid-1570s, represented a broad spectrum of theological and political positions. During the Interim, irreconcilable differences emerged between two groups: those who identified themselves as orthodox or Gnesiolutherans, and those they opposed, labeled as followers of Philip Melanchthon, the Philippists. One reason for the split could be traced to Melanchthon's compromising position during the Interim, but theological differences on the nature of Christ and the eucharist also divided the two groups.

The strongholds of the Gnesiolutherans were the universities of Jena and Tübingen. The party consisted of theologians and their political supporters who had bitterly opposed the Interim. Convinced of the imminence of the apocalypse, Gnesiolutherans condemned theological and political differences in uncompromising language, and produced a vast polemical literature. They opposed secular intervention in matters of the Church and saw themselves as the true heirs of Luther. Through their publications and sermons on the Devil and on the Antichrist, Gnesiolutherans popularized an apocalyptic theology among broad segments of the populace, and enjoyed substantial political power in Lutheran Germany.

In origins far from homogeneous, the Philippists included many students of Melanchthon at Wittenberg: a few were theologians, but more numerous were jurists, physicians, and humanists. They belonged to a generation with formative experiences between 1520 and 1540. Strongly influenced by Erasmian humanism, approving of learning and charity and weary of doctrinal polemics, Philippists resembled humanist circles of an earlier, preconfessional generation. They believed in the innate goodness of Man and his capacity for regeneration through piety and learning. They advocated moderation in matters of theological precision, and conceded primary authority in moral and religious reforms to the secular magistrates.

Their conversion to Calvinism resulted in part from deliberate exclusion by orthodox Lutherans, as was the case with Zacharias Ursinus, the author of the Heidelberg Catechism, a Philippist who converted to Calvinism in the Palatinate, or Johann Sturm, the rector of the Gymnasium in Strasbourg, drawn to Swiss theology in part because of his bitter fight with Johann Marbach, the senior Lutheran pastor in the Alsatian city.

Developments in Electoral Saxony in the second half of the sixteenth century played a crucial role in the transformation of Philippism and cryptocalvinism into the "Second Reformation." During the first twenty years of Elector August's long reign (1553 – 86), he struck a fine confessional balance, tolerating both Philippists and Gnesiolutherans at his court in Dresden. Dr Georg Craco, a student of Melanchthon, was his trusted chancellor; Caspar Peucer, Melanchthon's son-in-law, served as the elector's personal physician; and the court preacher, Christian Schütz, showed strong Calvinist sympathies. Opposing them stood a strong coalition of Lutheran nobility and clergy. In 1574, an anonymous tract espousing Calvinist eucharistic theology appeared in Leipzig. Outraged at this open challenge, orthodox Lutherans convinced the elector of a Calvinist plot in Saxony and furious at his councillors for their alleged deception, he ordered a merciless purge of all Philippists in Saxony: the chancellor Craco died in prison under torture; Peucer and Schütz were imprisoned until 1586; professors, pastors, and officials suspected of Philippist sympathies were purged; hundreds went into exile. Elector August then charged orthodox theologians to articulate a Formula of Concord, leading to the acceptance of the Book of Concord in 1580 by all Lutheran princes and cities as the definition of orthodoxy.

The Saxon purge of 1574 dispersed Philippists to other Protestant territories. Some openly avowed their conversion to Calvinism, such as Christian Pezel, who played the leading role in Bremen's turn to the Reformed Church. Remarkably enough, sympathy for Calvinism in Saxony revived after the death of Elector August in 1586. His heir, Christian, showed a strong aversion for the Lutheran clergy and a predilection for Calvinism; the most powerful man at court, the chancellor Dr Nikolaus Krell, shared his master's feelings. Aided by a small group of like-minded professors, pastors, and officials, Christian and Krell planned a gradual transition from Lutheranism to Calvinism. Key appointments were made, Catholic vestiges in Lutheran rituals were eliminated, the clerical administration was reorganized to weaken its autonomy, and a new commentary on Luther's German Bible was prepared with ample biblical citations to support princely intervention in religious affairs. However, Christian's reform was dashed on the rock of aristocratic resistance. In 1588, the nobility refused to support the elector, who had rescinded the provision that all officeholders must swear to the Book of Concord. The court's policies also ran into stiff opposition from the estates and the populace. Christian's sudden death in 1591 unleashed a storm of reaction. Krell was arrested, imprisoned for ten years, and executed in 1601. On the heel of the 1574 purge of Philippists came a massive purge of suspected Calvinists. In 1592, the new regime required all officeholders to swear by the Formula of Concord and denounce the Calvinist confession of faith. In 1593, a riot broke out in Leipzig against suspected Calvinists among the city's political and economic elites.

Even though the Calvinist movement failed in Electoral Saxony, the developments between 1574 and 1594 were important for understanding the over all political and social character of German Calvinism:[1]

1 Unlike the popular enthusiasm for the Lutheran Reformation of the 1520s, the Calvinist movement in Saxony represented the work of a small minority whose plan was opposed by the majority of the populace, the Lutheran clergy, and the nobility. Christian's attempt to abolish exorcism in infant baptism ran up against widespread and genuine popular resistance. It seemed that Lutheranism had struck deep social roots in Saxony.

2 Humanists and jurists played the leading role in the movement at court. Sympathy for Calvinism was narrowly concentrated in the academic–civic elites in the large cities, especially Leipzig. Krell, a Leipziger himself, came from a magisterial and jurist family that had many members as big merchants; an in-law, Jakob Grieben the Younger, married a daughter of the tragic chancellor Craco. Andreas Paull, a privy councillor and ally of Krell, hailed from a magisterial family in Brunswick. Heinrich Ryssel, a leading Calvinist in Leipzig, was an immigrant from the Netherlands who founded the first factory in the burgeoning city. Another transplanted Netherlander in Leipzig was Heinrich Cramer, an entrepreneur in textiles and mining. In fact, the 1593 anti-Calvinist riot in Leipzig showed clear signs of class tensions. The Lutheran crowd consisted of small merchants, guild artisans and journeymen; their target, the Calvinists,

belonged to the economic and political elites of the city.

3 The failure of Elector Christian to carry out a Second Reformation in Saxony signaled the limitations of princely absolutism. The Calvinist party was essentially a court faction supported by the upper bourgeoisie in the major urban centers and by part of the academic elite. Orthodox Lutheranism represented both a political opposition of the nobility and the clergy in the *Landtag* (provincial estates), and widespread communal resistance at the popular level against the innovations of a centralizing state.

The Calvinist international

The revolt of the Netherlands and the French Wars of Religion gave a bitter confessional edge to longstanding dynastic conflicts in western Europe. Many German princes, by alliance or by marriage (the two often the same), participated in the international struggle between Calvinism and the Counter-Reformation. In the empire, the Dutch connection was strongest in the Wetterau. Count Louis of Nassau was a younger brother of William of Orange; and after the initial military setbacks in the Netherlands, William went into exile in Nassau–Dillenburg, bringing in his train a large number of Dutch noblemen and Calvinist preachers. The presence of William and Louis encouraged their brother, Count Johann VI of Nassau–Dillenburg (reigned 1580 – 1606), to adopt Calvinism. In 1582 Count Johann grafted the Middelburg Church Ordinance (from Dutch Zeeland) onto the existing Lutheran state church in Nassau. Through Nassau's preeminent position in the Wetterau Union of Counts, a loose confederation of small independent territories in the region, the counts of Solms–Braunfels, Sayn–Wittgenstein, Isenburg–Büdingen, and Hanau–Münzenberg all adopted the Reformed confession.

Dutch influence was also strongly felt in Westphalia, not least because of the spillover of the warfare between Spain and the Netherlands into neighboring northwest Germany. But the fear of an aggressive Counter-Reformation, embodied by the militarism of Spain and Bavaria's ambitious ecclesiastical politics, provided the more immediate reason for Westphalian princes in adopting

Calvinism. In the tiny Lordship of Büren, a strong Calvinist identity was crucial in preserving autonomy against a big and aggressive neighbor, the Bishopric of Paderborn under the Counter-Reformation bishop Dietrich von Fürstenberg. For Count Arnold of Bentheim–Tecklenburg, Catholic Cologne was the most formidable foe. In ousting Gebhard Truchsess, the Archbishop of Cologne who proclaimed himself a Calvinist, the counter-candidate, Ernst of Bavaria, appealed to the Spanish Army of Flanders for military aid. The Cologne War of 1583 drew Westphalia into the war in the Netherlands. When Ernst became Bishop of Münster in 1583, in addition to his archiepiscopal dignity at Cologne, the Counter-Reformation became an oppressive threat to Protestant princes in the region. In 1588, Ernst of Bavaria allowed Jesuits to settle in Münster; the same year, Count Arnold of Bentheim adopted Calvinism. When the Münster Jesuits took over the gymnasium, Count Arnold established a rival Calvinist academy in nearby Steinfurt, a part of his lands surrounded completely by Catholic territory.

For the Palatinate and the Upper Rhine, Calvinist Switzerland furnished a steady stream of theologians, jurists, books, and ideas. In the initial phase of the Calvinist Reformation in the Palatinate, Heinrich Bullinger and the Zürich Church were valued as the leading theological authority. Reformed Switzerland, however, was not the sole influence in the Palatinate. The composition of the professors and officials at the university and court in Heidelberg attested to the internationalism of Palatine Calvinism. They included men from many parts of Germany, from France and Italy. Most stemmed from bourgeois families, either from Heidelberg or from the south German imperial cities. The medicine professor Thomas Erastus (1524 – 83), who gave his name to a doctrine of state supremacy in matters religious, was a Badener. Among the Swiss were the pastors Theodor Marius and Valentin Winckler, Professor of Philosophy Johannes Brunner from St Gallen, and Johann Jacob Grynaeus from Basel, tutor to the young prince Frederick IV. From the eastern territories of the empire came the court councillor Otto von Grünrade from Saxony, the humanist Martin Opitz from Silesia, the Silesian Zacharias Ursinus (by way of Zürich), two younger Silesian theologians Bartholomäus Pitiscus (1561 – 1613) and Abraham Scultetus (1566 – 1624). Others migrated from Catholic territories: the theologian Hippolyt of Colli (1561 – 1612) from Lombardy, another Italian Emanuel Tremellino, and Kaspar Olevian from Trier. From the Upper Rhine came Dr Dietrich Weyer, *Oberrat*, whose father, Johann Weyer, court physician in Jülich, won fame as a spirited opponent of witch hunts. France was represented by Daniel Tossanus, second court preacher, son of a Lorraine pastor, previously active in Orleans. Natives of South German imperial cities included: Johann Hartlieb from Memmingen as *Hofgerichtsrat*; the Strassburgers, Johann Wilhelm von Botzheim, patrician and *Hofgerichtsrat*, and the humanist Georg Michael Lingelsheim.

For practically all German Calvinist principalities, the international character was further enhanced by military service in the Dutch and Huguenot armies. Politico-confessional alliances were often strengthened by dynastic unions, the most famous being of course the marriage of Count Frederick V of the Palatinate to Elizabeth Stuart, daughter of James I. Foreign Calvinist communities settled in Reformed German principalities, adding to the diversity of their population. Books and ideas also crossed national boundaries: Swiss theology strongly influenced the Heidelberg Catechism and the Palatinate Church Ordinance; and the organization of the reformed Church in Zeeland served as a model for the synodal–presbyterial organizations of the German churches.

The Calvinist state

Why did so many German princes adopt the Second Reformation? Did Calvinism function better, as an ideology of the centralizing state, than Lutheranism? How did German Calvinism compare to the Reformed churches in Western Europe? What "democratic" principles of the congregational churches, if any, survived in the princely Second Reformation?

For the princes who converted to Calvinism, religious and political concerns were inseparable in their personal motivations. Elector Frederick III explained his motive in the foreword of the 1563 Heidelberg Catechism:

We Frederick, by the Grace of God Count Palatine of the Rhine . . . make known to you herewith. In Our remembrance of

God's Word, and due to Our natural duty and inclination, We have finally recognized and undertaken to fulfill Our divinely ordained office, vocation, and governance, not only to keep peace and order, but also to maintain a disciplined, upright, and virtuous life and behavior among Our subjects, furthermore and especially, to instruct them and bring them step by step to the righteous knowledge and fear of the Almighty and His sanctifying Word as the only basis of all virtues and obedience, and also unflinchingly and with gladness of heart to help them gain eternal and transient wellbeing, to the best of Our abilities.

A century later, the 1656/7 Church Ordinance of Calvinist Lower Hesse also expressed this exalted view of the prince as *"summus episcopus"*: he was God's viceroy and a pious, patriarchal Prince of the Reformation. Politics and piety mixed naturally in this vision of a Christian society. In other cases, the political significance of conversion was more obvious. It has been suggested that Johann Sigismund (1572 – 1619), Elector of Brandenburg, adopted Calvinism in 1613 to strengthen his position during the Jülich–Cleves succession. Without doubt, the Calvinist communities and nobility in Mark, the part of the Duchy that passed on to Brandenburg, welcomed their new prince and coreligionist as a bulwark of their faith.

Enforcing confessional conformity and political centralization proved more difficult in Hesse–Kassel and Brandenburg. The confessional division in Hesse corresponded to the political fragmentation of the territory. After the death of Philip of Hesse in 1567, the land was divided into four, then in 1583 into three, and in 1604 eventually into two territories, Hesse–Kassel and Hesse–Darmstadt. The dynamics of confessional confrontation followed the rhythm of dynastic competition between the brothers and cousins. When Hesse–Darmstadt subscribed to the Book of Concord, the rival dynasty in Hesse–Kassel moved in another confessional direction. In 1603 Landgrave Moritz of Hesse–Kassel married Juliane of Nassau and in 1604, he inherited Hesse–Marburg. A year later, he proclaimed the Reformed Confession for his territory. But the Second Reformation in Hesse–Kassel met with strong opposition. In Marburg, Landgrave Moritz dismissed Lutheran professors in Marburg and abruptly introduced reformed

services. Claiming to be protecting their beloved churches from
iconoclasts, Lutheran burghers in the university town beat up
Calvinist ministers and professors. In Eschwege, the guilds had
their members swear to stay away from reformed services. In the
Landtag, the knights protested the introduction of Calvinism. In
most areas, civic and rural corporations protested their allegiance
to the traditions of Lutheran services. Calvinism in Hesse–Kassel
was essentially a reformation imposed from above: autonomous
community churches, as represented by the presbyterial–synodal
constitution in Western Europe, played an insignificant role.
Representative of this central confessional control was the importance of court preachers, who owed their appointment entirely to
the Landgrave.

The example of Hesse–Kassel points to a central characteristic of
the Second Reformation: "court Calvinism" rested on a limited
social basis; it was a reform imposed from above by princes and a
small crust of official-academic elite; confessional struggles often
reflected the contest between the centralizing state and the
traditional forces of a society based on estates and established
privileges. Nowhere was Court Calvinism more apparent than in
Brandenburg. Forewarned by the political and social unrest in
Hesse–Kassel, Johann Sigismund limited the Second Reformation
in Brandenburg to the conversion of the ruling dynasty. In his
Confession of Faith (1614), the elector renounced the right of the
territorial prince to enforce religious conformity on his subjects.
Thus unlike the situation in the Wetterau Counties or in the
Palatinate, the social impact of the Calvinist Reformation was
restricted only to the court in Berlin. Through the creation of a
system of court preachers and the appointment of Calvinist
professors to the University of Frankfurt-an-der-Oder, Johann
Sigismund hoped to implement gradually a thorough reformation
of religion and society. However, even these first cautious steps
met with violent opposition. When Abraham Scultetus (called to
Berlin from Heidelberg) announced his intention to reform church
services in the Berlin Domkirche in 1614, a riot broke out.
Berliners rushed to defend the church against the "iconoclasts."
They stormed the house of the Senior Court and Cathedral
preacher, Füssel; and when Markgrave Johann Georg tried to calm
the crowd, some began to curse him: "You black Calvinist . . .

you give permission to smash our pictures and hack our crosses; we are going to smash you and your Calvinist priests (*Pfaffen*) in return." In the face of such vehement protest, nothing was done to the Domkirche, except for Füssel's sermon denouncing the vestiges of papacy. Further steps of Calvinization were not undertaken until the reign of the Great Elector, Frederick William.

The outbreak of the Thirty Years' War signaled simultaneously the triumph and the decline of German Calvinism. When the Palatine Count Frederick V accepted the Bohemian Crown, Calvinism reached its political zenith in the empire. For a brief moment, three out of seven imperial electoral votes (Brandenburg, the Palatinate, and Bohemia) were controlled by Calvinists; from Heidelberg came Rosicrucian pamphlets with visions of a universal Protestant front against the Habsburg; the dream to elect a Protestant Emperor and to crush the Counter-Reformation seemed within grasp. Yet within two years, the armies of the Catholic League and the emperor had reconquered Bohemia; the Spaniards had captured Heidelberg and occupied the Palatinate; and Frederick had gone into exile. By the end of the war, the Palatinate was a vastly reduced state. For a smaller territory like the Palatinate–Zweibrücken the war wrought almost total destruction. Although the war destroyed Calvinism as a coherent political force within the empire, the Peace of Westphalia guaranteed the constitutional rights of Calvinists in Central Europe. Reformed communities survived princely ambition and the collapse of the Calvinist Palatine state. In the second half of the seventeenth century, Calvinism grew in strength in Brandenburg–Prussia, where toleration and confessional coexistence had replaced the militancy of the first generations.

The structure of the Calvinist Church

How did German Calvinism differ from west European Calvinism? Except for Calvinist churches in the Lower Rhine and in East Friesland, which adopted the presbyterial and synodal structure of the West European Calvinist churches, German Calvinism represented a mixed-type, heavily influenced by the territorial Lutheran state church, where the prince or territorial government exercised decisive power.

The "pure" type was exemplified by the Emden Church. The local congregations sent preachers, elders, and deacons to weekly meetings at the consistory; the consistories elected delegates to the *conventus classici* (convention of "classes") that met every three to six months; and delegates from the *conventus classici* attended the provincial synod. Although the calling of ministers for each level had to be approved by the next higher level, the congregation was the locus of authority.

The "mixed" type was found in the Palatinate, Hesse–Kassel, and the Wetterau counties (except for Nassau–Dillenburg), where secular authorities often intervened in church affairs. In these areas, existing Lutheran state churches simply absorbed the Calvinist Reformation. Secular officials of the *Kirchenrat* (Church Council) continued to control clerical appointments, synodal meetings, and the visitation of parishes. Any measure to limit the power of the prince, such as the case in Nassau, could only be achieved with the tacit agreement of the count. Lutheran institutions, such as the superintendency, the inspectorate, and the consistory, remained in Hesse–Kassel and the Palatinate. Unlike the Emden Church, officials in these Calvinist states appointed delegates to the *conventus classici*. The consistories had no right of excommunication; the congregations could not elect their own preachers; and the *conventus classici* existed only in name. Real control rested with the ecclesiastical officials of the central bureaucracy. Where the right of consultation existed, as in Nassau–Dillenburg, it was limited to senior members of the congregation. But even in Nassau, where theoretically, state intervention in the church had clear limits, in practice the magistrates exercised much more power. A Nassauer treatise, *On the Office of the Christian Magistrate* (1586), described the magistrates as "persons set by God above (*praeficit*) his people in this world, in order to supervise (*curet*) them through the exercise of equitable laws, and to preserve among them piety, justice, and peace." German Calvinism embodied the idea of *magistratus in ecclesia*, so familiar to the Lutheran state churches.

3

Catholic Germany

Until the mid-sixteenth century, Catholicism seemed like a lost cause in the empire. All of North Germany, except for Münster and Cologne, had been lost to the Reformation. In the south, most imperial cities had endorsed Protestantism; Bavaria was the only major Catholic territory. The situation for the bishoprics looked particularly precarious: Cologne was almost lost to Calvinism in 1583; in Bamberg, 105 of 190 parishes were Protestant by 1600, and in 1611, Catholics controlled a mere 150 benefices (out of a total of 536) in the diocese; in Eichstätt 209 parishes became Protestant; Osnabrück, Würzburg, Salzburg, Passau, Trier, and Mainz all had sizeable Protestant communities. The prospect for the Catholic cause looked grim in Habsburg lands as well. The Protestant Reformation had spread to most regions of the realm, with Upper and Lower Austria containing large pockets of Protestants in the towns, and with the feudal nobility, both Lutheran and Calvinist, entrenched in provincial assemblies and exercising extensive patronage in the rural areas.

The renewal of German Catholicism fell into three phases. The initial phase of the Counter-Reformation, c. 1550 – 1620, coincided with the strengthening of the Catholic confessional state, a process most visible in Bavaria and Würzburg. The two primary goals were essentially reactive: the reform of the Catholic clergy and the enforcement of confessional conformity. The instruments of reform rested in state institutions, and centralization of power took place in both secular and ecclesiastical states. During the second phase, c. 1620 – 60, a more confident and dynamic

Catholicism asserted itself in the empire. The Thirty Years' War witnessed the greatest feats of Catholic arms, but also the futility of force. More permanent successes were represented by conversions among the Protestant nobility and intellectuals. The religious orders also turned their attention to the popularization of the Catholic Reform, laying the groundwork for the implementation of the Tridentine decrees. The third phase, c. 1660 – 1750, represented Baroque Catholicism in its full splendor and glory. Through the imperial dynasty and the Schönborn bishops, Catholicism achieved its highest cultural expression in Central Europe. A concomitant popular Catholicism manifested itself in the revival of pilgrimages and sacramental devotion.

In the process of Catholic renewal, four factors deserve attention:

1 the building of the confessional state by both secular and ecclesiastical rulers
2 the Counter-Reformation as an European movement, implying the important role non-Germans played in the revival of Catholicism in the empire
3 the crucial part played by the religious orders, in particular, the Jesuits
4 the chronological extension of the Counter-Reformation into the eighteenth century.

Bavaria Sancta

In 1615 Matthäus Rader, a Tyrolese Jesuit in Munich, published *Bavaria Sancta* (Holy Bavaria), a hefty tome in praise of the historic and sacred destiny of Bavaria. Rader praised the land as having been blessed with a long line of saints, martyrs, holy monks, and pious rulers. Bavarian Christianization began with Charlemagne and came to fruition during the reign of Duke Maximilian, claimed Rader, who added the dedication of the Society of Jesus as a central force in this sanctification. A panegyric of the Counter-Reformation, Rader's work was a sign of the crucial importance of Wittelsbach lands in the Catholic reconquest, prominence which was achieved only after three generations of repression of Protestantism within the duchy.

During the 1540s and 1550s, the Bavarian priesthood, as elsewhere in Catholic Germany, accepted clerical concubinage and dispensed communion in both kinds. There was a good deal of fluidity and fuzziness in liturgy and religious practices; a Catholic hymn even had the verse that "salvation comes to us from Grace and Goodness, works do not help anymore." To reinvigorate Catholicism, Duke Wilhelm IV (1508 – 50) summoned the Jesuits to Ingolstadt in 1549. His successors Albrecht V (1550 – 79) and Wilhelm V (1579 – 98) continued the policy of Catholic renewal by centralizing power and enforcing confessional conformity among their subjects. The suppression of the Protestant noble opposition in 1564, the weakening of the estates, and the establishment of the Clerical Council (*Geistlicher Rat*) in 1570 represented the crucial steps in the consolidation of a Bavarian state Church.

Composed of officials and clerics, the *Geistlicher Rat* played the central function in creating a Catholic state. It supervised and disciplined the clergy by regular visitations. A disciplined, dependent clergy, in turn, acted as an arm of the secular state in controlling the Catholicism of all officials by issuing certificates documenting annual confession and communion. Officials, supported by the clerics, then enforced religious and political obedience among the populace.

Control was matched by persuasion. Under the Bavarian dukes, many new religious foundations dotted the land. In 1556, the Jesuits established a college in Ingolstadt, followed by colleges in Munich, Dillingen, Landshut, Landsberg, Straubing and smaller houses in Altötting and Ebersberg. In 1600 the Capuchins, a new order of Franciscans, settled in Munich, to be followed by twenty more foundations in Bavaria during the seventeenth century. Other male orders and new female orders, such as the Ursulines, also established houses in Bavaria.

In imperial politics, Bavaria, not Austria, took the initiative. Duke Maximilian I (not Emperor Ferdinand II), organized the League of Catholic princes and fielded the largest army to defeat Frederick V in Bohemia. Through the persuasion of Maximilian, Wolfgang Wilhelm of the Palatinate-Neuburg converted to Catholicism in 1613 and inherited the duchies of Jülich and Berg. In 1623, Maximilian's armies also conquered the Calvinist Upper Palatinate, ceded in perpetuity after 1648, and proceeded to recatholicize a stronghold of Protestantism.

The Bishoprics

A similar pattern of state building proceeded in the ecclesiastical territories. The prince-bishops faced obstacles also encountered by the Bavarian dukes: a feudal nobility, often entrenched in the cathedral chapters, the need to build a centralized church and discipline the clergy. Measures of reform during the first phase naturally tended to focus on internal discipline: the training of a new clergy and the establishment of new institutions.

In Trier, the heavily rural territory of the Archbishop remained Catholic, and a Calvinist movement in 1559 in the capital city failed to establish a foothold. Although the decrees of the Council of Trent were publicized in the archdiocese in 1569 and the first visitation was carried out subsequently, reforms ran up against entrenched clerical interests and widespread apathy. Archbishop Jakob III (1567 – 81) had direct or indirect patronage over 59 of 295 parishes in his territory; more than half (144 parishes) were under the patronage of cloisters or collegiate churches, bastions of noble and patrician privilege. Catholic reform depended on stronger bishops, one of the measures proclaimed at Trent. Between 1585 and 1595, Archbishop Johann VII von Schönenberg (1581 – 99) tried to limit the power of the chapter with the support of the papal nuncio. Indirect, long-term policies, however, were more effective than direct confrontations. The fortunes of Catholic renewal depended on the creation of a new clergy. In 1561 the Jesuits founded a college in Trier. From a modest beginning of 135 students, the number rose to 1,000 in 1577. Many of the students took clerical vows, with the Society picking the cream of the crop; others became officials in the territorial state, faithfully carrying out the policy of the Counter-Reformation; still others attended the Collegium Germanicum in Rome to return as high-ranking clerical officials.

Another cluster of ecclesiastical territories were the Franconian bishoprics of Bamberg, Würzburg, and Eichstätt. The Counter-Reformation began in earnest in the 1570s. In Bamberg, Bishop Veit II von Würzburg (1567 – 77) published the Tridentine decrees, summoned Jesuits to Forchheim, and sent promising young clerics to the Collegium Germanicum. In 1591, Bishop Neidhart von Thüngen dismissed all Lutheran pastors and officials, and forced his subjects to choose between professing the Catholic faith or exile.

The best known Counter-Reformation bishop was Julius Echter von Mespelbrunn, Bishop of Würzburg (1573 – 1617). Elected with a small majority in the cathedral chapter, Bishop Julius carried out the policy of recatholicization and centralization of power with determination. He undercut the power of the cathedral canons; he encroached on the enclaves of Lutheran Imperial Knights that dotted his territory; he expelled Jews; he established the Juliusspital in 1579 and a university in 1582; he issued a statute in 1584 to reorganize the diocese into 24 rural chapters for visitations; he proclaimed many mandates prohibiting work on feast days, blasphemy, and immoral conduct; he crushed a Protestant movement in the 1580s, exiling more than 600 Lutherans in 1586; he published a church ordinance in 1589 incorporating many Tridentine decrees; he summoned Jesuits, established a Clerical Council after the Bavarian institution, and carried out diocesan visitations.

Visitation records of the rural chapters reflect the success of Bishop Julius's reform. The most prominent success was the gradual improvement in the quality of the clergy. In Mergentheim, where 46 per cent of the rural clergy lived in concubinage (or under suspicion) between 1583 and 1599, the percentage dropped to 8 per cent for 1600 – 15, and 4 per cent for 1616 – 31. Book ownership increased over the years, as did the frequency of confessions for rural priests, from an average of 2 to 3 times a year in 1597 to 36 times in 1630. In all rural chapters, the clergy began to keep meticulous parish records after 1600. Judged by numbers alone, the Counter-Reformation had already triumphed in most rural chapters by 1605, with 100 per cent rates for Easter confessions and communion.

State building and religious conformity also went hand in hand in Münster. Early signs of Catholic reform were visible under Bishop von Hoya, who ordered the first diocesan visitation in 1573. Substantial progress did not get underway, however, until the coming of the Wittelsbachs. In 1585 the Cologne Archbishop Ernst of Bavaria was elected to the Münster see in addition to his other ecclesiastical dignities (Freising, Liège, Halberstadt, and Hildesheim). Under Ernst and his nephew Ferdinand, the model of the Bavarian confessional state was copied in Münster, leading to heightened tensions between Catholics and Protestants in the bishopric and a defensive alliance of the towns against the prince-bishop, his officials, and the nobility. The centralization of state power under the Wittelsbach bishops paved the way for the successful completion of the Tridentine reform under Bishop Christoph Bernhard von Galen (1650 – 78). During his episcopacy, Galen called 43 diocesan synods and composed many pastoral letters. He succeeded in eradicating the last traces of clerical concubinage and non-residency, while suppressing the last foothold of communal autonomy by subjugating the city of Münster in 1661.

The Catholic social order

Catholic renewal in the empire resembled the structure of the Calvinist Reformation. Both were reformations from above, emanating from princes, high officials, and the academic elite. Not surprisingly, the conversion of Protestant princes and intellectuals constituted an important tactic in the Counter-Reformation. In 1591 the contemporaneous conversions of Henry of Navarre, King of France, and Justus Lipsius, the greatest Protestant scholar, signaled a path to be trodden by others in the next hundred years.

The list of princely converts to Catholicism reads like a roll-call of the ruling Protestant dynasties in the empire. In 1613 Wolfgang Wilhelm, Duke of Palatine–Neuburg, converted to Catholicism and inherited the duchies of Jülich and Berg. In 1636 Frederick of Hesse–Darmstadt converted in Italy and was raised by the Pope to be the master of the Knights of Malta; he ended his life as the Cardinal-Bishop of Breslau. During the Thirty Years' War, Christoph Wilhelm of Brandenburg forswore Calvinism for Catholicism after his capture in battle, as did two princes of Nassau and several descendants of the Winter King, Frederick V. The trend continued after the Peace of Westphalia. In 1651, Landgrave Ernst of Hesse–Rheinfels and his wife the Countess of Solms deserted Calvinism for Catholicism. Christian August of Sulzbach turned to Rome in 1656. In 1697 the young elector, Friedrich August of Saxony converted. Other members of the Wettin family also turned to Rome: Christian August of Saxony–

Zeitz, a cousin of the elector, was one. In the eighteenth century, the Guelfs of Brunswick also yielded several converts: Johann Friedrich, the elder brother of Ernst August of Hanover, and Anton Ulrich of Wolfenbüttel. In staunchly Lutheran Württemberg, Carl Alexander converted in 1712 and in 1734 became the first Catholic duke after the Reformation; he was succeeded by his son, Carl Eugen, also a Catholic. Several members of the Lutheran Lauenburg family converted later in the century.

Conversions among the intellectuals were also numerous. Particularly gratifying for the Catholic world was the apostasy of sons of famous Protestant theologians. The jurist Dr Helfricus Ulricus Hunnius converted in 1631; he was the son of the theologian Aegidius Hunnius, one of the leading figures in promoting Lutheran orthodoxy in Württemberg and Hesse. Christoph Besold, Professor of Law in Tübingen, converted in 1635 and accepted an appointment in Ingolstadt. Perhaps the most famous intellectual convert in the seventeenth century was the Silesian, Andreas Scheffler (1624 – 77), better known as Angelus Silesius, celebrated for his beautiful lyrical poetry and his many Catholic polemical treatises.

The Counter-Reformation clergy

The Protestant Reformation depleted the ranks of the Catholic clergy. At the beginning of the Catholic renewal in the 1560s, there was a desperate need for qualified secular clergy. The work of Catholic reform fell mostly on the shoulders of the new religious orders of the Counter-Reformation, and of these the Society of Jesus occupied the pre-eminent position.

Before the widespread establishment of seminaries in German dioceses, the only reliable institution to train the secular clergy was the German College (*Collegium Germanicum*) in Rome. As the first of the many missionary seminaries (among which were the English and Hungarian Colleges), the German College, established in 1552, aimed to train young German Catholics in their future fight against Protestant heretics. In 1573 Pope Gregory XIII reorganized the German College, making it a strategic institution for his plan to recatholicize Germany. It was entrusted to the Jesuits in Rome and modeled after the organization and curriculum of the

Jesuit College. Alumni of the German College emulated the Jesuits in their work; these young German priests trained in Rome were to be weaned away from ties to particularist interests within Catholic Germany. Like the Jesuits, the "Germanists," as the graduates came to be called, constituted an elite, dedicated, and mobile force, ready to advance the cause of Catholicism in different parts of the empire. As Cardinal Giovanni Morone described Gregory's intention in a 1573 letter:

> It seems to me that His Holiness is well disposed to the deliberations to found this college because, like the Trojan Horse, many brave men will come forth from it, who, fired by Divine Grace, will convert parts of Germany or at least preserve those parts that are now Catholic.[1]

During the 1570s and 1580s, the Curia wanted to transform the German College into an exclusive institution for the Catholic nobility, in order to ascertain the future orthodoxy of noble cathedral canons and the security of German bishoprics. The Jesuits, however, successfully opposed the plan. They continued to recruit the most talented and dedicated young men, regardless of social class, and kept the German College open as an avenue for upward mobility for intelligent and committed young men from bourgeois families. A network of recruitment and placement linked Catholic Germany and Rome. Catholic princes and bishops in Germany often relied on the recommendation of Jesuits and selected students from Jesuit colleges for further study in Rome. The students, at least 20 years old, underwent a rigorous theological curriculum, spoke only Latin and Italian during their sojourn, and returned to positions reserved for them in the Church bureaucracy. Shaped by their Italian experience and contacts, the students returned to Germany with a vision of Catholic renewal shaped by the Roman Curia and the Jesuits, namely, that the confessional competition within the empire represented a universal struggle between orthodoxy and heresy that subsumed all local, particularist interest.

Between 1552 and 1797 3,899 students graduated from the German College (out of 4,143 enrolled students). Enrollment figures were highest between 1570 and 1610, followed by a drop from 1610 to 1660, and reached a second high between 1660 and

1740. Who were these students at the German College? In the first thirty years of the college, the students all came from non-noble families. Thereafter, the number of students from noble and patrician families increased steadily, at the expense of students from "common" backgrounds. Already by 1600, 41 per cent of all students were noblemen. By 1670 some 63 per cent of all students were inscribed as *nobiles*. The zenith of noble participation was reached between 1720 and 1740, when 75 per cent of all students were noble. In total, slightly more than half of all students between 1600 and 1800 stemmed from noble lineage. The great majority of the earliest alumni came from the Low Countries. The geographical focus of recruitment soon shifted to the Catholic northwest, to Cologne, Trier, and Mainz. In the seventeenth century, the proportion of students from South Germany and Austrian lands steadily increased.

What positions did the alumni occupy after their return to Germany? The majority joined the elite ranks of the secular clergy, as bishops, cathedral canons, and members of the episcopal curia (the suffragan bishop, the Official, and the General Vicar). In the first half of the seventeenth century, of 1,489 canons elected to the 24 Catholic cathedral chapters, 209 (14.9 per cent) were alumni of the German College; for the second half of the century, close to one-quarter (22.8 per cent) of all canons had studied at the college. The record for episcopal election is equally impressive. For the entire seventeenth century, one-quarter of all German bishops were alumni of the college; in the first half of the eighteenth century, the proportion increased to almost one-third.

Alumni of the German College represented the most reliable allies of the Jesuits. They occupied many of the key positions within the clerical bureaucracy and helped to push through reforms against the opposition of entrenched corporate interests within the German Catholic Church. In Trier, the suffragan bishop, Peter Binsfeld, was a graduate of the German College; a total of fifty alumni of the college occupied positions of influence in the second half of the sixteenth century. In politically fragmented Silesia, divided between Catholics, Lutherans, and Calvinists, the main force behind the Tridentine reform consisted of alumni of the German College, native Silesians and outsiders, who had been elected to the cathedral chapter of Breslau. In Münster, Bishop

Christoph Bernhard von Galen was opposed by a faction of canons who scorned the alumni of the German College as "soft, beardless, Italian comedians."

The Jesuits

The first Jesuits in Germany were not Germans. Peter Faber (Faure) was a Savoyard, as was Claudius Jajus (Jay), and the Spaniard Nikolaus Bobadilla. The Society had a modest beginning in Germany. The first Jesuit college was in Cologne (1544), followed by foundations in Ingolstadt (1549), Vienna (1552), Worms (1557), Straubing (1558), Augsburg (1559), and Innsbruck (1563). By the 1560s, when the Council of Trent concluded, the Jesuits already represented an important force in Germany. Divided into two provinces at first, the Rhineland and Upper German, the Society grew rapidly until the outbreak of the Thirty Years' War. The Rhineland Province had 113 members in 1565, 363 in 1600, 579 in 1614, and over 800 in 1626, the year when it split into the Lower and Upper Rhine provinces; the number of colleges grew from the original one at Cologne to 22. In 1563 the Upper German Province had 160 members, the number increased to 341 by 1600, 465 by 1611, and 820 by 1630; 20 colleges fell within the jurisdiction of the father provincial in 1630. A third province was created in 1563 to cover lands under the Austrian ruling house. In 1600 the Austrian province had become the most successful of the German-speaking Jesuit provinces, the number of Jesuits stood at 407; membership rose to 616 in 1616 and to over 800 in 1622. In the aftermath of the Battle of White Mountain (1620), a new province was created to hasten the recatholicization of Calvinist Bohemia; by 1636, the new province counted more than 600 members, while the Austrian province had 859 members in 1633. Together the two provinces covering the lands of the Habsburgs had 23 colleges.

As we have seen, the first Jesuits in Germany were foreigners – Italians, Frenchmen, Netherlanders, and Spaniards. Peter Canisius, composer of the first popular Catholic catechism, and called the "first German Jesuit," was actually born in Nijmegen at the border of the empire, at the cross-roads between German and Dutch cultures. But with the rapid spread of Jesuit colleges, the Society began to recruit new members from among their more talented and dedicated students. Who were the young men attracted by this new dynamic religious order? There exists, as yet, no comprehensive study of the social origins of German Jesuits. However, regional studies and selected biographies suggest a pattern of recruitment that may be typical of the larger picture. Jesuit recruits in the empire seemed to consist of young men from the middling to upper classes in urban areas. Family backgrounds spanned a spectrum of civic society that stretched from a commoner, artisanal milieu at one end to the patrician-magisterial elite at the other. Vastly under-represented were sons of peasants and noblemen. In Münster, for example, the Jesuits came from families that represented a wide range of civic professions: bakers, butchers, lawyers, notaries, merchants, civic officials, and magistrates.

The family background of three prominent Jesuits reflected the larger social pattern. Their different careers also represented three types of Jesuit activities during the Counter-Reformation. Johann Rethius (van Rheidt) (1532 – 74) was the son of a five-term Cologne Bürgermeister. After his entry into the society, this young patrician studied in Rome before returning to the Jesuit College in Cologne, his alma mater. A prolific writer of anti-Calvinist treatises, translator of the Greek Church Fathers, a historian, professor, and reformer of the Cologne Church, Rethius's career typified that of many Jesuit savants and pedagogues.

Paul Hoffaeus (1525 – 1608) was a Rhinelander like Rhetius. Born in Münster near Bingen of burgher background, he studied at the Jesuit College in Cologne, and was sent by the *patres* as one of the first students to the German College in Rome. He began his career as rector for the Jesuit colleges in Prague, Vienna, and Munich, rising to become the vice-provincial and then the provincial of the South German Province. From his modest family background, Hoffaeus became an important administrator in the German Society.

Still another career pattern was exemplified by Georg Scherer (1540 – 1605), a commoner from Tyrol. After attending the Jesuit college in Vienna, Scherer enjoyed great success as a court preacher to the Archdukes in Vienna; he served for a time as a confessor to the princes. In 1584, he won fame by a spectacular exorcism in the capital and ended his career in the Jesuit college at Linz.

As the careers of Rethius, Hoffaeus, and Scherer suggest, the success of the Jesuits rested on the diversity and flexibility of their activities. United by a common dedication to advance the cause of Rome, Jesuits were teachers, professors of theology, preachers, confessors to princes, army chaplains, and administrators. They published numerous treatises, attacking Protestantism and defending the Catholic faith; they wrote catechisms and schooltexts, created plays for students and princes, composed beautiful poetry and hymns; they organized and directed Marian sodalities, promoted recitation of the rosary and pilgrimages to Marian shrines; they preached, listened to confessions, and administered the sacraments to both the clergy and the laity; they undertook missions of conversions in rural areas, or even deep into Protestant territory; they pushed for reforms in cloisters; they served as preachers, confessors, and political confidants to princes; they exorcized demons; some hunted witches, others defended them. Theirs was an order that cut across the rigid social barriers of a society of estates, with an assigned niche for everyone. The Society represented an organization where talent, ambition, and dedication were rewarded, where commoner *patres* hobnobbed with mighty princes, and where the soldiers of Christ bridged the gap between the lower echelons of Catholic society and its ruling head.

Baroque Catholicism

The century after the Thirty Years' War saw the greatest achievement of German Catholicism. At the level of the *Reichskirche*, the remarkable Franconian dynasty of Schönborn set a tone of moderation and toleration. The progenitor of the Schönborn dynasty in the German episcopacy was Johann Philipp (1605 – 73), elected Bishop of Würzburg in 1642 and Archbishop of Mainz in 1647. As Archchancellor of the empire, Johann Philipp gathered around him a circle of Protestant converts. The Mainzer circle shared irenicist ideas with Leibniz and other Protestant intellectuals. With the security of the Catholic ecclesiastical states guaranteed by the Peace of Westphalia, Johann Philipp reversed the repressive policies of his predecessors: he prohibited witch hunts, condemned discrimination against Jews, and granted limited rights of public worship to Protestants in his territory. In 1647, he forbade forced conversions of Lutherans in Kitzingen; he issued an edict of toleration allowing Protestants to constitute their own community, in coexistence with Catholics. A nephew of Johann Philipp, Lothar Franz (d. 1729), was also elected Archbishop of Mainz (in addition he held the See of Bamberg). Three other Schönborns became prince-bishops: Friedrich Karl (d. 1746), Bishop of Bamberg and Würzburg, Johann Philipp Franz, Bishop of Würzburg (1719 – 24), and Franz Georg, Archbishop of Trier and Bishop of Worms.

The Schönborn era saw a great outpouring of artistic energy in Catholic Germany. The prince-bishops themselves were great palace builders and patrons of the arts. A wave of popular devotion, however, was just as characteristic of Baroque Catholicism. The age witnessed a revival of sacramental piety: renewed pilgrimages, Marian devotion, eucharistic worship, and commemoration of Christ's life. Religious energy expressed itself in a great outpouring of devotional literature, much of it in the form of published sermons, such as those by the popular preacher Abraham a Sancta Clara. In Bavaria and Austria, the Capuchins enjoyed great success as popular preachers. Religious orders undertook frequent preaching missions to remote villages. The period between 1680 and 1740 also witnessed the golden age of the Benedictine cloisters of South Germany and Austria.

Amidst this general climate of toleration came a shocking reminder of confessional conflict. In 1731, the Protestant estates (the *Corpus Evangelicorum*) at the Imperial Diet of Regensburg received a petition signed by 19,000 Protestants in the territory of the Archbishop of Salzburg. The petitioners described generations of persecution by the prince-bishops and demanded freedom of worship and the right to emigrate. In reprisal, Archbishop Leopold Anton Firmian (1727 – 44) ordered the expulsion of all Protestants from his lands. There was a long history of peasant protest and Protestantism in Salzburg. After the brutal suppression of the Peasants' War of 1525, Protestantism became the vehicle of social protest against the authoritarian ecclesiastical state. In 1684, several hundred Protestants had already been expelled from the Defereggental. The mass expulsion of 1731, however, caused an uproar among German Protestants because it occurred at a time when mercantilist interest and reasons of state called for confessional toleration. Most of the exiled Salzburgers settled in East

Prussia; others were absorbed by Protestant territories and cities in the empire; a few emigrated to North America. The example of Salzburg showed that the principle of confessional conformity and princely absolutism outweighed the considerations of state and toleration, even in the decades leading up to the *Aufklärung*.

4

The confessional state

The age of confessional conflicts coincided with the age of
absolutism. This chapter will examine the complex relationships
between state building, political modernization, and confessionalism. There is no simple correlation between a particular confession
and a political form. Recent research has shown that we need to
rethink traditional associations of the Counter-Reformation with
the absolutist state, Lutheranism with political conformity, and
Calvinism with democratic republicanism. For the imperial
dynasty, the Habsburgs, the Counter-Reformation created the
Danubian monarchy, and served, in turn, as an ideology of
Austrian imperialism. For Brandenburg, the rival of Austria in the
later history of Central Europe, the tensions between a Calvinist
ruling house and a Lutheran polity necessitated other configura-
tions of confessional politics. For the ecclesiastical state of Salzburg, the Counter-Reformation represented a policy of political
centralization and modernization, and its enemy was the Protestantism of the rural communes. Confessionalization also profoundly
affected the smaller German principalities, as they struggled to
emulate their more powerful neighbors, and to find a niche for
themselves in the politics of the confessional bloc. In adopting the
Second Reformation, politics and religion played equally important
parts in the calculation of the Wetterau counts.

"Pietas Austriaca"

The history of Catholicism in the empire was inseparable from the
fortunes of the Austrian Habsburgs. Catholic orthodoxy created the

Austrian state just as it had confirmed the boundaries of Bavaria. Unlike the Wittelsbach dukes, the Habsburg emperors did not preside over a unitary state; they had to contend with autonomous provinces inhabited by peoples of diverse tongues and religious beliefs. When Archduke Ferdinand became emperor, Protestantism still represented a formidable force in the hereditary lands of the Austrian Habsburg: Calvinists were entrenched in the estates of Lower and Upper Austria; and peasant uprisings in Upper Austria directly challenged the Counter-Reformation.

To impose unity on this political and ethnic mosaic, the personal piety of the Habsburgs was elevated to a public cult. Catholicism furnished the rites and symbols for the creation of a state ritual, in which the House of Habsburg formed the legitimating center of a Baroque theater of power. Emperor Ferdinand II embodied Austrian piety, both in his personal religious devotion and in his politics. In 1632, Ferdinand wrote *A Mirror of Princes* for his son, the future Ferdinand III, in which he admonished the crown prince to uphold the universal Catholic monarchy against Machiavellian power politics. The writings of Catholic intellectuals, lay and clerical, transformed this legend of imperial piety into a historical ideology. Guillaume Lamormaini, confessor to Ferdinand II, praised the emperor's humility before God. Nikolaus Vernulaeus, a student of Lipsius at Louvain, published *Three Books on the Virtues of the August Austrian Clan* (1640), *A History of Austria* (1651), and *The Light of Austria (Phosphorus Austriacus)* (1665). To celebrate the coronation of Leopold I, the Jesuit Nikolaus Avancini wrote a play, comparing the new emperor to Constantine the Great.

Rites of Counter-Reformation Catholicism underpinned Habsburg imperialism. Four central motifs in this Austrian piety were devotion to the eucharist, faith in the crucifix, Marian piety, and the veneration of saints. Processions, Jesuit drama, treatises, statutes, sermons, churches, and sacred objects acted out the ritual of imperial legitimation in a public theater of power and sanctity.

Universal imperialism rested on international support. Two Italian clerics first praised the eucharistic piety of the Habsburgs. In 1649 the Milanese Jesuit Hortensius Pallavicini published a work, *Austrian Caesars*; and in 1660 the Franciscan Didaco da Lequile, court preacher and historian in Innsbruck, issued his *On*

Matters Austrian. The two works recorded the legend of Rudolf, founder of the dynasty, prostrating himself before the eucharist during one of his trips: Pleased by Rudolf's piety, God blessed the fortunes of the house and, fed by the eucharist, metaphorically speaking, the dynasty grew in strength. Many examples of the personal piety of later Habsburgs were cited: the eucharist rescued Maximilian I on a dangerous trip; the kings took frequent communion in public; from Charles V onwards, the emperors, dressed in black, with pilgrim staff, followed the King of kings in Corpus Christi processions; and Ferdinand III knelt before the blessed host in open streets. After the Ottomans raised the siege of Vienna in 1683, a play was performed in Linz on Corpus Christi Day to celebrate this deliverance from the Turks. The play, *Another Bethlehem or Home of the Blessed Host*, explained that Vienna, being the eucharistic sanctuary, was invincible; and a covenant between the Habsburgs and the host defeated the infidels. The Sun, symbolizing Austria and the eucharist, triumphed over the New Moon of the Ottomans, "for just as the Sun in Heaven, here on earth is the Emperor."

The crucifix was another symbol of imperial sanctity. According to legend, Charles V led the way in dynastic piety. Lamormaini described Ferdinand II prostrating himself before the crucifix whenever Catholic forces faced defeat during the Thirty Years' War. Chaplains in the imperial army carried crucifixes with them into battle. Imperial devotion to the crucifix inspired noble emulation, as the Austrian state became a partnership between the Habsburgs and the great magnates.

Marian devotion represented a third motif of Austrian piety. Chivalric romanticism and Catholic devotion merged in the Cult of the Virgin. It was passed on in part by the Spanish court, where Ferdinand II spent his youth, and in part by Ferdinand's mother, Maria of Bavaria, a daughter of Wilhelm V, who had imbibed the fervor of Marian devotion at the Munich court of her father. Ferdinand erected a Marian column in Vienna imitating that in Munich depicting the immaculate conception. Ferdinand II swore allegiance to the Virgin as his "mother," and implored her patronage in his vision to recatholicize his lands. His son, Ferdinand III, dedicated all of Austria to her. The Marian cult united the cousin dynasties of the Habsburg and the Wittelsbach.

Altötting near Regensburg, the holiest of the Bavarian shrines, was a favorite pilgrimage site for Leopold I when he attended the imperial diets. Back home, Leopold promoted the shrine at Marienzell, near Vienna, where he went on pilgrimage seven times during his reign to honor Mary as the Empress of Austria. During the Turkish wars of the 1680s and 1690s, Leopold also sponsored many processions in honor of Mary in the imperial capital. Leopold's fervor was matched by that of his third wife, the Empress Eleonora Magdalena of Palatine–Neuburg. She was a member of "The slaves or serfs and servant-maids of Mary," an organization of devout noble women founded by Henriette Adelheid, wife of Duke Ferdinand Maria of Bavaria.

The Habsburgs promoted cults of saints from their own land. Ferdinand II was said to have been particularly devoted to German saints, saints who converted the Germans, and warrior saints. After the reconquest of Bohemia in 1620, the cult of Jan of Nepomuk was gradually elevated to a dynastic cult. Jan of Nepomuk, confessor at the Prague court in the late fourteenth century, was drowned by King Wenzel IV in the Moldau because he refused to reveal the queen's confession. After 1689, the Nepomuk cult was spread by the Bohemian nobility resident in Vienna. In 1729 Pope Clement XI conferred sainthood upon the Bohemian. Leopold I, Joseph I, and Charles VI all promoted this cult; and under Maria Theresa, it was elevated into a state cult in 1742 at a time of dynastic crisis.

Beyond the personal religiosity of the Habsburgs, "Austrian piety" also set a style for the imperial court that bound the provincial aristocracy to Baroque Catholic imperialism. A small group of aristocratic families in Habsburg lands, some converted from Protestantism, emulated imperial piety as an expression of their own status in the Habsburg Catholic state. Elevation to princely status represented the pinnacle of success. The best known example of this alliance of interest between the imperial dynasty and the Catholic aristocracy was of course Albrecht von Waldstein, or Wallenstein. As one of the earliest Bohemian noble families that supported the Habsburg and the Counter-Reformation, Wallenstein's fortunes rose rapidly until his dismissal and assassination by orders of Ferdinand II. Other families created more lasting achievements. The Liechtensteins, Lobkovices, Dietrichsteins,

Eggenbergs, Esterhazys, Auerspergs, Portias, and Schwarzenbergs were all magnates with vast lands and wealth. Imitating the imperial house, the Catholic nobility supported new religious foundations, enforced confessional conformity on their own subjects, and provided church dignitaries from their families. The common expression of Catholic devotion shown by the imperial dynasty and these families created the foundations of the Baroque Austrian state.

Religion and reason of state in Brandenburg–Prussia

In the nineteenth century, Prussia achieved hegemony in Central Europe and supplanted Austria in unifying Germany. The success of the Hohenzollerns in creating a rational, dynamic, and expanding state could be traced back to the conversion of Johann Sigismund in 1613. For the Hohenzollerns, Calvinism served a function similar to that of Catholicism for the Habsburgs: it represented a confessional ideology in the making of absolutism.

For Friedrich Wilhelm, the Great Elector (1640 – 88), the religious vocation of the Hohenzollerns and reason of state were synonymous. He expressed the belief in a divine vocation to rule in three testaments: a confession of faith (1642), his first political testament (1651), and the second political testament (1667), containing instructions for his successor. In surveying the history of the Hohenzollerns, Friedrich Wilhelm attributed the success of Johann Sigismund's politics to the reformed faith. The Great Elector warned his successor against a life of luxury and corruption, in vogue in other German courts. He condemned "mistresses, comedies, operas, ballets, masquerades, balls, feasting, and debauchery" and admonished the future ruler to lead a pious and ascetic life, as an example to his people and army. Piety of the Hohenzollerns would be rewarded by divine blessings. The existence and strength of the state depended on strict adherence to Calvinism by the ruling house.

The religio-political asceticism of the Great Elector was shaped by his Calvinist tutor, Count Alexander von Dohna. The Dohnas, a Junker family from East Prussia, exemplified the alliance between the Hohenzollerns and a small faction of Calvinist court officials. Alexander von Dohna was the eldest son of Count Friedrich, who had served the Winter King Frederick V, and the Prince of Orange. In fact, the Dohnas cherished a long tradition of ties to the Calvinist princes of Western Europe. A close advisor to Elector Johann Sigismund was Fabian von Dohna, who had previously served Henry of Navarre and the Elector Palatine. His nephew, Abraham, studied at Heidelberg under Scultetus and fought in the army of Prince Maurice of Orange in the Netherlands before entering Brandenburg service. Different generations of Dohnas served the Berlin court as privy councillors, diplomats, and generals. Through their Dutch connections, the ideals of neo-stoicism, crucial in forging a link between Calvinism and the reason of state for the House of Orange, also deeply influenced the Hohenzollerns. For the Brandenburg electors and their Calvinist ministers, Calvinism was not merely a personal faith, but the outward expression of God's work in the perfection of the state.

Faced with a Lutheran populace, a strong Lutheran nobility entrenched in the estates, and a Lutheran court faction, the Hohenzollerns tried to augment princely authority by furthering the Reformed religion. The creation of the Privy Council in 1604 by Johann Sigismund was due in part to the influence of Ottheinrich von Bylandt, Lord of Rheydt, a Calvinist nobleman from Cleves who had fought against the Counter-Reformation. The existence of a Calvinist faction among the privy councillors injected a more aggressive element in Brandenburg foreign policy. Under Elector Georg Wilhelm, the Calvinists advocated a policy of Protestant rapprochement, leading to the 1631 Leipzig meeting between Saxony and Brandenburg. They also argued for a more active foreign policy of resistance to the Habsburgs, thus helping to set Brandenburg's course as the major rival of Austria in later generations.

In addition to the Calvinist officials on the Privy Council, the Hohenzollern princes also created a small Calvinist clerical elite. These men constituted the nucleus of a new religious elite for the gradual calvinization of Brandenburg. In 1614 Johann Sigismund ordered the University at Frankfurt-an-der-Oder to admit Calvinists; many Silesian students enrolled subsequently. Foreign preachers predominated among the court preachers of the first generation. Before 1648, of the 12 ministers called to the Berlin Domkirche (Cathedral), only one man was a Brandenburger; three were Silesians; two came from the Palatinate and from Anhalt; Bremen, the Upper Palatinate, Pomerania, and East Prussia each supplied one. The earliest court preachers formed a small social clique in Berlin society. Nine of the twelve families were related by marriages. The widow of a deceased court preacher often married one of his colleagues. One son usually entered the ministry; others joined the civil service.

At first, the Privy Council exercised jurisdiction over the court preachers. Later, individual privy councillors, in conjunction with the consistory, supervised the court preachers, until the creation of the Department of Clerical Affairs in 1738. Outside of Berlin, twenty court preacherships were established in cities with residences of the ruling house, most of them during the reign of Friedrich Wilhelm. Until 1645, the Lutheran magistrates of Königsberg resisted the appointment of a Calvinist preacher, but they gave in eventually to the Great Elector. Aside from serving the religious needs of the Hohenzollerns, the ostensible reason for appointing court preachers, their presence in the various administrative centers also served the growing Calvinist official families. When Frederick the Great conquered Silesia, he appointed Calvinist preachers to lands where the Reformed religion had been suppressed by the Habsburg Counter-Reformation in the 1620s.

Presentations of candidates for the preacherships were made by the Department of Clerical Affairs. The electors (later kings) actually made the appointments. The preachers had to swear fealty to Johann Sigismund's Confession of Faith and later to Friedrich Wilhelm's 1664 Edict of Toleration. Preachers at the Berlin court traveled with the royal house and instructed young princes. Those in the provinces attended to the many cadet branches of the Hohenzollerns.

The formation of a centrally appointed Calvinist clerical apparatus weakened the Lutheran consistory. The senior court preacher had a seat on the Lutheran Consistory and could thus express a voice in the selection of Lutheran pastors, a clear provocation for the Lutheran clergy. As a group, they supervised school curricula and exercised theological censorship. In 1637, a Calvinist court preacher was appointed as a councillor of the Lutheran consistory in the Kurmark, to the chagrin of the Lutheran pastors. In 1665, a Calvinist president headed the same consistory. In 1713, the

German Reformed Church Directory was founded which took away the jurisdiction the Lutheran consistories had had over Calvinist preachers.

By 1648, the Calvinists in Berlin – in state service as officials and court preachers – clearly constituted a faction in high society. The Treaty of Osnabrück at the Peace conference of Westphalia protected Protestant subjects from forced conversions by their princes. The creation of court preacherships and the policy of active confessional toleration represented the only legal means open for the Great Elector to promote Calvinism in his lands. Friedrich Wilhelm welcomed Calvinist refugees. He planned to consolidate state power with the help of striving bourgeois families not tied to the Lutheran estate society of Brandenburg. In addition to Calvinists, the Great Elector encouraged non-Lutheran Protestant immigrants. The result was the consolidation of an international Calvinist elite at the service of the Hohenzollern state. Let us look at two examples of this Calvinist official-clerical elite. The son of the court preacher Christian Scholtz counted four nationalities among his grandparents (Silesian, Bremener, Bohemian, and Scottish). The privy councillor Karl Ludwig Selig was the son of the court preacher Moritz Selig; his grandparents came from Hesse, Switzerland, Bremen, and Brandenburg. The education of the Calvinist elite also reflected their internationalism; they studied at Leiden, Utrecht, Groningen, Oxford, Cambridge, Paris, Saumur, Geneva, Basel, Heidelberg, Marburg, as well as at the territorial universities at Frankfurt-an-der-Oder and Duisburg.

By the time of the royal coronation in 1701 (when Elector Friedrich III proclaimed himself Friedrich I of Prussia), the Calvinist elite stood at the pinnacle of society. Even Calvinist ministers from presbyterian background stood for a High Church in the Prussian state. Sons of court preachers filled all sorts of academic and civil posts, as high as the privy council. Intermarrying among themselves, the Calvinist elite maintained a distinct identity apart from the provincial Lutheran nobility.

Religious toleration in Brandenburg–Prussia was a creation of the reason of state. It reflected the limitations of Hohenzollern absolutism. Not only were the rights of Lutherans guaranteed by the Peace of Westphalia but the Great Elector's attempts to restrict Lutheranism met with opposition. In 1657 Friedrich Wilhelm refused to recognize the Formula of Concord. In 1662, he forbade his subjects to attend the university at Wittenberg, forcing some Lutheran pastors to leave Brandenburg in protest. As a long-term policy, repression had limited success. Toleration became the most secure safeguard for Calvinist gains in the land. The Hohenzollerns absorbed waves of religious refugees such as the so-called "secret Protestants" from Salzburg in 1684 and 1731, and the French Huguenots, expelled by Louis XIV after the revocation of the Edict of Nantes in 1685.

A Calvinist state religion was one of the weapons used by the Hohenzollerns. At the end of the seventeenth century, they entered into an alliance with the pietist movement in common opposition to Lutheran orthodoxy. There were three centers of pietist influence: Berlin, Halle, and Königsberg. For the pietists persecuted by orthodox Lutherans, the tolerant confessional politics of Brandenburg–Prussia promised the strongest support for the implementation of their moral reform. For the Hohenzollern state, the social activism of the pietist movement and its opposition to Lutheran orthodoxy, entrenched in the estates, proved ideal for the centralization of state power.

After Spener accepted the call to Berlin, he provided the moral and intellectual center for the pietist movement in Brandenburg–Prussia. It was the Frankfurt pastor's proposal for poor relief that first attracted the attention of the Hohenzollern. In Berlin, many discharged soliders and their families led a miserable existence. Spener criticized the unsystematic methods of private charity. In a treatise published in 1692, he advocated the establishment of factories and workshops to provide employment for the destitute and to promote the weaving industry. The poor were to be taught to read and write and through catechism lessons they were to be remade into pious Christians, disciplined workers, and obedient subjects. Work, not charity, was to solve the social problems created by the Prussian military state.

In the meantime, another center of pietism had developed in Halle. The new Prussian university at Halle was founded as a rival to the Saxon universities of Wittenberg and Leipzig, bastions of Lutheran orthodoxy. Due partly to Spener's influence, pietists at odds with the established state churches in other Lutheran territories received appointments in Brandenburg. An example was Gottfried Arnold (1666 – 1714), who came from a family of schoolteachers and pastors. He studied at Wittenberg, came into contact with pietists, and was influenced by Spener's ideas. Appointed Professor of History at Giessen in 1697, Arnold soon resigned his post. His mystical, spiritualist tendencies led him to convert. Called to the ministry, he became a court pastor in Allstädt in 1702. When Arnold refused to swear by the Formula of Concord required of all Saxon pastors, he was forced to seek Prussian patronage. In 1704 he became pastor in Werbern; in 1707 he was superintendent and clerical inspector in Perleberg. Arnold was famous for his four-part work, *An Impartial History of the Church and of Heretics*, published in 1700 in Frankfurt-an-der-Oder. In this detailed chronological narrative of church history from the first century to his day, Arnold argued for irenicism and criticized both the Catholic and Lutheran churches for their persecutions. Arnold dedicated his book to Elector Friedrich III, whom he praised for religious toleration. The negative assessments of the Lutheran church provoked the provincial estates in Magdeburg to call for censorship, a request that the central government in Berlin denied.

Another pietist called to Brandenburg was August Hermann Francke, a follower of Spener, Professor of Oriental Languages and a pastor at Halle, who had clashed with orthodox Lutherans in Leipzig. Francke set out to reform the moral life of his parishioners by enforcing strict church discipline. He established an orphanage and a school. His social ethics stressed self-improvement and social advancement through work and talent. He attacked orthodox Lutherans in his sermons and writings. Not surprisingly, the university and the town soon became deeply divided between orthodox Lutherans and pietists.

In line with a policy to weaken Lutheran orthodoxy and the power of the estates, the Great Elector and the Privy Council supported the minority pietists against their opponents. With the reform of the Prussian army and universal recruitment, Francke and his pietist reformers were drawn into the policy of state. Pietists served as army chaplains, taught the raw recruits the rudiments of religious discipline, and helped to instill obedience to God and to the state. An Army orphanage modeled after Francke's Halle orphanage was established in Berlin.

The Prussian state was remaking pietism in its own image, co-opting the ideas of social and moral reforms, while ignoring Francke's ecumenism. Francke and his followers became standard-bearers of Prussian absolutism because they relied on the state to suppress their opponents. Opposition to pietism was strongest in the estates. Pietism advocated a universal Christian ideal that cut across all social stations and classes. In Saxony and Prussia, however, the Lutheran Church was a church of the estates (*Ständekirche*). The churches were filled with tombstones, epitaphs, coats of arms, and flags of the nobility and the patriciate. Junkers carried swords into churches; they summoned pastors to their estates for baptism; they received communion according to rank precedence; and all possessed special places of burial. Moreover, the provincial nobility controlled many livings; the pastors they called usually came from the lower classes and were expected to preach acceptance of the social and political order. Quite simply, the Junkers and the urban patricians hated the social leveling tendencies of pietist conventicles and condemned pietists as "quakers." The split separated the Berlin Court and the provincial nobility. The ruling dynasty, noblemen at court, in the civil bureaucracy and the army, and bourgeois officials constituted the major supporters of pietism; the provincial Junkers, urban patricians, and orthodox Lutheran clerics were the chief opponents.

After 1701, when Frederick I embarked upon a policy of cultural and demographic colonization of East Prussia, he selected pietists for ministries in the eastern outposts and called pietist professors to the university at Königsberg. In the 1720s, pietism had achieved a pre-eminent position in the Prussian state: the movement, almost institutionalized, attracted those with talent, aspirations, and ambitions. Their opponents, once in the majority, described themselves as "the little flock of the orthodox." At the accession of Frederick II (the Great) in 1740, pietism had helped to make Prussia into the ascetic, disciplined, pious, and militaristic society that was to become the first among the German states.

Peasant resistance in Salzburg

The expulsion of Salzburg Protestants represented the final triumph of absolutism in the Counter-Reformation ecclesiastical state of Salzburg. With the exception of mining, agriculture and livestock raising were the major economic activities in this mountainous ecclesiastical state. The archbishop, the cathedral chapter, and the noble cloisters owned most of the land in the principality. Thus, the problems of implementing the Counter-Reformation became entangled with peasant resistance to a feudal noble regime that had its apex in the prince-bishop.

The peasant uprisings of 1525/6 won no concessions for Salzburg peasants, unlike their counterparts in neighboring Tirol. Cardinal Matthäus Lang, Archbishop of Salzburg, forbade peasants to carry arms, banned assemblies, ordered curfews, exiled disobedient subjects, and persecuted religious dissidents. From the beginning, Protestantism became a vehicle for social and political protest against the Catholic ecclesiastical authoritarian state. The so-called "secret Protestantism" in fact reflected an intense popular piety among Salzburg peasants. It represented the communal striving for salvation, a need ignored and met with suspicion by the aristocratic Catholic clerical regime. When the Counter-Reformation was adopted as a goal of the state, peasant communalism and popular collective piety found an alternative outlet in Protestantism.

After 1526, Anabaptists were active in every parish. Their presence was documented at least until the end of the sixteenth century. More numerous were the Lutherans, who turned to the neighboring imperial city of Regensburg for spiritual and political support. The Counter-Reformation began in the 1580s and represented efforts at political centralization. The capital was first affected: officials were required to swear by the Catholic faith; Lutheran burghers emigrated from Salzburg; confessional conformity was imposed on all teaching and first the Franciscans, then the Jesuits established houses in the city. Subjects who demanded communion in both kinds were expelled from the territory. The success of recatholicization coincided with the reach of the state: the Counter-Reformation first succeeded in the city of Salzburg, then extended to the other towns of the bishopric and the flatlands, but made slow and unsteady progress in the mountain villages and hamlets.

In 1588 Archbishop Wolf Dietrich von Raitenau (1587 – 1612) ordered that only Catholics could serve as city councillors and that all Protestants had to leave Salzburg. Parish priests were to send lists of recalcitrant burghers and troublemakers to the central government. Fearing infiltration of Protestant ideas from Regensburg, the archbishop forbade any unauthorized movement of the rural population. Raitenau's policies remained largely ineffective, for his successor Markus Sittikus discovered in a series of visitations between 1613 and1617 that clerical concubinage was still widespread among the rural clergy. In Radstadt, Pinzgau, Pongau, and Lungau, peasants rejected the missionary efforts of the Capuchins until troops were sent in. Some 9,452 converted to Catholicism, but 1,219 refused to swear obedience and many chose exile. During this second phase of the Counter-Reformation, catechisms, rosaries, confessional notes, and religious medals were distributed; confraternities were revived; and Protestant churches and graveyards were destroyed or reconsecrated. Civil officials and the clergy informed on each other. Priests kept records of church attendance and reported on dissidents.

Something more fundamental underlay this conflict between the Counter-Reformation and Protestantism. What went on was a protracted struggle between an aristocratic Catholic state, its power based in towns and the flatlands, and the peasants of the mountains, with their strong communal traditions, neglected by the official church for many generations, practising their own religion and ignorant of the doctrines of the Tridentine Church. The real problem, then, was popular religion, not Protestantism. At issue was the power of the state versus the rural communes. The Counter-Reformation could only be implemented when state authority extended into the remotest corners of the mountains.

The Catholic clergy embodied the symbols of the ecclesiastical state in the rural villages, thus anticlericalism amounted to a political offense. In 1652, the shoemaker Christoph Reiter and the innkeeper Hans Egger of Grossarl came under investigation. Egger had refused the service of the vicar at the funeral wake of his mother and had given the priest a black eye. Officials discovered Protestant literature in the shoemaker's home and exiled him. Suppression of dissent, however, only fanned anticlerical resentment. The last decades of the seventeenth century witnessed the first major clash between the absolutist state and the rural communes.

During the last quarter of the seventeenth century, the religion of the towns and flatlands was on the offensive. The prince-bishops tried to impose an ideal of moral and family life alien to mountain dwellers. For the first time, visitations in the 1670s and 1680s discovered the shocking rate of infant mortality in mountain villages (40 per cent) and a high rate of illegitimacy (30 per cent). Parish priests represented the footsoldiers of the ecclesiastical state in this campaign against mountain religion. The majority had studied at the seminary in Salzburg, forerunner of the university, where they had imbibed the values of the Counter-Reformation before being sent out to rural parishes.

The concern for state control extended to population movement. Due to the poverty of the mountain villages, many peasants worked as migrant laborers across the border in the empire. Some returned with Protestant ideas and literature. Officials and priests routinely investigated peasants who returned to Salzburg. The state targeted mobile groups for special investigation: traveling journeymen, soldiers, and beggars, who might infect the sedentary peasants with magical and Lutheran books. The fear of vagabonds prompted the state to crack down on roving youth bands. The campaign culminated in the "Jackl the magician trial" that lasted from 1671 to 1690. Vagabond youths were charged by the state with corruption by the mythical magician Jackl: they had fallen away from Catholicism, formed a demonic sect, openly defied God and the Virgin Mary, and did violence to the clergy. A total of 133 people, mostly young men, were executed as witches and magicians.

Repeated mandates against migrant work provoked mounting peasant resentment and anticlericalism. A major conflict took place in the Defereggental, one of the highest Alpine valleys between Salzburg and Austria. Population pressure had forced many in the valley to work as peddlars outside Salzburg. Many brought back Lutheran tracts and bibles and a homegrown "Protestant" religion took root in the valley in the early seventeenth century. This village religion represented an admixture of Lutheranism and Catholicism, a native creation of rituals and ideas compatible with the social and economic lives of the peasants. Outwardly, the peasants adhered to Catholic worship, but their unorthodox behavior and ideas came under suspicion in the 1660s when priests unfamiliar with the region reported their suspicions to central authorities. State investigations and repression provoked resistance.

Peasants gathered in inns to discuss religious and theological matters, to criticize Catholic rituals and the pope. Capuchin missionaries came to the valley with troops but failed to reconvert the mountain folk. In 1684 the prince-bishop Max Gandolf ordered the exile of all who refused religious obedience, ending a long tradition of peasant religion and communal autonomy.

Another center of resistance to the state was Dürrnberg in the vicinity of Berchtesgaden. Many peasants worked as part-time miners and woodcarvers, amongst whose ranks were the major Protestant leaders in the region. To enforce confessional conformity, officials dismissed dissidents from the mines and cut off outside contacts for the woodcarvers, who made toys for Lutheran Nuremberg, the center of the toy industry. Between 1686 and 1691, some sixty to seventy of the most active Protestants in Dürrnberg left for Nuremberg, Regensburg, and Württemberg. Their leader was the woodcarver Josef Schaitberger (1658 – 1733) who composed letters from Nuremberg to his countrymen encouraging them to resist the absolutist state.

In many villages of Salzburg, increased state repression turned passive resentment into active resistance to the Catholic Church. Innkeepers provided contacts between exiles, emigrants, and the home population. Many stayed away from mass during feast days; others openly criticized the clergy; the dying did not ask for extreme unction; and dances were held on holy days. The state reacted with more control: it offered gold for denunciations of dissidents; it imposed even stricter restrictions on travel and work; couples married without the clergy were exiled; and gypsies were declared outlaws. The central government in Salzburg ordered resident parish priests to conduct home visits and confiscate suspicious books, a task formerly entrusted to the mobile Capuchins, thereby creating new friction in the villages. Formerly, local officials were responsible for hunting down dissidents, now the parish clergy was pressed into state service.

Whatever social balance had existed between the clergy and the laity in the villages was destroyed by these new repressive measures of the central state. The case of Anton Geschwanter, a peasant of Hüttan, exemplified the escalation of conflict. On June 29, 1691, the vicar visited the 90-year old peasant and met with these harsh words:

Shame on you for starting this business of informing on us to the outside! To build the parsonage, the peasants worked more than 200 day shifts without pay. And now this is the reward. I have known 100 priests in my life and no-one has insisted that one should carry the rosary around. Where is it written in the Scriptures? Did our Lord command it? . . . Shame on you . . . You are worse than the court clerks. You undertake visitations yourselves and poke around in our houses . . . You are not worthy that one should take his hat off before you. . . . I do not believe in the pope, nor in Martin Luther: they are all the same to me. I believe in the God who has created me and the world, as it now stands, and who has redeemed me. Is that not the right faith?[1]

The vicar reported Geschwanter to the deacon and the old man was ordered to confess his sins against the clergy.

Under Archbishop Johann Ernst Count of Thun (1687 – 1709), even sharper measures were ordered, to ferret out Protestants. Instead of the traditional examination of faith, to which the peasants could answer without compromising their conscience, the prince-bishop required oath swearing to Catholicism. Offenders were incarcerated, paraded with placards, and publicly shamed in churches. In peasant society, where the oath represented the symbol of credit and honor, this repressive measure shamed whole families and hardened hatred. Instead of suppressing Protestantism, it increased opposition to the Catholic state.

The use of paid informants further added to village tensions. Hawkers, traveling merchants, beggars, family members, and poor women denounced others out of economic or personal motives. To the suspicious authorities, many things became signs of potential dissent: gatherings in isolated peasant houses, ownership of forbidden books, singing of unknown songs, absence during mass, negative comments about Catholicism, the prince-bishop, the officials, or the clergy, conversations in inns, business contacts with peasants in foreign Protestant lands, meetings in remote mountain paths, refusal to fast, absence of consecrated water at home, or even the smell of meat in noodles during fast days. If the local priest felt a conflict of conscience if he learnt of these things in confessions, the government sent in a priest from a neighboring parish or a Capuchin, accompanied by a law clerk, to visit and question the denounced person.

By 1720 there was a fundamental lack of trust between the people and the clergy. In 1727/8 Archbishop Leopold Anton Firmian (1727 – 44) sponsored a Jesuit folk mission from neighboring Bavaria to visit Salzburg over the objection of his parish clergy. The Jesuit missionaries had little success and described most peasants as indifferent to religion.

In 1731, a petition of 19,000 Salzburg Lutherans was submitted to the Protestant estates at the Imperial Diet in Regensburg. It described persecutions by the prince-bishop, demanded freedom of worship and the right to emigrate. Back home, Protestant peasants elected representatives and began to form embryonic organizations of more than regional dimensions. Hundreds of peasant representatives first met in Schwarzach in July 1731. Many of the leaders had been punished under the repression of the 1690s; they were middle or lesser peasants, not rich peasants, burghers, or craft masters. Small peasants also comprised the majority of the Protestant party (two-thirds of the 19,000 signatories); rich peasants tended to be solidly Catholic. When the archbishop sent court councillors to investigate, the peasants primarily presented economic grievances against state finances and only secondly religious demands. In truth, the Protestant movement comprised different factions: some used religion as a vehicle for articulating social and economic resentment, others clamored for actions against the clergy and appealed for outside military aid.

Despite government injunction, peasant leaders met twice more in Schwarzach and called for the avoidance of Catholic services. In consultation with the imperial government in Vienna, Archbishop Anton Firmian viewed the movement as a potential rebellion. With the help of Austrian troops, the prince-bishop arrested the leaders, disarmed Protestant peasants, and discovered a list of 17,000 Protestants. The unpropertied groups in rural society – servants, maids, and daylaborers – were immediately expelled. Propertied peasants were given a limited time to sell off their possessions and leave. Archbishop Firmian proclaimed his "emigration mandate" on October 31, 1731 despite the protests of the Protestant powers in the empire. In the aftermath, Jesuit missionaries were summoned to pacify the "infected" areas. Other religious orders established churches and monasteries in the mountain villages. The final triumph of Baroque Catholicism in Salzburg represented the victory of the absolutist state over the peasant communalism of the mountain villages.

Confessionalism and corporatism in imperial politics

In the previous section, we have discussed three examples of the complex relationships between confessionalism and absolutism in the Old Reich. We now turn our attention to examine the role confessionalization played in the political organization of smaller territories in the Holy Roman Empire.

In the age of absolutism, when powerful territorial states competed for hegemony in central Europe, the history of the smaller political entities is often overlooked. Nevertheless, the small territories comprised an integral part of the mosaic of imperial politics. In their effort to ward off the encroachments of powerful neighbors and to protect their constitutional right to be represented at the Imperial Diet, the rulers of these small territories made confessional politics a part of their overall strategy. The Wetterau was a case in point. In the late sixteenth century, several Wetterau counts consolidated power by adopting Calvinism and modernizing their petty states. The Second Reformation enhanced a sense of corporate solidarity among the counts, forged an alliance with the Dutch, and helped to secure a permanent position for these smaller political powers on the imperial stage.

The Federation of Imperial Counts of the Wetterau emerged at the beginning of the sixteenth century: it represented a regional organization for common representation in imperial politics, a forum for the regulation of internal disputes, and an institution for securing internal peace and mutual protection against external aggression. During the course of the century, the Wetterau counts came to be threatened by the process of territorialization. Mighty princes in the empire, often in the wake of the Reformation, set out to strengthen power by imposing an uniform system of law and confession on their subjects. The Count Palatine and the Hessian Landgraves went on the offensive by constantly meddling in the affairs of the counts, in order to extend the influence of the territorial states at the cost of the petty counties.

The Wetterau counts had no choice but to imitate the territorial princes and strengthen their own rule by abolishing the numerous particularist privileges, in an effort of political modernization. However, rural communes opposed increased taxation and the undermining of their traditional rights by a centralizing bureaucracy. Caught between powerful territorial princes and potentially rebellious subjects, the Wetterau counts also felt neglected by the emperors. Unable to find support among Lutheran princes to guarantee their political status within the empire, the Wetterau counts turned to Calvinism as a political solution.

Johann VI of Nassau–Katzenelnbogen and Ludwig of Sayn–Wittgenstein were the first Wetterau counts to convert in the 1570s. The change of confession, from Lutheranism to Calvinism, did not enjoy popular support. In Nassau, the introduction of the Reformed religion was an act of state. The Calvinist Church existed to legitimize the state. To reinforce the power of social control of the church, lay officials took an active part in synodal affairs.

From Nassau and Wittgenstein, Calvinism spread to other ruling houses of the Wetterau through family ties. In 1582 Konrad of Solms–Braunfels converted to Calvinism, joining the counts of Nassau and Wittgenstein in a triumvirate that dominated the politics of the Federation of Wetterau counts at the end of the sixteenth century. The Calvinist Wetterau counts sided with Gebhard Truchsess in the Cologne War of 1583 and defused internal confessional tensions by pointing to the danger of a Catholic Spanish invasion. After the end of the Cologne War, Calvinist counts in the Wetterau organized a general synod to help stabilize the Federation of Counts and to ensure Calvinist domination over their Lutheran counterparts.

Calvinist counts also led the way in political modernization. In 1578 Johann VI reorganized his government, modeling it after the large territorial states. The central bureaucracy was divided into branches for administration, finance, justice, and church affairs. The 1578 Dillingen chancery ordinance in turn served as the model for the other counties in the Wetterau. Although the process of political centralization had begun before the Reformation, the adoption of Calvinism gave a strong push in this direction, and the pace of reform was faster in the Calvinist counties. Johann VI pursued a mercantilist policy of promoting Dutch immigration and population growth. He wanted his lands to be populated with skilled artisans and disciplined workers. To that end, he created an impressive educational system that included village schools, schools for girls, and the academy at Herborn. The Nassauer educational system functioned as a model for subsequent educational reforms in Wittgenstein, Solms–Braunfels, Wied, Isenburg, Hanau, and Sayn. For Johann VI, the schools represented "seminaries of the republic": their mission was to instill internal discipline in children, to lay the foundations of social discipline, to honor God, and to produce the best soldiers. Self-discipline and consciousness of duty proved in the long run to be superior to coercion in making obedient subjects. Calvinism, or "a Christian regime," was to be the bridge between ruler and ruled. Johann VI and his son established a militia system in Nassau that led to the foundation of a self-defense union of Wetterau in 1595. Concessions to the peasants and patriarchal rule removed the potential danger of a popular uprising. A militia was both cheaper and more reliable than hiring mercenaries; it represented the only realistic option for the Wetterau counts wishing to have an effective defense at a time of rising military expenditures.

In sum, the influence of the Netherlands and disappointment with Lutheran princes prepared the Wetterau counts for accepting Calvinism. The change of confessions helped them close the gap in political modernization between their small counties and the large territorial states. Since they lacked the power of coercion that princes could muster, the Calvinist counts had to rely on education to inculcate self-discipline among their subjects. They also adopted a conciliatory policy toward the peasants to reach a sociopolitical consensus, one informed by the ethos of godly rule. The success of the Calvinist counts was reflected in the policy of their Lutheran counterparts in the Wetterau, who adopted similar measures of political modernization.

5
Cities and confessionalization

While territorial princes were enforcing confessional conformity, trying to shape their subjects into obedient and pious Christians professing loyalty to one ruler and one church, the inhabitants of imperial cities had a different experience. In 1548, many South German imperial cities were forced to tolerate Catholic worship by Charles V after the emperor's military victory against the Protestants. Excluded from the clause of "cuius regio, eius religio" at the 1555 Peace of Augsburg, imperial cities, as centers of trade and manufacture, attracted visitors and immigrants, rendering confessional uniformity an impossibility.

Regarding confessionalization, the 65 or so imperial cities came into four categories:

1 a group of evangelical imperial cities where the Interim was never introduced or was later rescinded
2 Catholic imperial cities, including those where Protestant minorities were tolerated
3 the handful of imperial cities divided between a Protestant civic community and a Catholic clerical compound
4 imperial cities where Lutherans and Catholics achieved legal equality.

Cities in the third category were relatively few. In the small imperial city of Isny, where the Reformation was introduced in 1531, the civic community remained Lutheran whereas Catholics inhabited the suburb around the cloister. A similar division marked Kempten, where the old city, the imperial city, was Lutheran, and the new city, the cloister quarter, was Catholic. For

the other three categories, we will examine the process of confessionalization in Strasbourg and Hamburg (category 1), Cologne
(category 2), and four South German imperial cities – Augsburg,
Biberach, Ravensburg, and Dinkelsbühl (category 4) – where
parity existed between Lutherans and Catholics.

Lutheran Strasbourg

Strasbourg was one of the imperial cities that accepted the Interim.
The restoration of Catholic worship, however, met with widespread popular opposition. Encouraged by tacit magisterial toleration, popular riots effectively put an end to public Catholic services
in 1559, resolving what Erdmann Weyrauch calls "a social system
conflict." None the less, a small Catholic minority existed in the
Alsatian imperial city.

In the second half of the sixteenth century, Strasbourg was a
very different city from the great center for intellectual dissidents
and religious refugees of the 1520s and 1530s. A new generation
of magistrates and pastors helped to consolidate Lutheran
orthodoxy, culminating in Strasbourg's signature of the Formula of
Concord in 1598. Lutheranism informed the self-consciousness of
the Strassburgers. Although the layfolk lacked the appetite for
doctrinal precision and polemical battle of their pastors, ordinary
citizens considered themselves "good Christians," as opposed to
"Jews, sectarians, papists, and Calvinists." They lampooned Jesuits
as *"Jesuwider"* (opponents of Jesus); and pastors called the spiritualist, Caspar Schwenckfeld, one-time resident of Strasbourg, "Caspar
Stinckfeld." Tolerated by the magistrates, Calvinist and Catholic
minorities suffered routine discrimination and abuse.

After 1560, when Catholic worship was restricted to three female
and three male cloisters, Catholic Strassburgers practiced their
religion in secret. Occasionally, magistrates investigated citizens
denounced for holding clandestine Catholic baptisms, marriages,
and attending mass in the countryside. In 1574, the magistrates
abandoned a plan to close down the remaining Catholic cloisters
upon weighing the negative political consequences to the city. In
spite of continued magisterial intimidation and fines, the Catholic
clergy still carried out baptisms at the homes of Catholic citizens.

Why were there still Catholics in this fiercely Lutheran city? It seemed that confessional purity concerned the pastors and the magistrates much more than the ordinary Strassburgers. Mixed marriages were not uncommon. Many Strassburgers married women from Catholic territories, including maids who came to work in the city. Between 1529 and 1681, the parishes in Strasbourg recorded at least 148 mixed marriages. Until 1635, the magistrates refused citizenship to Catholics and Calvinists; they further threatened those who wanted to marry Catholics with the loss of civic status. In 1635, however, due to the financial crisis of the war, the magistrates toyed briefly with the idea of admitting Calvinists and Catholics to citizenship.

In spite of vigilant denunciations by the Lutheran consistory, the small Catholic minority in Strasbourg persisted, with the help of visiting priests. In 1576, a Jesuit even slipped into a theological discussion organized by the local pastors and raised objections. In 1618, the city fathers fined the burgher Laurent Werner for having invited two Jesuits to dinner. During the Thirty Years' War, the magistrates refused to extend protection to visiting Jesuits, causing some of the fathers of the nearby college at Molsheim to be roughed up when they visited the market in Strasbourg. In 1667, the Jesuit Johann Ohneberg published an anti-Lutheran treatise with the Strasbourg printer Johann Welper. The enraged magistrates confiscated all copies and gave up trying to arrest Ohneberg only when the Jesuit was forewarned not to visit Strasbourg.

The Jesuits experienced a consistently hostile policy from the Lutheran magistrates. Unable to suppress Catholicism without infringing on imperial constitutional law, the city council, aided by the consistory, kept up a policy of harassment and tried to restrict all contacts between the Catholic clergy and its citizens. The situation improved for Catholics after the annexation of Strasbourg by France in 1681. Even then, Strasbourg steadfastly defended its Lutheran identity by restricting Catholic citizenship. In 1697, there were only 168 citizens among the 5,119 Catholics in Strasbourg, compared to 19,839 Lutherans and 1,523 Calvinists.

Hamburg

The 1529 Reformation was central to the self-image and identity of the Elbian city. The commemoration of the major Protestant events in Hamburg (1517, 1530, and 1555) provided perennial reminders of Protestantism's historical unity and legitimacy. The magistrates (in the Senate) subscribed to the Formula of Concord in 1580. The 1603 constitution further stipulated that orthodox Lutheranism was the foundation of the civic polity. Hamburg celebrated the centennial of the Reformation with special sermons, a *Te Deum*, festive music, the ringing of church bells, hymns, and declamations of Latin poems in the gymnasium in praise of Luther. One theme predominated in these celebrations: Lutheran solidarity against Rome. Praised as the modern Elijah who led the German people out of the "Egyptian captivity" of Rome, Luther was contrasted with the pope and the Jesuits, forces of the Antichrist. Pastors and magistrates exhorted the people of Hamburg to be obedient and pious in their struggle against "popery."

Unlike Strasbourg, the confessional consensus in Hamburg began to dissolve during the seventeenth century over the toleration of religious minority. The ruling elite in Hamburg consisted of wealthy merchants engaged in long-distance trade. The guilds, which had a strong representation in Strasbourg politics, played a subordinate and sometimes antagonistic role in Hamburg politics. Moreover, Hamburg, the great seaport, rose to economic prominence as the leading commercial and banking center of North Germany after the demise of the Hanseatic League. Its socioeconomic structure was thus quite different from that of Strasbourg. As a vibrant, cosmopolitan, commercial center, Hamburg had to compromise its pure confessional identity in order to accommodate foreign merchants and immigrants. The struggle between socioeconomic change and confessional uniformity was played out over the toleration of Jews, Catholics, and Calvinists, and between orthodox Lutherans and pietists.

The first Portuguese Jews arrived in Hamburg in the 1580s. By 1610, they numbered 116. For economic reasons, the Senate tolerated Jews as protected subjects. In 1619, at the opening of the new Hamburg Bank, Portuguese Jews owned no fewer than 28 of the 560 accounts. Although Hamburg Jews could not build a synagogue, their wealth and visibility still provoked widespread resentment. Led by Lutheran pastors, a popular movement forced the Senate to expel the poorer German Jews in 1649. The Senate promulgated ordinances to regulate the life of the Sephardim and to protect them against verbal and physical abuse in the streets. By the 1660s, the Sephardic community reached its maximum number of 600. Manoel Texeira, the international financier and most prominent member of the community, acted as the diplomatic representative of the Catholic Queen Christina of Sweden. Attempts by Jews to build a synagogue in the 1660s and 1670s were met by counter demands of the Lutheran clergy, that they convert. When a synagogue was finally built in 1673, the Senate was forced to close it down when the civic militia declared they could not protect the Jews in the event of a riot. In 1697, the city tried to impose a heavy tax on Jews to solve its financial troubles, driving many Jews to emigrate to Amsterdam, Altona, and Glückstadt. The rise of the Ashkenazic community partly compensated for the decline of the Sephardic community. But even in the early *Aufklärung*, the "enlightened Lutheran" attitude was still vehemently anti-Judaic. The official mind was guided by *Policey* (law and order) rather than by *Humanität* (humane concerns).

The first Catholics in Hamburg after the Reformation were merchant immigrants from Italy, the Iberian peninsula, and the Low Countries. The tiny Catholic community attended mass in nearby Altona, where the Jesuits had established a mission in 1594. The Catholic cause in Hamburg was championed by imperial diplomatic pressure. After 1630, Jesuits became chaplains to the Imperial Resident and exploited their diplomatic immunity to secure a firm foothold in Hamburg. The roughly 600 Catholics in mid-seventeenth century Hamburg were mostly poor. But the arrival of ex-Queen Christina of Sweden in 1655 gave Catholicism a different social character. Her ostentatious private chapel provoked hostility from the Lutheran clergy and citizenry. Led by Lutheran pastors, a mob demolished Christina's chapel in 1667 when she gave a sumptuous feast in her house to celebrate the election of Pope Clement IX. Communal resentment, fed by Lutheranism, was also aimed at the Habsburgs because the Catholic community was placed under imperial protection after 1675. Latent and intense anti-Catholicism expressed itself in polemical sermons given by the Lutheran clergy during the bicentennial of the Reformation in 1717. Two years later, when the Imperial Resident began building a larger Catholic chapel, a Lutheran mob destroyed the new structure and the Imperial

Residence. Hamburg's magistrates averted a military retaliation by an apology, a fine on the ringleaders, and the rebuilding of the chapel. Although the Senate would henceforth suppress any overt political actions against Catholicism in Hamburg, popular hostility endured and the feeling of Lutheran superiority remained strong in the Elbian city.

Most of the Calvinists in Hamburg were merchants and immigrants from the Netherlands. Protected by the Senate against sporadic protests by the Lutheran clergy, the Calvinists achieved a position similar to that of the Catholics: they did not enjoy the right of public worship, but could attend services in Altona and in the house of the Dutch Resident. In 1685, the influx of some 900 Huguenot refugees brought increased local anti-Calvinist polemics from at home and Prussian intervention for favorable treatment of the French. Toward the end of the seventeenth century, intra-Protestant irenicism was strongly opposed by the orthodox Lutherans in Hamburg, who waged a fierce struggle against the pietists.

The first major threat to clerical solidarity came in 1679 with the appointment of a pietist pastor, Anton Reiser. In 1684, Spener's friend, Johann Winckler, was elected pastor of St Michael's. The next year, Johann Heinrich Horb, Spener's brother-in-law, became pastor at St Nicolas. The issue of "separatist" lay conventicles provoked bitter clashes between pietists and orthodox Lutherans in the 1680s. Matters came to a head in 1693 when Horb distributed a Jesuit tract on education as New Year's greeting. His colleague, pastor Johann Friedrich Mayer of St Jacob, roundly denounced Horb. St Nicolas and St Jacob were two parishes very different in character. The more prosperous citizens, many of them big merchants, supported Horb and the pietists. St Jacob, the center of orthodoxy, was the parish of the lower classes. The guilds and the workers stood behind Mayer and the orthodox pastors. Eventually, the Senate gave in to political pressure and exiled Horb. However, the confrontation eventually led to a struggle for power between the commune and the Senate. In 1699, the communal party forced the Senate to abolish the property qualification for attendance at Senate meetings, substituting, instead, the simple criterion of Lutheran orthodoxy. The turmoil degenerated into anarchy in 1708, and was resolved only by the occupation of imperial troops and the promulgation of a new constitution in 1712 that gave both the citizenry and the patriciate voices in government.

Several central themes emerge from a description of these events. Confessionalism in Hamburg was inseparable from the political conflict between the commune and the patriciate, and between the clergy and the Senate. Two views of the polity, one advocating the purity of Hamburg's Lutheran identity, the other tolerating religious minority for the sake of economic prosperity, were championed by different social groups. Lutheran orthodoxy found its social support among the small merchants, shopkeepers, guild artisans, and the working men of the harbor; its political ideology was a communalism that opposed the worldly and oligarchic polities of the patriciate. Toleration, on the other hand, was less a coherent policy than a patchwork of contingencies, at least before the eighteenth century. Its strongest advocates were the patrician magistrates in the Senate – the commercial, financial, and legal elite that dominated city politics. In part, the patrician regime deeply distrusted clerical zeal. Theological controversies among Lutheran theologians in the 1540s and 1550s alerted the Senate to the dangers of an uncontrolled independent clergy. Even more than their Strasbourg colleagues, the Hamburg magistrates were keen on placing clerical matters under secular jurisdiction. The Senate quickly dropped the idea of a consistory. In 1593, the Senate abolished the position of the Superintendent, replacing it with the informal post of senior pastor. Nevertheless, through parish schools and public sermons, Lutheran pastors continued to contest the power of the Senate. The toleration of religious minority, originating as issues of clerical–lay conflicts, became sociopolitical issues when pastors urged the citizenry and the working classes to oppose the mercantile elite and the patriciate.

For the Senate, toleration emerged as a necessary mercantilist policy to promote Hamburg's prosperity. In the early seventeenth century, two new cities arose as economic competitors – Altona, under the rule of the Count of Schaumberg, and the Danish city of Glückstadt. The proximity of Altona was particularly worrisome because it permitted Jews, Catholics, Mennonites, and Calvinists

the right of public worship. Indeed, the creation of new mercantilist towns in the seventeenth century, where religious toleration, if
not confessional parity, was practiced, proved crucial in pushing
the imperial cities to greater toleration within their own city walls.

Cologne

Unique among the great imperial cities, Cologne remained steadfastly loyal to Rome. The university, the city council, the large
clerical establishment, and the printers were important forces in
the city's Catholicism. Moreover, during the early Reformation
years, the socio-political struggles that fed into the evangelical
movement in other imperial cities had already been resolved in
Cologne after the uprising of 1512/13.

The only serious Protestant challenge emerged in the 1570s and
1580s. Much of our knowledge comes from the extensive diary
kept by a Catholic magistrate in Cologne, Hermann von
Weinsberg (1518 – 98), who scornfully called the Catholic clerics
"fat swine who all live in sauces." Writing in 1561, Weinsberg
did not see the Reformation year 1517 as a decisive year of
Christian schism. For many Catholics of his generation, the
confessional boundary was still fluid before the 1580s. Rather,
brutality in the name of confessional allegiance was for Weinsberg
and his contemporaries the bane of civility. The city council did
not decide until 1562 that all magistrates must be Catholics, a
resolution that was not enforced until the late 1570s. For example,
the patrician Ailff von Straelen, a Protestant, sat on the city
council from 1539 to 1579, as did the Lutheran Gerhard
Honthum, who was re-elected eight times between 1555 and
1576. Beginning in 1579 the city council began to reject non-
Catholic candidates elected by the urban corporations (*Gaffeln*).
Nonetheless, 10 of the 22 *Gaffeln* in Cologne elected Protestants to
the city council between 1576 and 1595. Weinsberg's *Gaffel*
(Schwarzhaus) was distinguished as a stronghold of Protestantism.
The moderation and toleration of traditional Catholicism in
Cologne could also be directed against the Counter-Reformation.
On occasion, Weinsberg saved his bitter comments for the Jesuits.
According to him, commoners in Cologne were open to Protestant
teachings, but the ruling elite was almost solidly Catholic and

forbade any open Protestant activity in the city. Likewise, the city council cracked down on other religious minorities. Throughout the sixteenth century, the authorities relentlessly hunted down Anabaptists. In 1565, they imprisoned 63 Anabaptists, beheading those who refused to abjure. In 1595, 17 Anabaptists were imprisoned and expelled.

The enforcement of confessional conformity in Cologne reflected the less tolerant attitude of a new generation of magistrates. The 1570s witnessed a new turn. In 1571, the city council uncovered and suppressed a native Calvinist community; two other reformed communities of Walloon and Dutch refugees from the Netherlands continued in clandestine existence into the seventeenth century, keeping their own records. A fourth Protestant community of Lutherans was also in existence.

Protestants were tolerated within the city walls of Cologne only with restricted rights. In 1616, the city council declared that Protestants could not become full citizens and hence could not purchase houses. In 1660 the magistrates tried to attract wealthy Protestant merchants to reside in Cologne but continued to discriminate against non-Catholics. For example, in 1674, the council levied a 0.5 per cent protection tax on the ninety nine Protestant heads of households, most of them rich merchants engaged in long-distance trade. Protestants could not worship in public, and had to cross the Rhine to attend church services in Mühlheim. During the 1690s, when Brandenburg and Palatine–Neuburg troops helped to defend the city against the armies of Louis XIV, the city fathers allowed Protestant services for the troops but rescinded toleration immediately after the war.

Nevertheless, the Protestant minority was quite visible by the early eighteenth century. In 1705, visitors reported seeing 500 to 600 Protestants attending services and singing hymns in a court-yard. Once again, the magistrates put pressure on the Protestants, restricting the business activities of all non-citizens (i.e. Protestants). In 1714, the city council publicized a new ordinance for all residents (*Beisassen*) of Cologne: they were to bear the same civic burdens as citizens, but were treated as aliens in business, being restricted to long-distance trade. In reaction, the Protestant merchant community complained to the Imperial Diet in Regensburg and to the Imperial Chamber Court.

Another group of ten Protestant families moved to Mühlheim at the invitation of Count Palatine Johann Wilhelm, who granted them full religious and civic liberties over the passive resistance of the petit-bourgeois Catholic Mühlheimers. The Calvinists established factories and commercial houses, laying the foundation for economic growth in Mühlheim during the eighteenth century. Its population grew from 763 (those over 10 years old) in 1708 to 3,062 heads in 1784. Cologne, conversely, experienced an economic decline, and its population sank from 43,000 in 1715 to under 40,000 in 1775.

Bi-confessional imperial cities

A number of imperial cities in the South were confessionally mixed communities. Catholics and Lutherans achieved a kind of balance in that the Peace of Augsburg guaranteed their legal rights. Neither citizenship nor political office was automatically denied to members of the minority confession, as it was in Lutheran Strasbourg or Catholic Cologne. These bi-confessional imperial cities were all located in Swabia: Ulm, Donauwörth, Kaufbeuren, Leutkirch, Augsburg, Biberach, Ravensburg, and Dinkelsbühl. During the 1530s and 1540s, the evangelical movement swept these urban communities, leaving only a small minority of Catholic patricians entrenched in city government. After the Protestant defeat in the Schmalkaldic War, Charles V restored Catholic worship in these cities and changed the civic regime by dissolving guilds and instituting patrician regimes. In Ulm, Kaufbeuren, Donauwörth, and Leutkirch, the Protestants maintained power, even after the partial restoration of Catholicism; in Augsburg, Biberach, Ravensburg, and Dinkelsbühl, however, the Catholic patrician minority determined city politics in opposition to the majority Protestant citizenry. In 1552, the revolt of the Protestant princes sparked temporary guild and Protestant restorations. With the abolition of the Interim in 1552 and the Religious Peace of Augsburg, a delicate confessional balance was restored in the four cities, and except for Dinkelsbühl, where confessional tensions led to violent confrontations, religious accommodation succeeded.

After 1555, Catholicism made slow but steady progress. Between 1555 and 1648, the proportion of Catholics in Biberach rose from 3 per cent to 12 per cent; similar increases were 15–25 per cent for Dinkelsbühl, 10–30 per cent plus for Augsburg, and 35–50 per cent for Ravensburg.

The principle of confessional equality functioned in many aspects of civic life. In spite of the constitutional provision that only Catholics could serve in Augsburg city government (a clause of the 1548 political reform of Charles V), Protestants and Catholics achieved a rough numerical parity in officeholding. Between 1555 and 1628, the number of Protestants in the city council numbered annually between 18 and 23; the number of Catholic magistrates fluctuated between 22 and 27. Confessional conflicts sharpened during the Thirty Years' War, due to external pressure. In 1629 and 1630, when Catholic arms seemed triumphant, there were twenty nine Catholic magistrates to sixteen Protestants. In 1631, reflecting Emperor Ferdinand's Edict of Restitution, Protestants were purged from the magistracy. For the next three years (1632 to 35), however, the Swedish occupation purged Catholic magistrates instead, against the protest of Lutherans in Augsburg. From 1635 to 1648, the Catholic League reconquered Augsburg, instituting a pure Catholic regime. After the restoration of peace, political parity was again established between the two confessions in Augsburg.

For the ruling elite in Augsburg, confessional toleration reflected the structural cohesion of the oligarchy and political consensus. Two factions dominated Augsburg politics after 1555: the families focused around the patrician clan Welser, confessionally mixed and tolerant, and the smaller faction formed around the Fugger, more openly Catholic. The first priority in civic politics was the maintenance of religious peace. Both clans – the Welser and the Fugger – their allies and clients had an interest in promoting the economic prosperity of the city and of their banking houses. In foreign policy, Augsburg steered an imperial, neutral course, avoiding allegiance to confessional blocs, in order to safeguard her extensive commercial and financial assets.

Confessional toleration in civic policies manifested itself in all aspects of daily life. The magistrates exercised careful supervision over both the Lutheran and Catholic clergy, censoring any polemical expressions. In civil affairs, they maintained strict impartiality. Until about 1580, mixed marriages were very common.

After the coming of the Jesuits, confessional lines hardened. Nevertheless, Catholics and Protestants worked side-by-side in guilds and markets, and lived peacefully in the same neighborhoods. In Augsburg, many Protestant parents sent their children to the Jesuit College, both for its excellent academic reputation and its free education. With few exceptions, social welfare did not discriminate between confessions. The Protestant orphanage in Augsburg and the Catholic House for abandoned children were located next to each other. This spatial juxtaposition was even more remarkable when it came to houses of worship. After 1548, Protestants and Catholics shared parts of church buildings for their respective services, without apparent tensions. Such was the case for the Parish Church of St Martin in Biberach, the Carmelite Church in Ravensburg, and the cloister Church of St Ulrich in Augsburg.

Toleration, thus, characterized the general tone of life in these bi-confessional imperial cities. Confessional conflicts did occur, such as in 1583, when Protestants resisted the introduction of the Gregorian Calendar, but even in the years of confessionalization, 1580 to 1648, conflicts often resulted from external factors and not from tensions within the civic community. The fear of bloodshed united magistrates and burghers in their pursuit of peace, toleration, and prosperity, blessings that separated their urban communities from the struggles between the territorial states.

Mercantilism and toleration

Joseph Lecler has written the standard work on toleration in early modern Europe (*Toleration and the Reformation*, 2 vols, London, 1960), in which he traces the growth of religious toleration into religious liberty as reflected in the intellectual currents of the period. Equal in importance to the intellectual history of toleration is the study of confessional plurality within the context of economic and political history. The coexistence of different confessional groups was often the direct result of the "reason of state" and its accompanying policy of mercantilism.

Perhaps the most poignant example of the use of religious toleration to gain power was the rise of Wallenstein. Without question, the "Generalissimo" owed his early career to loyalty in the Catholic Habsburg cause. But in his spectacular rise to power Wallenstein started to part ways from Ferdinand II, who pursued a rigid confessional politics, on the advice of his Jesuit confessor, Guillaume Lamormaini. To build the largest and most powerful army in Europe, Wallenstein employed military talent regardless of confessional allegiance. One of Wallenstein's closest and most trusted commanders, Hans Georg von Arnim, was a Lutheran. For the two years when Wallenstein ruled Mecklenburg as duke, he left the territorial Lutheran church in place, replacing only the ducal chapel (Calvinist) with a Catholic one. It was precisely the confessional neutrality of Wallenstein's enormous military machine that frightened his fellow Catholic ideologues and ultimately led to the warlord's downfall. The lesson of toleration, however, was not lost on the princes of the empire, particularly after the devastation of the Thirty Years' War. Religious toleration attracted immigrants, new sources of manpower and wealth, a lesson Prussia learnt well. To promote prosperity, other princes created enclaves for religious minorities in their otherwise confessionally uniform states.

Accepting religious exiles, however, did not necessarily imply religious toleration; the orthodox Duke Johann Friedrich of Württemberg allowed persecuted Lutherans, but not others, to settle in his mining town Freudenstadt. More significant in the early modern period were cities that owed their foundation or growth to religious refugees. These "cities for exiles" (*Exulantenstädte*), as Heinz Stoob calls them, were a new type of urban community created by princes for the sole purpose of attracting religious exiles.[1]

Neuwied

Neuwied was the most prominent example of these new cities. In the last years of the Thirty Years' War, Friedrich von Wied (1618 – 98) chose the village of Langendorf on the right bank of the Rhine as the site for his new residence. To attract settlers to the new residence, Friedrich, a Calvinist, proclaimed in 1648 that all immigrants, irrespective of their religious belief, could worship in peace in their homes. Friedrich also promised to exempt all immigrants from labor service, rescind feudal servitude, create a free market, grant tax concessions, and allow citizens of any confession to build houses and qualify for the civic magistracy The "Neuwied privileges" proved especially attractive for the sectarians excluded from the Peace of Westphalia. In the 1650s Mennonites settled in Neuwied. In 1680, Friedrich extended the original privileges to eight Mennonite families who sought refuge from persecution in Jülich. In the "concession letter" of 1680, Friedrich explicitly bound his heir and the Reformed Church not to persecute Mennonites. By 1699, there were eight Mennonite families among the 152 households in Neuwied. The separatist community grew after 1740, and by 1770 counted 125 Mennonites out of 2,905 residents that included by then the Moravian Brethren, Hutterites, and other separatist communities.

Mannheim

Other communities were created to accommodate Calvinist refugees: Count Philipp-Ludwig II of Hanau–Münzenberg founded Hanau in 1597; Friedrich IV, Count Palatine founded Mannheim in 1607. Mannheim belonged to the type of rationally planned early modern German city, with rectangular city blocks marked off by long straight streets cutting across the city. It was founded to promote industry and commerce in the Palatinate by attracting Calvinist refugees from the Netherlands. In 1652, elector Karl Ludwig appointed the merchant Heinrich Clignet as city director. In 1655, he gave permission to Hutterites to settle in Mannheim, a privilege extended in 1663 to Socinians (Anti-Trinitarian followers of Faustus Socinus) expelled from Poland.

Glückstadt

Christian IV, King of Denmark and prince of Schleswig–Holstein, founded Glückstadt on the Elbe in 1617 as a rival port to Hamburg. Its inhabitants were listed under "nations," with Netherlanders of all religious persuasions living under one registration. Portuguese Jews and Germans were likewise tolerated in Glückstadt. Mennonites, Quakers, Jews, Lutherans, German Calvinists, Remonstrants, and Counter-Remonstrants all enjoyed the freedom of worship; they had the right to wear costumes of their choice, and to follow the ceremonial and dietary customs of their community. In addition, Mennonites did not have to swear the civic oath and carry arms.

Frankenthal

In the second half of the sixteenth century, Frankfurt had the largest refugee community from the Netherlands, with roughly 13 per cent (c. 2,000) of the population in 1562 of foreign origins. While the civic elite welcomed immigrants who brought money and skills, the Lutheran pastorate and the artisans resented the presence of so many non-Lutheran foreigners. When the Palatinate turned to Calvinism in 1562, Netherlanders in Frankfurt moved en masse to Palatine towns. Frankenthal was the leading destination, where Walloons and Flemings constructed their own communities and enjoyed broad economic freedom. In the first two decades of Frankenthal's foundation, the population increased fivefold; by 1600, the number of inhabitants was approximately 1,200, a figure that included many German Calvinists.

Neu-Hanau

As the first planned settlement for refugees from the Low Countries, Neu-Hanau was intended to be an economic rival to Frankfurt. In spite of the xenophobia of the Lutheran populace, Frankfurt continued to attract many refugees from the Netherlands. Between 1585 and 1595, the decade of heaviest immigration, some 4,000 refugees resided in Frankfurt, of whom half had gained citizenship. The presence of many international merchants and manufacturers from Antwerp led both to rapid economic growth in Frankfurt and to the domination of the city's commerce by Calvinist Netherlanders. Their effort to gain religious expression met with hostile resistance from the Lutheran community and measures to curb Calvinism. In the nearby County of Hanau–Münzenberg, Philipp Ludwig II, a Calvinist, extended hospitality to the Dutch Calvinists, over the objections of his subjects, granting them religious liberty and extensive economic privileges in return for settling in a new section of Hanau. Out of the 300 families that pledged to emigrate from Frankfurt to Neu-Hanau in

1597, only about 120 families actually made the move. Demographic growth fluctuated widely in the first years of the new community, depending on the economy, the plague, and the climate of toleration in neighboring Frankfurt. By 1609, Neu-Hanau had between 2,500 and 2,800 residents. Population and economic growth stagnated during the second decade of Neu-Hanau's existence. The new community did not attract as much capital, and the original plan of a pure Dutch Calvinist settlement gave way to an influx of poorer German artisans. In the end, Neu-Hanau did not become a serious rival to Frankfurt, but functioned as a satellite town to the powerful imperial city.

Altona

In 1602, Count Ernst of Holstein–Schaumburg founded Altona on the model of Neu-Hanau. At that time, two thousand Netherlanders resided in Hamburg (5 per cent of the total population), but did not have the right of public worship. Count Ernst, a Lutheran himself, granted Calvinists religious liberty in Altona in order to lure away Dutch capital and compete with Hamburg. He also granted privileges to Mennonites, Jews, and Catholics. Mercantilist calculation, rather than religious toleration, was at the heart of Schaumburg policy; in 1594, Count Ernst's predecessor, Adolf XIV, had allowed the Jesuits to settle in Altona in exchange for money. After 1602, financed by Dutch Calvinist and Mennonite capitalists, textile workshops and sugar refineries sprang up in Altona; and this "artisan village" became a hated competitor to the guilds in Hamburg. The foundation of Altona as an *Exulantenstadt* undermined the Lutheran city of Stade, which had tolerated Dutch and English merchants in the sixteenth century. It was, however, a long way from being a serious rival to Hamburg. In 1620, Altona's population stood at 1,500, the majority Calvinists, with c. 200 Jews and a small number of Mennonites. Only under Danish rule in the late seventeenth century did Altona grow to be second in rank behind the capital city of Copenhagen.

6
Culture and confessionalism

Coercion alone cannot explain the success of confessionalization. True, the Lutheran, Catholic, and Calvinist state churches relied on visitations, denunciations, and control to elicit conformity and discipline, but equally important was the element of persuasion, expressed by a multiple array of cultural media to create distinct confessional cultures. In other words, confessionalization in early modern Germany was more than a process of "social disciplining," that molded burghers and peasants into obedient subjects, it also represented a creative process of acculturation, one that reinforced the differences between the many Germanies.[1]

To understand this process of confessional acculturation, we need to examine the forms, content, and production of this vast array of cultural material: theater, poetry, hymnals, spiritual and "folk" songs, paintings, catechisms, sermons, legends, and all sorts of books – biblical, devotional, prayer, household guides, almanacs, historical, and others. The importance of confessionalism to the development of early modern German culture can hardly be overemphasized. According to one estimate, about 44 per cent of the book market in the seventeenth century consisted of religious books.[2] We would find a considerable amount of interconfessional cultural borrowings, especially in music and theater, but on the whole, distinct Catholic, Lutheran, and Calvinist cultures can be identified. Much is still unknown, although scholars of folklore and Baroque literature have recently erected many signposts of research. The great gap in our knowledge is the social history of culture: the questions of literacy, book ownership, the sociology of reading, patronage, and the history of meaning do not as yet have definite answers. The following summary, then, is necessarily tenuous, but should suggest the central importance of acculturation in the formation of confessional identities.

Baroque Catholicism

Three major characteristics are evident in the creation of a Counter-Reformation culture in Germany. First, it was an international as well as a regional movement. The Rhineland, the Spanish Netherlands, and Bavaria constituted the heartland of this movement, but works by French, Spanish, and Italian authors also featured prominently in translation. Second, in terms of the social conditions of its production and reception, Baroque Catholicism in Germany was decidedly non-bourgeois, in sharp contrast to the culture of Lutheran Germany. The German Baroque represented a culture created primarily by clerics, in academic institutions or under court patronage, for consumption by the official elites, both lay and clerical, of the Catholic states. Finally, the Counter-Reformation consciously re-established cultural links with late medieval Christianity, reviving traditional sacramental devotion in order to mobilize popular support for the Catholic cause.

Mainz and Cologne were the two most important Catholic strongholds in the Rhineland. Through their universities, printing presses, and Jesuit colleges, the two cities developed a network of exchange that extended to include Catholic South Germany and the Spanish Netherlands. Due to its proximity to Frankfurt, site of the largest book fair in Europe and the center of Lutheran printing, Mainz developed into the Catholic center for book censorship. The Imperial Book Commissioner, Valentin Leucht (c. 1550 – 1619), carried out his work in Frankfurt and was an ardent supporter of the Counter-Reformation. In addition to his role as censor, Leucht also popularized many Catholic devotional tracts. He edited and translated into German the *Eight Books of Saints* by Tilman Bredenbach (b. 1526), canon of St Gereon in Cologne. This collection of miracles and legends of saints transmitted many exempla compiled by the twelfth-century Cistercian Caesarius of Heisterbach. The work served as a defense of the miraculous efficacy of the Catholic Church against attacks by Protestants.

Another censor laboring for the cause of the Counter-Reformation was Johannes Ludwig von Hagen (1580 – 1649), chancellor of the University of Mainz. Appointed Apostolic Book Commissioner, a position first established during the reign of Rudolf II, Hagen collaborated with the Vatican in controlling the export of Protestant books to Italy. Between 1623 and 1649, Hagen corresponded regularly with the Roman Curia, supplying Rome with catalogues of the Frankfurt Book Fair and acting in general as the "controller" of Catholic publishing in Germany. During the 1620s, in cooperation with the papal nuncio in Cologne, Hagen tried to suppress Calvinist publishing.

The political fragmentation of the Empire and the juxtaposition of the confessions made effective censorship by and large impossible. Only in Bavaria – where the building of a centralized confessional state had made early progress – did secure territorial boundaries protect Catholic cultural hegemony. In 1565 Duke Albrecht forbade the sale of books published by non-Catholic printers. The ordinance proclaimed that:

> henceforth namely no bookseller, whoever he may be, resident or alien, may secretly or openly peddle or sell books, be they in Latin or German, that deal with theological matters, in which the Holy Scriptures are discussed...and interpreted, or [books] that defend this or that teaching and confession, likewise no books or hymnals . . . [are to be] brought into the land, except for those printed in the following cities and country: Munich, Ingolstadt, Dillingen, Mainz, Cologne, Freiburg in Breisgau, Innsbruck, Paris, Lyon, Venice, Rome, Florence, Bologna, Antwerp, Louvain, and Spain.

The mandate also specified the prohibition of non-religious books published by Protestant printers. The Clerical Council oversaw the enforcement of censorship in all of Bavaria except for the university town of Ingolstadt, where a member of the theological faculty, a Jesuit, exercised control. Border checks, especially of merchandise from Nuremberg, house searches, inspections of bookshops, book burnings, and fines were measures that endured until the end of the Old Regime in Bavaria.

Cologne was the most important center for the production of Catholic books between 1525 and 1660. In 1590, twenty presses were turning out Catholic literature, more than in any other German city. Major Catholic printers, such as the firm of Gymnich, enjoyed reciprocal publishing arrangements with Catholic printers in Münster, Paderborn, and Mainz. The Rhine served as a trade route between Catholic Germany and the Spanish Netherlands; Catholic literature produced in Douai, Antwerp, and Louvain was rapidly reprinted in Cologne and Mainz. The Jesuit Martin Delrio, born in Antwerp and professor at Louvain, achieved fame with his erudite treatise against magic and witchcraft, *Six Books of Inquiry on Magic* (*Disquisitionum Magicarum Libri Sex*), first published in 1599 in Louvain and reprinted twenty five times by 1755, including eleven editions in Germany. Other Netherlanders won fame in Germany through their publications, such as the Jesuit Johann Maior, whose anthology, *The Great Mirror* (*Magnum Speculum*) (Douai, 1603), was reprinted in Cologne until 1747.

Since Latin was the international language of learning, Latin works published in Italy, France, or the Spanish Netherlands were frequently reprinted in Catholic Germany. But the Counter-Reformation also provided for the absorption of Spanish culture through German translations of the writings of the major Spanish religious figures.

Aegidius Albertinus (1560 – 1620), a native of Deventer, the most prolific translator of Spanish works, was the secretary of the Bavarian Aulic Council in 1593. In all, Albertinus compiled and translated fifty two works: they fall into four categories

1 "mirror handbooks" for the various social estates
2 didactic histories, entitled *The Theater of Human Life* or *Theater of the World*
3 books of consolation such as Pedro de Ribadeneira's *Treatise on the Tribulation* (*Tratado de la tribulacion*)
4 hagiographies, such as Antonio Gallonio's *Life of St Philip Neri* (translated from the Italian) and Pedro Malón de Chaides's *Conversión de la Magdalena* (*Conversion of the Magdalene*).

His list of translated authors included Antonio de Guevara, Mateo Alemán, Alonso de Orozco, Pedro Sanchez, Francisco de Osuña, Luis de León, Juan de la Cruz, and Pedro de Ribadeneira. The Wittelsbach court strongly supported this literary effort to promote Spanish religiosity. Duke Maximilian himself commissioned the translation of the *Life of St Philip Neri*. Another project was paid for by Duke Wilhelm, and Maria, the duke's sister, wife of Archduke Karl and mother of Emperor Ferdinand II, praised Albertinus for his pious labor. Court ladies, lower clerics, village curates, lay brothers, low ranking noblemen, officials, and burghers were among the readers of these translations – people unlearned in Latin, but who formed the mainstay of the Bavarian Catholic state.

Another important "cultural middleman" was the Westphalian Matthäus Timpius (Timpe) (b. 1566), who was active in promoting the Catholic cause, first in Osnabrück and then in Münster, as a schoolteacher in the gymnasia. Himself an extraordinarily prolific writer, with at least sixty three polemical and devotional treatises to his credit, Timpius contributed decisively to the dissemination of the writings of Luis de Granada, of which there were already thirteen German translations before 1620. As one may expect, Cologne was the center for the distribution of Spanish books in the Catholic northwest, both in the original and in translations; the publishing house of Martin Nutius in fact specialized in handling Spanish books.

The popularity of Spanish authors is quite understandable. For Catholics, Germany was a land teeming with heretics; Spain stood as the bulwark of Catholicism, a land that gave more saints to the Catholic Church in the sixteenth century than any other Catholic country: among the Spanish saints, Teresa de Avila and Juan de la Cruz enjoyed notable receptions in Baroque Germany.

Before 1650, works by the two Carmelite saints appeared only in Latin translations in Germany: in 1626, after Teresa was blessed, Matthais Martinus Wacquier published a Latin edition of her writings in Cologne; in 1639, the first Latin edition of Juan de la Cruz appeared in Germany. The first German translation of St Teresa was by Matthias, Prior of St Arnold in Würzburg, a Bohemian convert; the two volume work was printed by Heinrich Pigrin in Würzburg and distributed by the Cologne bookman Jodocus Kalchovius. This translation went through five editions, the last reprinted in 1756 in Augsburg. Partial translations of St Teresa appeared later, sometimes secondhand from the Italian; all of the translators were clerics, many of them Jesuits. The translator of Juan de la Cruz was the Bohemian Carmelite, Modestus a Sancto Joanne Evangelista; the work appeared in print in 1697, just before the Spaniard's canonization.

Teresa's work enjoyed a much wider reception than that of her disciple. Her early canonization created the groundwork for a popular reception. Several biographies and hagiographies were prepared in the early seventeenth century: in 1620, Matthias Martinez translated into Latin an early biography by the Jesuit Francisco de Ribera, *Vida de la Madre Teresa de Jesus*, first published in 1590 in Salamanca; in 1622, Philip Kissing's German translation of Martinez's Latin edition was published in Cologne. The century from 1650 to 1750 represented the height of Teresian and Juanian reception in Germany. But on the whole, the influence of the Carmelite mystics on Counter-Reformation German Catholicism was limited. The Discalites, naturally the major promoters of St Teresa and St John, came to Germany relatively late; they settled in Cologne in 1613, in Vienna in 1623, and in Würzburg in 1627. The writings of the Silesian convert, Angelus Silesius, reveal a good deal of mysticism. But this type of Christocentric eroticism transcended confessional boundaries; Spanish mysticism also showed its influence in the poetry of the Lutheran Georg Philip Harsdörffer, and through Silesius and Harsdörffer, the Carmelite mystics exercised an indirect influence on Johann Arndt and on pietism.

The domination of Catholic Germany by the clergy was near total in theater, one of the greatest achievements of Counter-Reformation culture. Previous centuries had left a theatrical heritage of medieval passion plays, carnival farces, and humanist school drama. During the early Reformation, the Protestants adroitly adapted various dramatic devices to propagate their message. The theater, then, represented a powerful medium of cultural and confessional propaganda, and evolved, over the centuries of confessionalization, as one of the chief instruments for the propagation of faith.

The theater united two aims of the Counter-Reformation: it served a didactic purpose in helping students to learn their Latin or catechism; it also represented, through the histrionics of sensuality, the earthly embodiments of the struggle between heresy and orthodoxy, sin and virtue, Devil and God. Undoubtedly, the Jesuits were the greatest playwrights of Catholic Germany. Between 1555 and 1665, Jesuits produced 323 plays in Germany, an important corpus for Catholic self-expression. Generations of Catholic school boys were brought up in the Jesuit theatrical

tradition: they and their parents participated as actors and spectators of this vast repertoire of Catholic glory and salvation. With
each college producing five to eight plays each school year, Jean-
Marié Valentin estimates that some 120 – 50 Jesuit plays were
performed annually in the seventeenth century. Since hundreds if
not thousands of spectators viewed each of these performances in
open air theaters, the immense success of Jesuit theater is apparent.
The 1591 curriculum (*ratio studiorum*) of the Society of Jesus
spelled out the purpose of this school drama: "[the theater] would
thus accommodate all actions toward the intended goals of the
Society, to move souls to detest evil mores and depraved habits, to
flee the occasions of sins, to greater desire for virtues, and to
imitate the saints . . ."

Based on her study of South German Jesuit drama, Elida Maria
Szarota divides Jesuit theater into five periods. Conversions formed
the central theme in the plays of the first period (1572 – 1622)
when episodes from Church and secular history furnished the stuff
for dramatic creation. Compositions included plays on the conversions of St Paul and St Augustine, the stories of Constantine the
Great, Julian the Apostate, the Byzantine Emperor Mauritius, and
Charlemagne, cycles of biblical plays on Joseph, the Theophilus
drama on the Virgin Mary and on the demonic pact, and plays on
the life of St Hildegard, Ignatius of Loyola, and Francis Xavier.
The reflection of divine glory in individual decisions and heroic
acts informed the themes of these productions. During the second
period (1623 – 72), confessional and political conflicts, centering
around the events of the Thirty Years' War, predominated in
Jesuit drama. The transience of life became a central motif in the
culture of the High Baroque. Two new themes characterized Jesuit
drama of the third period (1672 – early eighteenth century): one
group of plays portrayed the struggle between Catholics and Turks;
another dealt with familial themes, dispensing Catholic wisdom on
the problems of rearing children, parental love, and conjugal
behavior. The next period (to 1730) saw productions of Jesuit plays
with world historical themes and with portraits of the new
Catholic ideal of the prince. During the last period of Jesuit drama
(1730 – 73), the ideas of the *Aufklärung* began to influence Jesuit
dramaturgy as well.

The enormous success of Jesuit theater cannot be adequately
explained by its anti-Protestant themes, although these were

important in the earlier plays, and in the Jesuit theater of the Rhineland and the northwest. Rather, Jesuit theater emphasized positive values: the need for wisdom, the desirability of learning, and the glory of piety. In *Otto Redivivus* (Act II Scene 1), composed by the Dillingen father Georg Stengel in 1614, it was Catholic learning, not Catholic arms, that was to be the weapon against heresy, as Charles V and Pope Clement VII agreed. A theater sophisticated in staging and production, supported by generous donations from noble patrons, Jesuit drama reflected a self-conscious Jesuit dramaturgy that used the natural world and its artistic representations as media for religious teaching.

To understand the success of Jesuit drama, let us examine one particular production. In 1580, several Jesuits, including the playwright Jacob Pontanus, were entrusted with establishing a college in Augsburg, an imperial city governed by a Catholic patrician regime, but with a large Lutheran populace. During the 1582/2 academic year, the *patres* produced a play about "the Egyptian Joseph," both to demonstrate their pedagogic success and to avoid a direct polemical confrontation with the Lutherans. The *History of the College* and the *Litterae Annuae,* the annual reports submitted to the General in Rome, left a record of the performance. The spectators were of different ages, social status, and confessions. Women also attended and Lutheran schoolteachers were invited and some went; the leading ecclesiastical and civic dignities were in prominent attendance. Staged in the open air, in the courtyard of the college in fact, the play accommodated hundreds of spectators. The Duke of Bavaria, the Fuggers, and noblewomen donated costumes for the production. Seventy-five students took on the roles, including female ones; the performance lasted from noon to four. The plot and summaries of scenes were translated into German in the brochure; Latin, of course, was the language of the actual dialogue. The five-act play told the Bible story of the betrayal of Joseph by his brothers and his eventual return to Jacob. In the first act, the allegorical figure of Envy tempted the brothers to sell Joseph. In the Egyptian acts, there was even a seduction scene, with titillating language about "*pudicum corpus.*" Figures from classical Roman theater and carnival plays appeared in the roles of the "peasant" and "merchant," providing comic relief. The drama conveyed the message of the

Catholic doctrine of free will, guided by Divine Providence, and ultimately responsible for decisions between good and evil acts. *Egyptian Joseph* was a great success: it assured the goodwill of the burghers and attracted Protestant students to the college.

Bavarian and Austrian Jesuit theater assumed increasingly a laudatory function of Wittelsbach and Habsburg piety. In 1578, Munich Jesuits staged *Josaphat* to celebrate the marriage of Duke Wilhelm V to Renata von Lorraine. Many of the performances in Munich were no longer confined to the schoolyard but staged in the Marienplatz. Jesuit theater drew in the city just as the city engulfed the stage. The cast grew from a few dozen to hundreds: in 1575, some 1,000 actors participated in the play *Constantinus Magnus*; in 1577, 1,700 took part in *Hester*. Dramatic characters became allegories for living princes. In 1617, on the coronation of Ferdinand as King of Bohemia, the Jesuits in Graz staged *Joseph the Patriarch* to honor their erstwhile pupil and patron. In the play, "Piety" helped the patriarch Joseph-Ferdinand conquer a lion, the emblem of Bohemia. The play ended in a triumphal procession, in the manner of a Renaissance *trionfo*. The biblical Joseph, as father to the chosen people, was an allegory of the pious patriarch, a figure central to Jesuit political theory, as expressed in *Ten Books of Politics* by Adam Contzen, confessor to Duke Maximilian of Bavaria. The service of Jesuit theater in the cause of the confessional state could not have been more explicit than in the 1635 Ingolstadt play, *Drama of Tilly and Friedland,* that praised the Commander of the League armies, while justifying the recent assassination of Wallenstein.

As a school that taught the sensual experience of truth, the Jesuit stage showed the beauty and excellence of virtue, the ugliness of sin, and the triumph of faith. Historical process and worldly events were the symbols of the history of salvation. A twofold involution dissolved the boundaries between stage and life, actors and spectators: as the whole world became a stage in the moral theology of the Counter-Reformation, with sins and virtues from history informing books entitled *Theatrum mundi* or *Theatrum vitae humanae,* Jesuit theater in turn was a symbolic ritual representing that wider field of symbols, life itself. Just as the stage depicted the lives of saints and sinners, Catholics and heretics, heroes and villains, the spectators were invited to reflect on the "moral histrionics" of their own lives. Protestants were enjoined to convert; and if the reports of the various Jesuit colleges are accurate, Jesuit theater scored occasional victories in securing Protestant conversions. Catholics were encouraged to remain steadfast, prompted by dramatic representations of the martyrdoms of Mary Queen of Scots (staged in 1594 in Ingolstadt), St Thomas More (1631), or the Jesuit missionary Titus in Japan (staged in Augsburg, 1622/9). Jesuit dramaturgy aimed at transcending the boundary between stage and life. The truth of theatrical symbolism was manifest, as when a maid in Bamberg converted, to the glory of the Catholic cause, after she had seen the 1622 performance of *John of Damascus*, convinced of an actual miracle effected on stage, having witnessed the cutting off of John's hand and its healing by the Virgin Mary. Such was the power of living visual sermon on the simple folks. The actors – the most able and socially prominent students – played out roles written for them by the *patres*, in training for their later roles in the larger Catholic world historical drama, as princes, ministers, officials, soldiers, scholars, missionaries, martyrs, and priests.

In Munich and Vienna, Jesuit theater assumed the character of court culture and ceremony, binding the nobility to the Wittelsbach and Habsburg courts. Elaborate costumes, staging, and music became important elements in late Jesuit drama. The *Oratory of Philothea*, performed in 1634 in Munich, was actually an opera rather than a play. In 1653, the Munich Jesuits celebrated "Austrian piety" in a musical drama, on the occasion of a visit by Emperor Ferdinand III. But the function of Jesuit theater in court culture gradually receded in the second half of the seventeenth century, when classical opera, with more explicit allegories of imperial and royal apotheosis, better reflected the courtly fashion for more secular pleasures. Jesuit theater itself took on a more popular character after the Thirty Years' War, as Catholic culture in general reached down to the lower social orders. In 1649, a "Joseph play" was performed in German by the Confraternity of Young Journeymen, a nonacademic Marian congregation attached to the Munich Jesuits.

The Jesuits were the most prominent creators of the theatrical culture of Catholic Germany; other clerical orders readily imitated their success. Most notable among this secondary tradition was the Benedictine Baroque theater in Salzburg. In 1618 the Salzburg

Benedictines founded a gymnasium and wrote schoolplays for their students. In the 1670s, during the height of the Salzburg witch hunt, the monks produced a number of "witchcraft plays."

A number of archbishops were patrons of the Salzburg theater, including Archbishop Max Gandolf, himself a playwright. The golden age of this theatrical tradition was the second half of the seventeenth century, with ancient mythology providing much of the dramatic material. In Bavaria, the cloister theater of Ettal and Rottenbuch exercised an important influence on the Oberammagau Passion Play.

The importance of noble cloisters in the cultural life of Bavaria and Salzburg underscored the poverty of Catholic bourgeois literature. The counterparts to cloister theater, monastic schools, and libraries were the Jesuit colleges, which were urban institutions no doubt, but hardly bourgeois. Book ownership, so characteristic of Protestant civic culture, was highly concentrated and exclusive in Catholic Bavaria. In the eighteenth century, Bavarian monasteries owned over 1.5 million books; even a relatively small cloister such as Polling had over 80,000 books. In comparison, the Court Library in Vienna, the largest in the German-speaking world, stored 170,000 books; Berlin and Göttingen each had 150,000; and the Court Library in Munich had 100,000.

If a poetics of saintly heroism represented the rhetorical trope for the persuasion of the Catholic elite, then a didactics of Christian humility characterized the acculturation of the people. After the mid-seventeenth century, the academic neo-Latin culture of the Counter-Reformation yielded to a greater concern for popular didactics and religious culture for the lower social orders. At the center of this missionary undertaking was the catechism. Like many other aspects of confessional culture, Catholic Germany followed the lead of Protestants; Peter Canisius's catechism, for example, was influenced by Luther's catechisms. In later catechistic endeavors, the Counter-Reformation proved to be more ingenious, employing theater, folksongs, poetry, and sermons to reach down to the lowest social order.

Not surprisingly, the Jesuits were the pioneers. As the seventeenth century progressed, other religious orders took up the missionary work initiated by the Jesuits earlier in the century. The theater, a demonstrated success of Jesuit pedagogy, was used experimentally in Cologne to teach catechism. Between 1625 and 1654, Jesuits in Cologne performed 26 plays in catechism schools for boys and girls. In addition to the basic catechistic material, the Jesuits worked in a good deal of anti-Protestant polemic, depicting Cologne as the defender of the faith and Saxony as the land of heresy. Young children played allegorical roles that represented virtues and sins; other roles were assigned for "Spain," "Lutheranism," "Calvinism," "Church," "Germany," "Austria," "Saxony," "the Society of Jesus," and "Cologne."

Stories of Christian virtues and Catholic miracles conveyed to the simple folk the worldview of the Counter-Reformation. Songs and sermons repeated this message of salvation. German Catholics recognized early the power of songs in spreading the Lutheran movement. The Jesuit Adam Contzen warned his reader that "the hymns of Luther kill more souls than his writings or declamations" and urged Duke Maximilian of Bavaria to promote Catholic songs to defend the faith.

Earlier Catholic hymnals imitated Lutheran success; both Michael Vehe's 1537 hymnals and Johann Leisentrit's 1567 *Spiritual Songs and Psalms* included some well known Protestant hymns. But with the publication of Nikolaus Beuttner's *Catholic Songbook* in 1602, confessional purity became the stand for Catholic musical culture. The Jesuits led the first wave in confessional songwriting: eight *patres* published eleven editions of Latin and German spiritual songs between 1605 and 1633; the famous playwright, Jakob Bidermann, was one of the compilers. Best known of all Jesuit songwriters was Friedrich Spee, courageous in his condemnation of witch hunts. The Jesuitical-ascetic approach came to the fore in the catalogue of good works for sanctification and neighborly life. In the "songs of virtues," Spee praises good works, while condemning heresy:

> Schäm dich; schäm dich, du fauler Christ
> Der du so faul im guten List
> Merck hie der Ketzen List.
> Der dir das Gifft geblasen ein
> Man könn ohn Werck wol selig sein.
>
> You lazy Christian, for shame, for shame
> You who are in good tricks so lame

Hark the heretics' tricks
whose poison has gotten you fixed
one could be holy without works.

In the eucharistic song:

Vns last das Heylthumb, vnd Monstrantz
(Weil Ketzer es verhönen)
Mitt manchem schönen Blumenkrantz
Nach alter andacht krönen.

Let us the sanctuary and monstrance crown
for heretics hold them in derision
with many pretty flower crowns
in good old devotion.

While pre-Reformation songs were revised, Jesuit songwriters like Spee and Georg Vogler composed new lyrics and melodies. Some sang of saints' legends; others praised virtues; yet a third group narrated miracles: all aimed to teach the rudiments of Catholic moral theology, using the vernacular and dialects.

As we have seen, Jesuits dominated the first period of songwriting. After 1625, other religious orders, especially the Observant Franciscans, joined in this musical missionary movement. The Franciscans in Bosnia and Herzegovina, the border zone between Germanic and Slavic cultures, established a seminary for folksongs in order to compose spiritual songs in the manner of folk epics. The establishment of a permanent Jesuit Folk Mission in Tirol in 1718 prompted another period of Jesuit hymn composition that lasted until 1773.

The material for these songs often came from sermons, devotional books, and poetry. The various cultural media repeated essentially the same narrative of salvation. Songs about the Holy Family provided a social model for the simple folk; they could readily identify themselves with grandmother Anna, housefather Joseph, the holy couple, or with the child Jesus. Another cluster of song themes glorified the good: saints, especially of the Society of Jesus, knightly crusaders, and powerful noble patrons of the Church. Jesuits composed many songs of noble saints for the emulation of the lower social orders; they also promoted songs about patron saints of particular social groups, such as those celebrating the peasant saint Isidor of Madrid or St Notbert, patron saint of servants.

Catechistic songs represented musical narratives in verse; story-telling was the central act of religious propagation. It is perhaps difficult for us to imagine the attraction of sermons for Baroque Germany. But it was a time when storytelling provided one of the main forms of entertainment. Sermons differed little in form from storytelling: successful "folk" preachers, such as Abraham a Sancta Clara, built their sermons around saints' legends, exempla, and dramatic narratives of sins and virtues.

The printers of the Counter-Reformation furnished many editions of medieval sermons. Miracle stories, legends of saints, horror tales of the Devil, compiled by Caesarius of Heisterbach and Vincent de Beauvais in the Middle Ages, passed on from the Counter-Reformation to the Baroque through successive generations of compilers – Tilmann van Bredenbach (1526 – 87), Valentin Leucht (1550 – 1619), Martin von Cochem (1634 – 1712), and Abraham a Sancta Clara (1644? – 1709). The title of Leucht's 1614 compilation bespeaks the essence of this narrative transmission – *Viridarium Regium illustrium miraculorum et histo-riarum* – Leucht explained in German that

> [the book] is a royal pleasure garden, wherein God has effected magnificently the most splendid miracles and histories to confirm the true faith, in all past times, in famous places, regarding sacred matters, foremost those of the Holy Eucharist, of Holy pictures, of miraculous apparitions, of liberality, of glorious victories, of the wounds of the pure Virgin Mary and other saints, also of the lofty virtues of virginity, and the freedoms of the clergy, etc.

The "folksy style" of a Martin von Cochem or an Abraham a Sancta Clara agreed in essence with the more erudite Latin devotional works written by Jesuits and Benedictines for the court nobility. As two distinct media, German and Latin conveyed to different social orders the same message of Catholic salvation. These writings can claim little originality: they heaped familiar examples, stories, legends, and morals one after another. The examples are pieces of a larger mosaic: the repetitions create a structural unity to refresh the Catholic folk in a timeless, unchanging unity, one that stretched from the Middle Ages to the eighteenth century. Authority, not originality, was the key in these works.

A bilingual Catholic culture reflected the propagation of faith according to social orders. Catholic Germany created its own neo-Latin literature; and the Bavarian dialect remained the standard vernacular well into the eighteenth century, when Protestant Germany had long led the way in the creation of a national literature. To a certain extent, Latin–German bilingualism also characterized the cultural life of Protestant Germany, as catalogues of the Frankfurt Book Fair clearly reflected. In 1637, for example, 53 per cent of all books published in Germany were in Latin and 45.5 per cent were in German; in 1658, the respective percentages were 58.5 and 39.[3] In Bavaria, the readership for Latin books included educated laity outside of the academic and ruling elites. In 1614, the Jesuit Emmeran Welser, sponsored by Duke Maximilian, established the Golden Alms, a foundation in Munich that distributed free spiritual literature. Similar foundations were later set up in Dillingen, Constance, Lucerne, Würzburg, Cologne, Graz, Tyrnau, and Vienna. The catalogues of the foundation in Munich recorded the sponsorship of both Latin and German books:[4]

Until the late eighteenth century, Catholic Germany possessed a distinctive culture, with a coherent worldview, expressed in its

Table 6.1

	Latin	German	% of Latin
1614	7	32	18
1673	35	133	21
1698	70	229	23
1722	135	300	31
1734	140	346	29
1749	142	320	31
1766	172	369	32

own languages and forms. Undeniably aristocratic, Baroque culture depended on princely and noble patronage for the production of religious drama, the printing of devotional literature, and the erection of magnificent palaces and churches. Further down the social orders, a "popular Baroque" flourished in pilgrimages and sermons, as the Church extended its cultural mission to shape the lives of the common folk. Elements normally associated with bourgeois civility – literacy, book ownership, and family values – appeared submerged in this noble–popular bipolarity. These values seemed more characteristic of the culture of Protestant Germany, where reading and family life became the focus of religious expression.

Luther and Lutheranism

The person, life, thought, and history of Martin Luther comprised the core of a complex legacy for Lutheran Germany. Even during Luther's lifetime, images of the reformer served as propagandist devices to further the cause of the evangelical movement. In popular pamphlets, woodcut illustrations, and broadsheets, Luther appeared as a holy man of God, prophet, and Christian scholar. Often, Luther was depicted with a halo, linking him with a late medieval tradition of saint worship so powerful in the popular imaginations of the early sixteenth century. Three main images of Luther predominated in Lutheran propaganda: the heroic Luther on the world historical stage as presented by Flaccius in *The Magdeburg Centuries* (1559 – 74); the folksy Father Luther figure in Johann Aurifaber's *Conversations of Luther* (*Colloquia Lutheri*) (1566); and the orthodox, doctrinally correct Luther as in Hoe von Hoenegg's sermon cycle *Sanctus Thaumasiander et Triumphator Lutherus* (1610).

The connection between world history and Luther biography dates back to the first decades after the Religious Peace of Augsburg. In 1566, the pastor Johann Mathesius published his sermon cycle as *Luther's Histories* (*Luther Historien*). In 1571/2, Cyriacus Spangenberg, the Gnesiolutheran and early Protestant Church historian, composed *The Cither of Luther* (*Cithara Lutheri*), in which Luther is depicted variously as knight, man of God, prophet, apostle, evangelist, and angel of the Lord.

In addition to narratives of Luther's heroic deeds, delivered in sermon and in print, Luther's life began to appear on stage around the turn of the century. Composed by officials, pastors, and schoolteachers, these Luther-plays aimed to strengthen confessional loyalty during a time when Calvinism was making significant inroads into Protestant–Lutheran territories and when the Counter-Reformation was geared for confrontation. In his 1593 play, *Luther Revived (Lutherus redivivus)*, Zacharias Rivander (1553 – 94), pastor and Superintendent in Bischofswerda, composed a comedy to parody the endlessly irksome eucharistic disputations between Lutherans and Calvinists, and between Gnesiolutherans and Philippists. Rivander looked back to an age of heroic simplicty and religious convictions in Luther's time, in mock contrast to the doctrinal quarrelsomeness of his day. In 1600, Andreas Hartmann, chancery secretary in Merseburg and former subnotary in the Consistory at Dresden, composed a play, *Curriculum Vitae Lutheri,* to dramatize the scenes from Luther's monastic life, his confrontation with the emperor, and his sojourn at the Wartburg.

The centenary of the Reformation inspired many artistic representations of the *"vita Lutheri."* Heinrich Kielmann (1581 – 1649), co-rector of the gymnasium in Stettin, wrote a school comedy of Tetzel's indulgence peddling (*Tetzelocramia. Eine lustige Comoedie/von Johann Tetzels Ablasskram*) to mock the Roman Church. But the most famous schoolplay performed in that centennial year belonged to the pen of Martin Rinckart: *The Christian Knight of Eisleben (Der Eisslebnische Christliche Ritter)* was put on by students of the gymnasium in Luther's birthplace. The celebration of the Reformation centennial was simultaneously a defense against Catholic assaults; Rinckart composed his Luther plays in order to combat the enormous popularity of Jesuit theater. In *The Christian Knight of Eisleben,* Luther is cast in the role of a prophet, predicting the end of the world; and the humble town of Eisleben takes on world historical significance as the true Bethlehem of contemporary Christian Europe. The Lutheran faith had to be defended not only against Jesuits but also against Calvinists. Rinckart traced the "genealogy" of Calvin back through Zwingli to Karlstadt and the radicals of the 1520s whom Luther had roundly condemned. Rinckart planned *The Christian Knight of Eisleben* as one in a cycle of plays on the life of Luther. Two plays, *The Public and Miraculous*

Shaming of the Blasphemer Johann Tezel, and *Confusing Indulgences* commemorated Luther's entry onto the world historical stage. During the 1625 centennial of the Peasants' War, Rinckart composed *Seditious Warning or the Ravages of the War of Rustics,* a play about the life of Thomas Müntzer. Four more plays were planned but never finished: *Magnanimous Luther* on his appearance at the Imperial Diet of Worms, *Luther Desired,* on the pre-history of the Reformation, *August Luther,* and *Luther Triumphant.*

The genre of Luther-biography or hagiography arose in the context of bitter confessional polemics. For Lutheran pastors and schoolteachers, it became imperative to depict a glorified Luther to counter Catholic vilification. The Dominican Johann Cochlaus set the tone for the Counter-Reformation's image of Luther. Catholic broadsheets and legends of the late sixteenth century, printed in both German and Latin to appeal to all social classes, created the image of Luther as magician whose success was due to the devil's help. In the 1579 Jesuit play, *The Triumph of the Archangel Michael,* Luther was conjured from hell and transformed into the figure of Lucifer. Catholic propaganda did not spare Luther's parents: Hans was depicted as a devil and his mother a bathmaid. Consequently, Lutheran counter-propaganda emphasized the human virtues of Luther within the context of an idealized Protestant household. A 1617 broadsheet published in Augsburg shows Hans and Margarethe in dialogue: Luther's parents appear as godfearing, pious, and solid German burghers, praising God's creation and the natural order in human society, namely "the regime of the Household" (*das Haus Regiment*), wherein pious parents could raise pious children. The suggestion that Luther's adult achievements could be traced to his family upbringing appealed to the heart of Lutheran social ethic. Unlike medieval Catholic saints who renounced family to lead lives of severe asceticism, the *vitae Lutheri* emphasized his pious upbringing, his successful education, heroic actions, and peaceful death — virtues inseparable from a solid burgher existence.

Another tradition in the *vita Lutheri* emphasized the hagiographic. The instigator of this genre was the Wittenberg professor Paul Eber (1511 – 69) who had studied with Melanchthon. Beginning with the 1550s, Lutheran calendars were printed to popularize legends and stories of Luther's life. One of the most popular example was Andreas Hondorff's "The Calendar of Saints" (printed in 1573 and 87):

> That is: A special daily House and Church History/ in which the sacred teachings and the lives, witnessing and sufferings of martyrs are described and put into order in the common calendar throughout the year.

In the calendar, Luther appears in the company of saints and Protestant martyrs; his life stories are introduced at places reserved for the saint of the day.

In early modern Germany, there clearly existed a Luther-cult in Protestantism. Promoted by the leaders of the Lutheran Church, Luther was represented as a prophet, holy man, and instrument of God. Legends of Luther's life persisted well into the nineteenth century. Some stories sounded similar to Catholic legends of saints' lives. The famous story of Luther's confrontation with the devil, when the bible translator threw an ink-pot at Satan, inspired generations of later visitors to view the ink stain in Luther's study on the Wartburg. Another tradition associated incombustibility with pictures of Luther and the house of his birth, a conscious counter, no doubt, to Catholic folk customs of burning Luther and his wife Katherina in effigy. The magical notions attached to the Luther-cult, as R. W. Scribner has suggested, represented the displacement of late medieval religious ideas in early modern Lutheranism, and indicate a historical continuity often overlooked.

One of the greatest cultural achievements of the Lutheran Reformation was the creation of a rich musical tradition. Luther himself wrote many new verses to traditional hymnal melodies. Hymn singing, in fact, became a moving and powerful experience in communicating the evangelical messages. In congregations, hymn singing reinforced the collective solidarity of established evangelical communities, fortifying members in their faith, as Luther's famous hymn, *A Mighty Fortress is our God,* testifies eloquently. In private, hymn singing expressed individual piety, often in the face of Catholic repression, as was the case with a citizen in Münster, denounced and fined for singing Lutheran hymns in his garden after the restoration of the Catholic regime. In any event, the hymn became an indispensable form of personal piety, the hymnal and hymn singing symbols of Lutheran confessional identity.

Spiritual singing in Lutheran Germany fell under two categories: church hymnals and private devotional songs. The former was regulated by ecclesiastical authorities for fear of doctrinal contamination. In 1543 Luther himself warned against "false hymns," composed by "false masters," inspired by the devil:

> Viel falscher meister itzt Lieder tichten
> Sihe dich für, und lern sie recht richten
> Wo Gott hin bawet sein kirch und sein wort
> Da wil der Teuffel sein mit trug und mord.

> Many a false master now writes a song
> Take heed, and judge them right or wrong
> Where God His Church and Word builds
> The Devil his with tricks and murder fills.

Up to the early eighteenth century, numerous church ordinances and reports warned against the singing of new hymns. Church hymnals in Lutheran Germany remained constant and geared to a fixed canon of hymns approved by Luther.

The primary function of church hymns was to consolidate a sense of confessional identity. In addition to earlier anti-papal hymns, others directed at Calvinism enriched the repertoire in the second half of the sixteenth century. In 1585, for example, to commemorate the fiftieth anniversary of the introduction of the Reformation in Pomerania, a hymn expressed Lutheran hatred for Calvinism:[5]

> Der Calvinisten Tück und Rank
> Lass Herr gehen den Krebsgang
> Ihr arge List gar nie besteh
> Und ihr Rat wie der Schnee vergeh,
> Dass deine liebe Christenheit,
> Dich lob in alle Ewigkeit.

> Malice and tendril of the Calvinists
> May the Lord make retrograde
> Their wicked ruse may not sustain
> And their counsel melt away like snow,
> So that thy beloved Christianity,
> May praise thee in all eternity.

Or, in the explicit words of Cyriacus Spangenberg (1528 – 1604), who edited and commented on Luther's hymns, "children sing songs against the two archenemies of Christ and his Holy Church." The one, papacy, Spangenberg equated with "the whole Antichrist gang of papist bishops, cardinals, monks, priests and nuns, and...all seducers of false teachings: Interimists, Adiaphorists, Sacrament-enthusiasts, Anabaptists, Calvinists, Osianderists, Schwenckfeldians, Stancavisten, Servetians, Sabbathers, Davidites, Majorites, Synergists, etc..." The other, the Turks, included "all tyrants...who opposed the open truth of the Gospel with violence."

Most Lutheran congregations, it seems, did not possess printed hymnals. Many parishioners could not read music or were illiterate; churches often lacked money for organs. In practice, choirs led in singing, followed by the congregation. The rather limited methods of musical expression in the Lutheran service belie a rich musical culture in private devotion. Whereas church hymns excluded all but doctrinal purity, private spiritual songs satisfied individual needs for private, domestic devotion.

In Lutheran Germany chamber music scores and household songbooks (*Hausgesangbücher*) of motets were often published together with devotional literature. Spiritual songs, together with catechism and family prayers, occupied a central place in Lutheran household worship (*Hausandacht*), the family devotion so lovingly prescribed by Luther and a multitude of devotional tracts. The first Lutheran house songbook, *A Handbook* (*Enchiridion oder eyn Handbuchlein*), was published in Erfurt in 1524. Sometimes, church hymns were transposed for house songbooks. Early songbooks were written for solo voices, to be accompanied by recorders or pipes. But by the late sixteenth century, private singing had given rise to a rich chamber music culture, as witnessed by the publication of Leonhard Lechner's *New German Songs for Five and Four Voices* (Nuremberg, 1582). The songs told of love of the eucharist and the Passion of Christ; their themes reflected the larger domestication of piety, characteristic of the culture of Lutheran Germany. During the seventeenth century, religious music played a crucial role in civic life. Musical literacy came to be expected of the educated Lutheran burgher. The hymns of Paul Gebhardt and the music of Heinrich Schütz in the seventeenth century laid the foundation for the glorious compositions of a Johann Sebastian Bach.

The visual arts also served as an early ally of the evangelical movement. Lucas Cranach the Elder and Younger, father and son, painted portraits of Luther and supporters of the Reformation. Paintings, engravings, and woodcuts from their workshops, and those of other painters, created a heroic Reformation iconography, with themes depicting the papal Antichrist, and allegories of Lutheran doctrines of justification and grace. In fact, the visual arts remained an important expression of Lutheranism well into the seventeenth century, as seen in the many artistic objects created for churches, cemeteries, castles, town halls, and private houses. Much of this art work has been destroyed over the centuries, thus creating obstacles for historians in reconstructing the context of artistic creation and representation. But recent scholarship has shown the tremendous significance the visual arts had for the self-expression of Lutheran Germany: Robert Scribner has studied the woodcuts of the early Reformation movement and analyzed the semiotics of pictorial communication; Kristin Zapalac has examined representations of judgment scenes in late medieval and Reformation Germany, with particular reference to Lutheran Regensburg, to argue for a magisterial self-consciousness of paternal good government; and Hartmut Mai has looked at ecclesiastical paintings in Saxony–Thuringia as expressions of Lutheran doctrines.

The question of literacy in Lutheranism suggests its essential character as bourgeois culture. Our knowledge of literacy, book-ownership, and reading is still fragmentary, but recent research points to rewarding avenues of scholarship. Erdmann Weyrauch has studied private book ownership in Lutheran Brunswick and Kitzingen in the sixteenth and seventeenth centuries. His conclusions suggest widespread book ownership among the middle strata of urban society. A sample of 48 Brunswickers who left behind books in their estates between 1600 and 1660 included 15 brewers, 14 merchants, 13 artisans, 3 soldiers, 2 innkeepers, and 1 apothecary. Together they owned 1,034 books (12 had 5; 16 had 6 – 20 books; 20 had 21 – 50; and one smith had 122 books). In

Kitzingen, 55 burghers bequeathed books; they included 38 artisans (7 vintners), 7 civic officials, 4 innkeepers, 3 merchants, and 2 apothecaries. Their libraries came to 691 books. Theology and piety were the favorite subjects (50.6 per cent of Brunswick books and 64.5 per cent of Kitzingen titles): actual reading matter included bibles, sermons, prayer books, and catechisms; at least 13.5 per cent of the Brunswick titles and 12.8 per cent of the Kitzingen theological titles were by Luther. Among non-religious books, history, medicine, classical texts, handbooks, and guidebooks formed the major categories.

The vast array of titles and sheer diversity of subjects, as exemplified by books published in Strasbourg between 1480 and 1599, should alert us to the danger of obfuscating the boundaries between religious and secular cultures. There were, however, several categories of books distinctive of Lutheran Germany: readings for girls, prophetic literature, and books of wonders (*Wunderbücher*). Books written for girls reflected Luther's concern for their education. Most titles were clearly intended for curricular use in girls' schools, such as Johann Agricola's 100 catechismic questions for the German Girls' School in Eisleben (1528), one of the first publications in this genre. Another example was Andreas Musculus's 1569 compilation of biblical sayings in a text for the Girls' School in Erfurt. Other titles expounded on feminine virtues for young Christian women. Examples included *The Little Flower Wreath of Honor for Christian Girls* (Prague, 1581), written by Lucas Martin, that "illustrates and explains all their virtues by little wreaths of flowers." Another title, Christoph Heitfeld's *Mirror of Godliness for Girls* (1602), interpreted Luther's *Little Catechism* to inculcate Lutheran ideals of femininity. Themes are rather predictable in this genre: the books praised "feminine" virtues of humility, chastity, obedience, and simplicity, or they prepared young women for marriage. Gender roles overlapped to a great extent in Lutheran and Catholic "feminine literature," with the notable emphasis on the pre-eminent virtue of chastity in the devotional literature of the Counter-Reformation. As a rule, the genre was created by men – pastors and schoolteachers, and served as a counterpart to the genre of "House Father Books," composed for the benefit of the Lutheran paterfamilias.

A unique feature of Lutheranism was its apocalyptic fervor. The preoccupation with prophecy reflected more than eschatological differences between the Lutherans on the one hand, and Catholics and Calvinists on the other. Interest in "last things" provided much of the energy for the initial evangelical movement; numerous prophecies and prophets sustained this apocalyptic fervor in Lutheran Germany into the early seventeenth century.

Luther himself was deeply interested in eschatology. He and his contemporaries understood their age as the last in human history. The death of the reformer and the imposition of the Interim in the late 1540s appeared as the long-awaited signs of the apocalypse, when the Antichrist would reign temporarily over the godly, until their deliverance by the Second Coming of Christ. In the 1550s, collections of prophecies by Luther appeared regularly in print. In 1557 Peter Glasner of Dresden published 120 of the reformer's prophecies; by the 1574 edition, the number of prophecies had grown to 200. Biblical and ancient prophecies also fueled Lutheran eschatological fervor. In his 1556 publication, *A Catalogue of Testimonies to the Truth*, Flaccius enlisted 400 historical witnesses in his confessional camp, with alleged prophecies against the errors of the papacy. Still another sign of the imminent end was nature herself, thus all unnatural or supernatural phenomena took on apocalyptic meaning. Between 1556 and 1567, Job Fincel, Professor of Philosophy at Wittenberg, published a series of three lengthy treatises on miraculous signs.

The failure of Lutheran education and church discipline to mold a people in the image of the pastors further deepened this apocalyptic pessimism in the second half of the sixteenth century. A mood of decline, an *Untergangstimmung*, permeated the flood of popular prophetic literature: the people refused Christian discipline; the Turks grew ever stronger; forces of the Antichrist battled beleaguered Christianity in the guises of papacy, Calvinists, and dissenters. Interest in prophetic reckoning reached its peak around the turn of the century: scholars and pastors attempted to correlate history and prophecy; astronomers tried to predict the exact end of the world. Amidst various conjectures and general confusion, the ecclesiastical establishment was particularly alarmed by popular apocalyptic fervor. Young girls and teenagers in Lutheran Germany

saw angels and fortold the future. Local pastors committed these
stories and prophecies to print, inspiring, perhaps, more vivid
imaginations. Self-proclaimed prophets roamed around, winning
the confidence even of Lutheran pastors. In 1606, Noah Kalb, a
baker in Ulm, claimed in a revelation that he was indeed Noah the
prophet, at first beguiling the local pastors until the magistrates
had him executed. In Nuremberg, a man called Philipp Ziegler
was inspired by Rosicrucian writings to declare himself a spiritual
monarch. An uncle and nephew, Esaias Stiefel (d. 1627) and
Ezechiel Meth (d. 1640), became radical spiritualists in Thuringia,
targets of repression by Lutheran authorities. For the ecclesiastical
establishment and magistrates, these events reminded them of the
radicalism of the early Reformation. The first decade of the Thirty
Years' War saw the last effervescence of popular apocalypticism.
The tide, however, had turned against apocalypticism, at least in
official Lutheran Germany. In 1634, Nicolaus Hunnius wrote *A
Comprehensive Account of the New Prophets*, in which he lambasted the
popular enthusiasm for prophecies. After mid-century, prophecy
survived as a minor current in the popular religious culture of
Lutheran Germany. The parting of ways between learned and
popular culture can be traced in writings on comets. The late
sixteenth and early seventeenth centuries witnessed the height of
this genre, in which the appearance of a comet was interpreted as
an apocalyptical sign. Until the 1630s, both popular pamphlets
and learned treatises shared in the same moralistic–didactic discourse. Thereafter, learned treatises became more astronomical and
"scientific," whereas popular tracts still retained their moralistic
tone.

Schools

Education was one of the most important instruments of enforcing
confessional conformity. Luther exhorted princes and magistrates
to establish schools for teaching boys and girls the rudiments of
Christian doctrines, for inculcating discipline, piety, and morality,
and for shaping model Christian subjects. When the Reformation
took hold, evangelical ordinances were promulgated, establishing
schools to plant deep roots of evangelical reform. Gerald Strauss
has recently suggested the limitations of the Lutheran pedagogic

reform. He argues that the initial enthusiasm for spontaneous moral regeneration gave way to a pessimistic view of the incorrigibility of human nature. Hence, control, discipline, and authority became the cornerstone of "Luther's house of learning." A few scholars have questioned this conclusion, but the evidence, compiled by Strauss from school ordinances and visitations, clearly points to the use of education for enforcing confessional conformity.

One can safely argue that institutionalized education was in essence confessional education. The catechisms of the different churches, together with various devotional and polemical material, constituted the core of the primary school curriculum. The 1593 ordinance for the Girls' School in Lutheran Göttingen illustrates the fundamentally confessional nature of primary education. Drawn up by pastor Theodor Fabricius and the clerical ministry of the city council, the ordinance governed the administration and curriculum of the school, attended by girls between the ages of 6 and 12. The purpose of the school, as the ordinance specifies, is

> to initiate and hold girls in propriety (*zucht*) and the fear of God. To fear God, they must learn their catechism, beautiful psalms, sayings, and other fine Christian and holy songs and little prayers, so that they can both read and recite them. For propriety, they must learn to love God's Word, to honor their parents, to guard themselves against disobedience, improper talk and gestures, the temptation to steal and lie, and to turn indolence into work, reading, writing, sewing, in order they are kept busy and forget thereby other frivolities . . .

Judging by the pedagogic principles of our time, Lutheran education appears repressive. Nonetheless, its achievements were considerable. Lutheran Germany enjoyed a higher rate of literacy than Catholic Germany, and provided education for broader segments of society than Catholic Germany, with its emphasis on the education of the elites. Primary education in Augsburg serves as an example. In 1623, there were 20 Protestant and 4 Catholic schoolmasters. In total, they taught 1,550 Protestant children (826 boys and 724 girls) and 240 Catholic pupils (118 boys and 122 girls). The Catholic–Protestant student ratio was 1:6, much lower than the proportion of Catholic inhabitants (c. one-quarter of the population). The territorial states and cities in the Protestant north spent more money on primary education than for example, Catholic Bavaria, in spite of the perennial complaint of Protestant schoolmasters for higher pay. Indeed, by comparison with primary education in Bavaria, Protestant schools reached wider segments of society and established the foundations for a broad reading public in the eighteenth century.

The first Bavarian school ordinance, promulgated by Duke Albrecht V in 1569, aimed at eradicating Lutheran texts and schoolmasters from the territory. The central bureaucracy in Munich took over supervision of primary education from the estates, but left the communities to raise funds for the schools. Confessional conformity was the guide of Bavarian education. To that purpose, the dukes ordered the clergy to supervise local schoolmasters and instructed the *Rentmeister* (fiscal officials) to include in their *Umritt* reports, when they travelled around in their districts, descriptions of pedagogic conformity in their district. Still, at the end of the sixteenth century, many schoolmasters were still using Lutheran texts. The failure of control was due in large measure to the state neglect of primary education. Ducal patronage showered the Jesuit colleges with money and favors, but funds were not forthcoming for the education of the simple folk. Bavarian education divided sharply between Latin and German schools, a gulf that separated the elites and folk of the Counter-Reformation state. In the 1613 instruction to the Rentmeister and in the 1616 *Landrecht* (territorial laws), Duke Maximilian ordered a reduction in the number of German schools because the state lacked sufficient personnel for effective control of all existing ones. The estates bitterly opposed this proposal, arguing that "one who could neither read nor write his mother tongue was as schooled as a dead man."

Unlike Lutheran schoolmasters, many of whom had some university training, Bavarian schoolmasters were recruited mainly from the lower strata. Most had to work at another job to supplement their meager income. The situation was bleak. In 1643, the one Latin and two German schoolmasters in Wasserburg all took on other employment, as choir master, notary, and clerk. Of 344 children between the ages of 5 and 13, only 148 (43 per cent) received any instruction. Educational institutions for girls existed only for the elites in the cities. After the Thirty Years' War, several convent schools were founded in Munich to accommodate girls from elite civic families and the nobility. Otherwise, there seem to have been no formal opportunities for the education of girls. The school ordinances of Landsberg (1612) and Pfaffenhofen (1656) both ignored education for girls.

In 1659, Elector Ferdinand Maria replaced the 1569 school ordinance. With slight modifications, it was renewed in 1681, 1738, and governed Bavarian folk education until the late eighteenth century. Confessional vigilance remained the overriding goal: schoolmasters were to give Sunday catechism classes and required to report to the local clergy the religious progress of their pupils and their family background; only Peter Canisius's catechism, and not Protestant material, could be used for instruction. In the vision of the Bavarian state, its subjects would grow up in "truthfulness, honor, reserve, gentility, obedience, and humility"; the duty of the schoolmasters, hence, was to punish "frivolity, whim, disobedience, lying, and malicious gossip." The resources available to the state for this ambitious mission of "civilizing" the vulgar folk proved wholly inadequate. By the eighteenth century, in the Catholic Aufklärung, there was an awareness that Catholic primary education lagged far behind Protestant Germany. The educational reforms of Bavaria and Austria in the Enlightenment finally substituted literacy and prosperity for the entrenched goals of confessional control.

Universities

As a result of the Reformation, German universities became incorporated into the confessional territorial states and suffered, in the process, a gradual erosion of their former corporate autonomy and international reputation. From funding, faculty appointment, lectures and student activities to publishing, princes and their officials intruded more and more into institutions of higher learning, turning the medieval *universitas* into a regional institution for the training of clerics, schoolteachers, and officials to staff the bureaucracies of the territorial states. In their respective territories, professors of theology specified doctrinal precisions for state churches, jurists composed legal opinions for princes, and students prepared for careers in the ecclesiastical and government bureaucracies.

As definitions of confessional orthodoxy turned more precise, the universities became confessional institutions of the territorial state. In Lutheran Germany, the pre-eminence of Wittenberg, the bastion of the Reformation, fell victim to intra-confessional disputes after the death of Luther. Melanchthon and his followers dominated the theology faculties of Wittenberg and Leipzig. To counter the influence of the Philippists, Moritz of Saxony founded a university in Jena in 1547, and called Flaccius to the chair of theology. During the 1560s and 1570s, Jena witnessed bitter academic fights between Philippists and Gnesiolutherans. In the end, orthodoxy triumphed. In the second half of the sixteenth century, Wittenberg and Jena represented rival camps in Lutheran Germany, bastions of Philippism and orthodoxy, respectively. Published as an alternative to the Wittenberg edition of Luther's writings, the twelve volume Jena edition of the *Works of Luther* (1555 – 8) reflected orthodox exegesis and became the standard edition for the Lutheran Church after the demise of Philippism. As a territorial university, Jena trained officials and pastors for Saxony–Weimar, and boasted among its distinguished faculty in the seventeenth century the theologian Georg Calixt (1586 – 1656) and the physician-historian and polymath Hermann Conring (1606 – 81).

In the German southwest, Tübingen University was the most important academic institution for the consolidation of Lutheran orthodoxy. Jakob Andreae (1528 – 90), chancellor of the university, was the prime mover behind the Formula of Concord. Together with the consistory, the theology faculty exercised censorship over the writings and sermons of the Württemberg clergy. For example in the early seventeenth century the pansophist and alchemical movement in Württemberg, centered around the writings and person of Johann Valentin Andreae (1586 – 1654), came under the suspicion of the university theologians. In 1622 the theologians denounced Eberhard Wild, printer in Tübingen. A search turned up mystical and Schwenckfeldian tracts; Wild was fined 200 gulden and the books were confiscated. In their zeal to combat Catholicism and heresy, Tübingen theologians exceeded at times the limit set by the dukes and the consistory in Stuttgart.

Lucas Osiander the Younger (1571 – 1638), appointed Professor of Theology in 1619, specialized in anti-Jesuit polemics. The mystics within the Lutheran Church presented the theologians with another target. Osiander and Theodor Thumm (1586 – 1630), also Professor of Theology, published treatises that attacked Valentin Weigel and Johann Arndt. But when the polemical zest of the Tübingen professors threatened to provoke a rift within the ranks of Lutheran orthodoxy in 1619, the consistory intervened and ordered Osiander and Thumm to end their heated theological debate with Balthasar Mentzer, theologian at the newly founded University of Giessen, another stronghold of Lutheran orthodoxy. Thumm got himself into more trouble in 1625 when his attacks against the Dillingen and Ingolstadt Jesuits included criticisms of the Spanish Habsburgs. Ferdinand II complained to Duke Johann Friedrich of Württemberg who, to placate the emperor, put Thumm under temporary arrest, fined him, and confiscated his books. Even in the cause of confessional struggles, professors of the territorial universities were on a short leash.

The political subservience of the university to the confessionalized territorial state was perhaps nowhere clearer than the Lutheran university at Helmstedt in Lower Saxony. Founded by Duke Julius of Brunswick–Wolfenbüttel in 1576, Helmstedt trained generations of pastors and officials for the Guelf Saxon territories. In 1578, Duke Julius, a Protestant, allowed two sons to take Catholic orders in preparation for gaining lucrative episcopal dignities. Sharply criticized by other Lutheran princes for his "betrayal" of the Reformation, Julius refused to recognize the Formula of Concord and favored theologians who justified princely power at the expense of confessional conscience. Between 1580 and 1640, a distinct school of Helmstedt theology developed, under the guiding intellect of Georg Calixt, appointed Professor of Theology in 1614, a school that opposed prevailing Lutheran orthodoxy. On one hand, Calixtinism advocated the supremacy of princely power in theological and ecclesiastical affairs, on the other, it criticized the mystical and emotional elements in Lutheranism, arguing from the posture of academic logic and rationality. Only theologians of the "Calixt School" received appointments in the Lower Saxon principalities of the Guelf line. Helmstedt represented one end of the spectrum of Lutheran theology, where political subservience to the prince constituted the central idea of intellectual discourse.

The increasingly provincial outlook of the confessional university is best illustrated by the history of the theological faculty at Lutheran Marburg, a university founded by Landgrave Philip of Hesse in 1531 as a rival institution to Erfurt. Born before the Reformation, the first generation of theologians taught from 1527 to 1540; they had a diverse and cosmopolitan outlook, and maintained close ties to Wittenberg. But the second generation of theologians, born between 1510 and 1540, entered teaching between 1540 and 1575, were already all trained by a territorial university (*Landesuniversität*). Most had studied only at Marburg, and the former intellectual connection to Wittenberg was lost. By the third generation, born around mid-century and reaching the professoriat in the last quarter of the century, all except one (Aegidius Hunnius) were Hessians. Most of the third generation theologians moved to Giessen in 1605, when Marburg became a Calvinist university; and among these Balthasar Mentzer, as we have seen, enjoyed the widest recognition for his numerous polemical publications.

The history of Catholic higher education in Counter-Reformation Germany reads like the success story of the Jesuits. Shortly after the Society had established itself in the Empire, the fathers aimed to take over the theological and philosophical faculties of all remaining Catholic universities, while leaving the medical and law

Table 6.2

Universities	Takeover of Faculties		Takeover of Chairs	
	Philosophy	Theology	Philosophy	Theology
1549 Ingolstadt	x (1585)			2
1556 Cologne				1
1561 Trier	x	x		
1562 Mainz	x	x		
1582 Würzburg	x	x		
1620 Freiburg	x			3
1628 Erfurt				1
1629 Heidelberg	x	x		

Source: Adapted from Karl Hengst, *Jesuiten an Universitäten und Jesuitenuniversitäten. Zur Geschichte der Universitäten in der Oberdeutschen und Rheinischen Provinz der Gesellschaft Jesu im Zeitalter der konfessionellen Auseinandersetzung* (Paderborn, 1981), 298.

faculties in the hands of laymen. Table 6.2 demonstrates their ubiquitous presence in Catholic universities.

In addition to their presence at well-established universities, the Jesuits, with the generous support of their princely patrons, also founded new universities. These new "Jesuit universities," with only two of the four traditional faculties (theology and philosophy), stood directly under the General in Rome but functioned, in effect, as territorial universities. They could be found in Paderborn (1616), Molsheim (1618), Osnabrück (1632), and Bamberg (1648). The university at Dillingen was transformed into a Jesuit institution in 1563, but the elevation of the Jesuit College in Münster to a university never came about. In the German-speaking lands of Central Europe, Jesuit professors taught at every Catholic university. Where they failed to take over entire faculties, due to the opposition of lay scholars or other religious orders, the Jesuits still ensured they had a decisive influence, by founding gymnasia and thereby educating new generations of scholars who might one day teach at the universities.

Calvinist higher education achieved intellectual distinction for its close ties to foreign universities. Nevertheless, the history of Calvinist universities and academies was still a part of the history of the Calvinist territorial state. Heidelberg, the leading Calvinist university of the sixteenth century, lost its pre-eminence when the Spanish conquest of the Palatinate resulted in a purge of the faculty. Among the remaining Calvinist academies, Herborn clearly enjoyed the greatest prestige.

Founded in 1584 as the pinnacle of a territorial system of Calvinist education, Herborn owed its constitution and finances to Johann VI, Count of Nassau–Dillenburg. The academy functioned, from the beginning, as a Calvinist *Landesuniversität*. When Calvinists left the universities of Marburg in 1605 and Heidelberg in 1621, Herborn became, by default, the leading German Calvinist institution of higher learning in the seventeenth century. Several distinguished scholars taught on the faculty during Herborn's heyday from 1584 – 1629: the theologian Kaspar Olevian, lured away from Heidelberg, the philosophy professor Johann Piscator, crucial in the Ramus-reception in Germany, Johann Althusius, later syndic of Emden and author of a major work on federative politics, and Johann Alsted, whose seven-volume encyclopedia of knowledge paved the way for much later scholarship.

Herborn professors fought in the front lines of the intellectual battle between confessions. Students from the Rhineland and Bohemia attended Herborn. Many Bohemian noblemen in the service of the Winter King in 1620 had attended Herborn, as did Amos Comenius, who witnessed the subjugation of his beloved land by the troops of the emperor and the Catholic League. In the summer of 1629, following the publication of the Edict of Restitution by Ferdinand II, the faculties of law and philosophy at Herborn turned into centers of Calvinist intellectual resistance against the Counter-Reformation. Under Johann Mattaeus and Johann Heinrich Bisterfeld, professors at Herborn, many academic disputations expounded on Calvinist theories of tyrannicide. Herborn suffered much during the Thirty Years' War, when the county of Nassau was devastated by warfare, and it never quite recovered its former academic reputation after 1650.

Herborn's major contribution was in training pastors and officials for the calvinization of the Wetterau counties. Not only did Herborn represent the apex of a new system of *Volksschulen* (German schools, as opposed to the Latin-speaking gymnasia) in Nassau, established by Count Johann to discipline his subjects, its students — sons of professors, chancery officials, and pastors — provided the personnel for the spread of the Second Reformation in the Wetterau.

7
The moral police

As princes and magistrates displaced the Catholic clergy in reforming the new Protestant churches, they also inherited increased power and responsibility to police the morality of the common people, a task that authorities had been arrogating to themselves well before the Reformation. With the religious division of the empire, attempts to enforce confessional uniformity by the many territorial rulers intensified the effort to enforce order in society and in the household. Thus one of the consequences of the Reformation and Counter-Reformation was the imposition of social discipline by the early modern state, in a process which displayed a parallel development in Lutheran, Catholic, and Calvinist territories. This official view of religiosity and morality is best summed up in an anonymous treatise, *On the Office of the Christian Magistrates*, published in 1586 in Calvinist Nassau, but applicable in essence to all three major confessions. The author advanced the idea of a double contract, between God and the Chosen People, and between the Ruler and the People. Hence the Ruler was both a godly magistrate and a servant of God. "A magistrate," the treatise declares, "is a person whom God has appointed to preside over his people on earth, in order he might oversee the execution of just laws, and in order that piety, justice, and peace are upheld among them." The three orders in a Christian society, according to the author, consisted of the church, the household, and the public office (*ecclesia, oeconomia, politia*).

In his Lutheran, Calvinist, and Catholic guises, the Christian magistrate issued numerous statutes and mandates regulating the household: some prescribed the varieties of sexual deviancy and their punishments; others enjoined family members to uphold the patriarchal household; many condemned luxury at weddings, baptisms, and burials; still others decried magical healings, blasphemies, and swearing; not a few upheld the correct faith and practice. By the second half of the sixteenth century, all the institutions of this moral regime were in place. The Lutheran territories had their consistory courts, marriage courts, and regular parish visitations; the Catholic states created clerical councils and instituted visitations; the Calvinist states and communities resorted to moral supervision by the elders and preachers in synodal, provincial, and class meetings. In spite of considerable differences, these institutions functioned in essentially similar ways. Staffed by a mixed secular–clerical personnel, they had a twofold mission: the enforcement of confessional conformity against external groups and the supervision of moral conduct internally.

In analyzing this process of social and moral disciplining, a distinction must be made between state sanctions and church discipline. Except for libertines and free-thinkers, all Christians believed in maintaining a certain degree of church discipline. Separatist communities persecuted by the state, in fact, upheld the strictest discipline, as did communal congregations, such as Württemberg pietists and Emden Calvinists. Internal church discipline was not synonymous with state coercion. Nevertheless, in territorial states, the official church and the government worked hand-in-glove in enforcing moral and social discipline through legislations and sanctions. Confessionalization brought together state coercion and church discipline, and created an intersection between the history of sin and the history of criminalization.

A vast amount of records generated by these institutions of the moral regime has survived: they document the slow march of official confessions at the expense of popular religion and demonstrate, to a surprising extent, widespread and tenacious popular resistance to the imposition of state control. Historians have mined some of these documents to reconstruct the process of confessionalization or to study the nature of popular religion. But until more systematic investigations are undertaken, it is impossible to generalize from case studies about the degree to which the state succeeded in imposing a moral regime on its subjects. I have selected from numerous local studies several examples to illustrate this process of social disciplining. By describing the institutions of the moral police as they actually worked, I hope to indicate both the successes and limitations of the early modern confessional state in imposing official religion and to compare the effectiveness of Calvinism, Lutheranism, and Counter-Reformation Catholicism as instruments of social control.

Calvinist church discipline

Moral discipline was most effectively enforced among urban congregational Calvinist communities, due to a high degree of internal cohesion and communal participation in the supervision. The urban communities of Calvinist Rhineland and Emden demonstrated a high degree of moral supervision by the presbyters, as well as self-discipline and censure by the church members themselves.

The Calvinist movement spread to the East Friesian seaport of Emden in the 1550s. A massive influx of Dutch Calvinist refugees during the early phases of the Netherlands uprising turned this city into a "German Geneva." Although they formed a powerful community, the Calvinists never dominated city politics the way their coreligionists did in Geneva. The Reformed Church existed side by side with Lutheran and Anabaptist communities. In the mid-sixteenth century, a small group of Christians fluctuated between the Anabaptist and Calvinist communities. Records of the Calvinist congregation are extant from the mid-1550s and are being systematically analyzed by Heinz Schilling to study the impact of Calvinist church discipline on the shaping of bourgeois morality.

The presbytery consisted of pastors and elders elected by the community. In weekly sessions, the leaders of the church discussed a wide variety of subjects, as reflected in the minutes. Activities of the presbytery fell into four categories:

1 A huge amount of energy was absorbed by matters external to the community concerning politics, secular government, the economy, work, social behavior of church members, contact with other Protestant communities, and general counseling.
2 Consultation over welfare, health, marital, and familial affairs constituted another category of activity.

3 Items proper to the Reformed Church included the administration of the community, the election of elders, the calling of pastors, theological controversies, book censorship, and relationship with other Calvinist communities.

4 Under church discipline, the presbytery discussed doctrinal deviancy among members, their public and private behavior, violence and strife, proper codes of dress and entertainment, familial conflicts, and sexual deviancy.

The relative importance of these four categories of activity changed over time. In the mid-sixteenth century, when the community was consolidating itself, problems of doctrinal orthodoxy and the public behavior of church members occupied the greatest attention of pastors and elders. Surprisingly, cases of sexual misconduct were relatively few, comprising only 8 per cent of all individual items of business during 1557 – 62. The proportion increased substantially after the 1650s and comprised the majority of items of church discipline in the eighteenth century. It seemed that the presbyters punished men on account of prostitution and marital infidelity with more frequency in the sixteenth, and unwed mothers almost exclusively by the early eighteenth century.

While the presbytery functioned as an institution of moral control, it would be misleading to emphasize only its repressive character, at least in the sixteenth century. Church members voluntarily accepted discipline. In many cases, the community brought up charges of immoral conduct and pressured the presbyters to take action. Fundamental to the success of the Calvinist moral regime, at least in freely constituted congregations, was its underlying character as a community of worship. Thus, admittance to communion depended on the moral rectitude of the individual church member, a condition whose responsibility lay with the individual primarily, with the community exercising secondary supervision. The presbytery also functioned as a kind of social agency: it helped settle marital disputes; it punished male householders for sexually exploiting their maidservants; it prescribed moral economic conduct; it censored verbal and physical violence among church members; and distributed welfare to the needy. The element of repression seemed to have been more characteristic after the mid-seventeenth century, when the Emden presbytery identified sexual offenses as a major target of censor.

The relative degrees of repression and voluntary self-discipline have to be measured against the relationship between the Calvinist communities and the state. In the Duchy of Jülich–Cleve, the reformed churches, originally voluntarily constituted, became in the course of the seventeenth century more integrated into the Brandenburg state. The records of the reformed church show an increasing cooperation between state coercion and church discipline.

For the Calvinist communities in the Rhineland, there are almost continuous records of the meetings of the various church bodies from the seventeenth century: the communal meetings, the "classes" conventions, the provincial synods, and the general synods. In the Rhineland, the individual Calvinist communities were first organized in synods in the late sixteenth century (Jülich, 1570; Cleve, 1572; Berg, 1589); in 1610 a general synod met in Duisburg, to which the County of Mark joined the following year.

Let us examine the enforcement of confessional and social discipline as reflected in the records of the provincial synod of Cleve. In 1609, on the eve of the Jülich-Cleve succession crisis, the division of parish control in Cleve was as follows:[1]

Catholics: 75 parishes, 39 cloisters, 32 chapels

Calvinists: 14 parishes, 15 chapels/housechapels

Lutherans: 9 parishes, 7 chapels/housechapels

For the Calvinist Church, the communities in Cleve were divided into three "classes" – Duisburg, Cleve, and Wesel. The local presbyters, called *"consistorium,"* sent their preachers and elders to the "class convention" which decided on matters unresolved at the community level. The pattern of delegation and subordination was repeated at the next higher levels, at the provincial and general synod. It is important to note, however, that unlike the Lutheran Church, local Calvinist communities in the Rhineland retained a high degree of autonomy and occasionally came into conflict with higher councils. Socially, prominent burghers and noblemen were heavily represented in the Calvinist Church, whereas Cleve Lutheranism consisted of peasants and lower strata citizens. In cities like Duisburg and Wesel, the Calvinists were in control of the city council. Except for a small number of communities under noble patronage, the Calvinist Church in Cleve corresponded to the classic model of the communitarian synodal church.

The provincial meetings moved between Wesel, Cleve, Emmerich, Rees, Duisburg, Goch, and Kalkar. Preachers and elders represented the local communities. It is instructive to note the items of business at the provincial synods that dealt with moral and confessional discipline; the following is a representative sample:[2]

1610: Cleve brought up a case of one brother cursing another; the synod instructed the community to admonish him to desist and to cite him before the class convention if he did not; Xanten questioned whether children must recite their catechism in public; an adulterer in Rees was to be warned, failing repentance, of excommunication.

1611: In Xanten, a young journeyman set up house with a maid and got her pregnant. The preacher asked him to marry her or send her away; he did neither. He was to be shunned.

1612: A preacher in Gennep left after a bitter dispute with the community over low pay and Arminianism. Disciplinary actions were to be taken against the Remonstrant preacher.

1613: In Berg an ex-priest was confirmed as preacher but returned to Catholicism. It was resolved that in the future, converts must be under a period of probation. In answer to a question from Wesel regarding mixed marriages: if a Catholic priest would not acknowledge a mixed marriage, the provincial synod would still give a marriage certificate to the Calvinist partner.

1617: Instructions to preachers to protect their communities from the teachings of Arminius and Vorstius.

1620: Discussions of grievances from Sevener and Xanten concerning Catholic and Calvinist children attending schools of a different confession (provincial synod welcomed Catholic children but lamented Calvinist children attending Catholic institutions).

1621: Adopted a resolution of the Wesel class convention that couples who lived together before matrimony were to be disciplined; their children were not to receive baptism.

1622: Adopted a resolution of the Duisburg class convention that a widow could remarry after nine months, a widower after six months.

1624: Visitation procedures specified: inspectors to visit the classes and to determine whether the synodal acts were enforced;

grievances to be heard. Admonition against Jesuit polemic from Emmerich.

1625: Wesel asked guidance concerning the case of a Calvinist invited to stand as a godparent to a Lutheran child; resolution to leave it up to the conscience of the individual church member.

1630: After the Dutch victory over the Spaniards in Wesel, the provincial synod called for the final reformation in Cleve; a collection was taken up to support Calvinist preachers and schoolmasters exiled from the Upper Palatinate by Bavarian troops.

1633: Deliberated on measures to prevent Catholic converts to Calvinism from relapsing; resolved in Wesel to ask Duke Georg Wilhelm to prevent Anabaptists from returning to Cleve from the Netherlands.

1634: Complained to the duke about mixed marriages, Anabaptists, and Catholic processions.

1637: Reading of the Wesel Class Convention admonition against engaged couples having sex.

1638: Petitioned the duke to abolish "disorderly feasting and drinking," especially during sermons, and to suppress common law marriages.

1639: Provincial synod suspected Bremeners of training preachers tainted with Arminianism and warned the communities that the calling of preachers had to be approved by the classes. Petitioned the duke to suppress Socinians exiled from Poland. Took up the case of Bürgermeister Heinrich Schmidt of Duisburg who had married his niece; the two and their child were excommunicated.

1642: Reading of three letters by Elector Friedrich Wilhelm of Brandenburg, promising support and protection against Lutheran and Catholic encroachments. Provincial synod to reply with gratitude and obedience; considered the case of an adulterer who had lived with the niece of his wife then with a maid.

1643: A priest in Xanten went to a dying Calvinist and gave him extreme unction after the man was unconscious; later he spread the news that the man had converted. Asked the government to prevent any such actions in the future (the priest was punished).

1647: Petitioned the Elector to confiscate the vicaries of two priests who kept common law wives and to give the money to the Calvinist Church.

Two salient trends stand out from this selective survey of the records of the Cleve provincial synod: First, the exercise of moral supervision over the household was constant and focused on the regulation of sexuality. Secondly, the church hierarchy found its own resources increasingly deficient in the enforcement of moral discipline and in competition with other confessions. Consequently, it appealed to the state, represented by the Calvinist House of Brandenburg, to reinforce the means of confessional and moral coercion. The suggestion that social disciplining was by no means merely a moral regime imposed from above by the state has enormous implications for the social history of confessionalization. In Calvinist Rhineland, a social–religious elite actively collaborated with a Calvinist state to impose their vision of Christian morality and political order. Membership in the Calvinist elite – the elders and deacons of the churches – often reinforced one's standing in politics and society or served as a rung in the ladder of upward social mobility, as Heinz Schilling has documented for the Calvinist churches in the Netherlands. The enforcement of a moral regime thus can be interpreted as an effective means of social control, exercised by the socially privileged over the lower orders in society.

Counter-Reformation Catholicism

The overriding goal of the Catholic states was the re-establishment of Catholic orthodoxy. Hence, confessional uniformity superceded moral discipline as the primary aim of social control. Two examples must suffice to support this argument: Bavaria, surely the most successful of the Counter-Reformation states, and the bishopric of Osnabrück, confessionally divided between Catholics and Lutherans.

The evangelical movement had penetrated every sector of Bavarian society by the mid-sixteenth century, winning adherents among the nobility, citizenry, rural artisans, and literate peasants. The Reformation was stopped only by a concerted policy by the Bavarian dukes, who undertook to repress particularist privileges and popular will by the twin policy of enforcing Catholic orthodoxy and consolidating central state control. The dukes crushed a Protestant noble opposition, ordered inspections of schools in 1558 – 60, and held hearings to ferret out Protestants in the capital city of Munich between 1569 and 1571. Backed by the state, confessional conformity was gradually re-established in the cities and flatland of Bavaria, but official religion was resisted more effectively in the mountains of Upper Bavaria. The tiny lordship of Aschau–Wildenwart near the Chiemsee was a case in point.

Religious dissent was tolerated by the nobleman Pankraz von Freiberg, Lord of Hohenaschau, son of an Anabaptist mother sympathetic to the Reformation. Briefly imprisoned in Munich in 1565, Pankraz and his descendants ignored repeated mandates from Munich to enforce Catholic orthdoxy. For the next thirty-five years, many complaints were brought before secular and ecclesiastical authorities (the bailiff in Burghausen and the Abbot of Herrenchiemsee), in which the inhabitants of the lordship were denounced as "Lutherans." In 1596, a religious commission investigated charges that the inhabitants refused Catholic sacraments. In 1597, Duke Wilhelm V sent Jesuits on a "folk mission" to Aschau–Wildenwart. In March 1601, secular and ecclesiastical authorities carried out another visitation. A list of 18 questions were composed; suspects were interrogated as to their religious upbringing, their confession and communion, baptism of children, their understanding of the eucharist and of the Catholic clergy, their knowledge of prayers and creed, and so on. Encouraged to denounce their neighbors, the questioned men and women faced the option of submission or exile.

Eight men and two women faced the commissioners: the men ranged in age from their late thirties to an 85-year old; the women were both widows, one over 80 years old. Four of the men were serfs of the Lord of Freiberg, one was a hunter, another a law clerk of the nobleman, and another a knifesmith. Some of them professed Protestant beliefs, having grown up in Protestant households (five out of ten) or educated by a Lutheran schoolmaster, but their answers reflected more an eclectic mixture of skepticism, materialism, and simple faith that differed fundamentally from the doctrinal and ritualistic precision of the official Catholic religion. Popular religion, in the specific locality of Aschau, seemed to suggest an admixture of Lutheran ideas and traditional beliefs and practices.

Many had avoided Catholic services due to the absence of a Lutheran pastor – the 80-year old Lucia Z. had not gone to confession and communion in twenty years. On the question of eucharistic theology, the answers showed a spectrum from complete ignorance to traditional understanding of the eucharist. Some professed ignorance of what the priest offered up at mass; others claimed they only prayed to God in heaven and not at the altar; others expressed skepticism on transubstantiation. Two men, brothers, "understood nothing about original sin." One man "knew nothing about the Holy Christian Church or the pope, processions, imploring saints, purgatory and so forth. He only believed in God." Others were more cautious, claiming they believed in the Catholic Church but doubted the existence of purgatory. Another man told his interrogators that both Catholics and Lutherans would go to heaven. This tolerant attitude apparently reflected the reality of village life: husbands and wives, parents and children of different faiths had no difficulty living together. Anna A. professed ignorance but then stated that she prayed to God alone and not to the saints. None of the ten were prepared to denounce anyone else. Faced with the threat of exile, the majority submitted themselves to the Catholic Church but asked that they be exempted from oath swearing. The authorities followed up their interrogation with more visits in the next two years: a Jesuit confessor dispensed "confession certificates" to the "converts." Only an overt demonstration of state power secured external conformity in the mountain lordship.

Of the hundreds of political entities in the Holy Roman Empire, the bishopric of Osnabrück in Northwest Germany possessed a unique constitution. The Reformation had left its mark in the territory: the metropolitan city of Osnabrück was mostly Lutheran, while the rural parishes were confessionally mixed, with the dividing lines often running through the same parish. During the Thirty Years' War, Catholic and Protestant armies battled over the region, and no fewer than five official religious reforms were variously decreed by the Catholic prince-bishops and by the occupying Swedish army. The Peace of Westphalia stipulated that the episcopal see was henceforth to alternate between a freely elected Catholic bishop and a Protestant ruler, selected from the house of Brunswick-Luneburg. In the city of Osnabrück, the two civic churches remained Lutheran, but the two collegiate churches were Catholic. In the rest of the territory, twenty eight parishes belonged to the Catholic Church, seventeen were Lutheran, and eight served both confessions. Visitation minutes kept by the episcopal government between 1624 and the 1680s offer detailed information on the confessional situation in rural parishes. Not only do these records document the progress of confessionalization, they also reveal the great gap between official and popular religion, even when the latter had been nominally integrated into the confessional regime of the state.

In 1624/5, Albert Lucenius, General Vicar of the bishopric, undertook a diocesan visitation. Having previously served in Cologne, and imbued with the Tridentine spirit, Lucenius was disheartened by the confessional confusion in the territory. Most of the clergy could not be classified simply as "Lutheran" or "Catholic." Of the 73 parish clerics, 19 – 20 were definitely Lutheran, 13 – 14 were Catholic in the Tridentine sense, and the rest fell into a vast gray zone. Professing Catholicism, these parish priests kept common law wives, dispensed communion in both kinds to the laity, and did not administer confirmation or extreme unction. Half of all clerics had succeeded their fathers in their parish livings. The laity, like their curates, also fell into a wide range of confessional consciousness, ranging from militant Lutherans who resisted recatholicization to the majority, who professed ignorance in matters holy and religious. Among the Catholics, folk religion retained many of its traditional practices. In Bersenbrück and other parishes, for example, statues or pictures of the Virgin Mary played the central role in a fertility rite to celebrate marriages. Processions were led by a flag bearing an image of Mary to the house of the newly wed. Entering the house, the flag was carried around the hearth, a picture of Mary was then placed on the conjugal bed, and a crucifix on the table, to ensure marital harmony and fertility.

When the Counter-Reformation attempted to do away with tradition, the church hierarchy met with strong resistance. Parishioners insisted on the right to communion in both kinds, claiming they adhered to Catholicism "in the manner of the land."

The confessional confusion of the Thirty Years' War forced the laity to be self-reliant in matters affecting their own salvation. The clergy came and went, depending on the fortunes of the armies. Between 1625 and 1628, Catholics purged Lutherans from parish posts; in 1633, when the Swedish army arrived, Catholic priests were dismissed. Within a generation (1624 – 50), most parishioners had seen two to five switches in official religion. The frequent changes in clerical personnel, in rituals, and doctrines must have irritated some and left the vast majority confused or indifferent. The only consistency in these years was the criterion for official appointments. Only professed Catholics or Lutherans were respectively appointed by the different territorial rulers, down to the level of the bailiff (*Vogt*). The gulf between the village and the state was thus not only one between local self-government and central bureaucracy, but also between an amorphous popular religion and a self-conscious official confession. One consequence of this dichotomy, as reflected in the bias of the official documents, was widespread popular anxiety. Confronted by the state, few people openly expressed their opinions and convictions. The profession of religious ignorance represented in fact both a result of confessional confusion and a strategy for self-protection. The community of Oesede thus stated to the visiting officials in 1639 that "on account of our ignorance, we poor peasants and laypeople do not understand the fundamentals of religion and are uninformed about things necessary for our salvation and sanctification." As to what the villagers actually thought, we know as little as the outsiders who sought to impose official state religion on the peasants.

The confessional picture resembled a jigsaw: over three-quarters of the communities had sizeable religious minorities (over 10 per cent); confessional divides ran through parishes, villages, households, and families; mixed marriages were quite common. Social status, age, and gender had little correlation to confessional allegiance. The only salient feature in this diverse confessional landscape was represented by the parish villages. These settlements functioned as "central places" for the scattered villages and hamlets in the parish; rural artisans constituted an important demographic element and were overwhelmingly Lutheran. This pattern of rural division – between market villages and farming settlements –

suggested and confirmed the generally urban character of Lutheranism within the territory.

Catholicism made some headway during the second half of the
seventeenth century. But reports of religious indifference or
confessional eclecticism were frequent enough, in both Lutheran
and Catholic parishes, to cast doubt on the success of the
confessional state. Two examples will suffice. In 1680, the
Lutheran pastor of Lintorf complained of many who never attended
church services. Many parents sent their children to tend cattle
rather than to Sunday schools. Admonished by their pastor, the
parents threatened to send their children to Catholic mass, and
warned that "if one should consider using church discipline against
them," they would convert to another faith. The second example is
from the parish of Ankum. In 1668, the parishioners – a Catholic
majority with a sizeable Lutheran minority – jointly complained to
the cathedral chapter about their curate, "a man who speculate[d]
more on the depth of the beer barrel than on the mysteries of the
Gospels." Instead, the community asked for the cathedral vicar
Johann Eberhard Schultze, who had recently preached in Ankum,
"and whose sermons and singing were listened to with joy by both
Catholics and Evangelicals." In addition, the Ankumers asked the
headman of Northoff, a Lutheran, to write a letter of support to
demonstrate their deep dissatisfaction "with such a pastor who
absolutely cannot care for their souls and salvation."

These two examples represented a general attitude among the
rural population in late seventeenth and eighteenth-century
Osnabrück. To the men and women of the villages, official religion
played a small role in their lives. Some simply ignored religion,
threatening conversion if church discipline should impinge on their
private lives. Others took salvation into their own hands, ignoring
the categories of confession, ritual, and doctrine, caring only for
good moral conduct among their parish clerics. Most seemed to
show a great deal of flexibility, toleration, and eclecticism in
confessional matters, in sharp contrast to the professional precision
of the clergy. In recatholicized churches, Lutherans did not
withdraw from parish life: they sat in the same pews, long in the
possession of their families, put in their share of church maintenance, and served as overseers of the church. They attended mass,
went on processions, and sometimes even carried pictures of saints.

At heart, they remained firm in their Protestant beliefs. In the long run, not even the confessional state could triumph over the forces of tradition and communal coexistence in the rural villages of Osnabrück.

Popular resistance

Resistance to the imposition of official religion took many forms, and they were not restricted to opposition to the Counter-Reformation. In all territories of the empire, officials and clerics of the early modern state encountered a populace more or less determined to retain control over their own lives, including religious matters. Examples of popular resistance in Calvinist Hesse–Kassel, Nassau–Dillenburg, Lutheran Württemberg, and Catholic Würzburg argue for a common pattern of conflict between popular religion and official confession.

When Landgrave Moritz of Hesse–Kassel introduced Calvinism in his land, he encountered widespread resistance. In 1608, the government sent officials and preachers to investigate reports of resistance in six villages in Eschwege. They questioned 749 men and women (40 men did not show up) and recorded reasons for refusing communion and disobeying their prince. In speaking their minds, the villagers pleaded confusion, anxiety, or steadfastness to traditional Lutheran beliefs.

The reasons most frequently given by villagers for the refusal to receive communion included the following: their conscience had not compelled them to receive communion; many had fights with neighbors, such as Hans Mansshen, who had not received communion in twelve years due to a *"Feindtschaft"* (feud); many did not attend because their neighbors did not go; some were used to Lutheran catechism and ceremonies; some excused themselves on account of illness; a few wanted to emigrate; several cited schism among the theologians; many were confused, such as Anna, the widow of Hans Rumpf, because the same pastors said communion was host and then it was bread, or Georg Wursteschmidt, who claimed that three years ago he had received communion in three ways in three consecutive weeks, now he was utterly confused; two men, Baltzer Compenhans and Asmus Deistung, compared themselves to Nicodemus (the irony perhaps was not lost on the

Calvinist preachers). Dissenters included village elites as well:
Nicolaus Wagener, former bailiff at Scharfenstein, said that
according to Luther's catechism, the breaking of bread denied the
presence of Christ, although he acknowledged that the landgrave
had the welfare of his people at heart. Jacob Reymann, stepbrother
of the Superintendent, stated that he had learnt his Lutheran
catechism forty years ago and intended to stick with it. Bürgermeister Georg Freundt pledged loyalty to his Lutheran beliefs in
spite of the fact that this was his eighth inquisition; it should
suffice to the officials he was a Christian, and not a Turk or Jew.
And then, there was the distrust of the clergy, as expressed by
Claus Eckhart who had lived through five pastors and had not
learnt his Decalogue.

Calvinism came to Hesse–Kassel relatively late, but even in
Nassau–Dillenburg, one of the earliest Calvinist German states,
there was considerable and persistent resistance to the moral
regime imposed by the state. In 1600, the County of Nassau–
Dillenburg had roughly 50,000 inhabitants. The government
integrated the presbytery into its system of social discipline in the
rural areas. Selected initially by secular and ecclesiastical officials,
the elders in the communities were replaced every three to four
years. They met regularly with the pastors in the community to
enforce the Ten Commandments and suppress magic. The Police
Ordinance of Nassau–Dillenburg was in fact based on the Ten
Commandments; and a parallel structure of church and state
institutions enforced moral discipline:

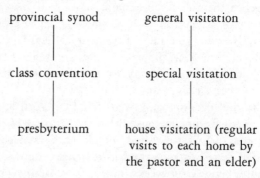

An interlocking system of control was set in place: the visitors,
representing the state, questioned the laity about the pastors, then

asked the pastors about the elders; the latter, together with the pastors, were to inform on the moral conduct of the entire community. Ideally one elder was appointed for twenty to thirty households. Instructions provided for the keeping of presbyterial books (baptismal, catechism, and communion lists), subject to inspection.

Visitation records showed that the elders were responsible for getting the children to attend catechism, for maintaining order during sermons, and for providing poor relief, although there was much resentment against vagabondage and charity-giving among the villagers. Often, the elders themselves missed church attendance, according to reports from pastors. Occasionally, the pastors accused them of sexual misconduct, magic, witchcraft, and drunkenness. Some villagers did not see any difference between the Catholic Tithe Court (loathed as an instrument of tyranny before the Reformation) and Calvinist church discipline. Many elders did not understand the nature of their posts; often they refused to serve, claiming "they did not want to earn ingratitude."

The moral regime of the state had its clear limits because it was in direct competition with another moral system: the village as an autonomous unit of ethical–economic behavior, defined by neighborly mutual help, and anchored in the family and community. Most villagers were unwilling to serve as elders because their roles as moral guardians of the state earned them the hatred of their neighbors, who despised them as traitors and informers. Wilhelm Zepper, one of the visitors of 1596, wrote of the problem in enforcing social and religious discipline:

> Those who should be exercising, leading, and administering discipline and church decorum in accordance with their selection and office, however, are anxious that they would be held and labeled as informers and traitors by their neighbors, and would earn much ingratitude, great resentment, and invite hatred and enmity from many upon their own heads.

Indeed, those who served as elders often found themselves and their families isolated in their neighborhood and village community, being refused help and sustenance by neighbors, and in a few cases, physically attacked. Treading a fine line between the community and the state, the elders exercised an ambiguous authority in the service of a resented state.

The authority of early modern government was also quite limited in consolidated, confessionally uniform territorial states such as the Duchy of Württemberg. With a population of 300,000 to 400,000 in the sixteenth century, Württemberg represented a relatively centralized state, where the Lutheran Reformation had strengthened the constitutional position of the urban and rural elites.

Based on his survey of over 7,200 *Urfehde* (a document issued upon the release of a person from official custody, by which he swore to accept his treatment and not to undertake further redress) for sixteenth-century Württemberg, R. W. Scribner has come to the conclusion that the early modern state encountered insurmountable obstacles in enforcing justice and order. Official mandates – whether they affected religious, criminal, or economic matters – could only work with the co-operation of the local elites and the acquiescence of the populace. In the villages of Württemberg, these decrees were often resented as defending the interests of the elites.

Local resistance to official religion took many forms. It ranged from the refusal to receive communion to separation and rejection of the official church. In 1587, the 80-year old Lienhart Seitz from the village of Holzheim refused to receive communion, even when threatened by officials that they would let him die and be buried like an animal. The old man did not find it in his heart to forgive an enemy and hence refused the sacrament of peace, even in the face of coercion. Or take the example of Hans Weiss from the village of Necktartailfingen. For repeated violations of his oath, the village authorities reported to the local bailiff, who had Weiss's right hand chopped off. Thereafter, Weiss refused to take communion. When questioned by the pastor, Weiss confessed to his hatred for the authorities and contradicted the pastor in denying the existence of the devil. He ended up in jail.

Non-attendance of church services could signify active resistance, and not just indifference, as the above examples testify. Throughout the old regime, Württemberg pastors continuously complained of absences during services. An even more serious challenge to the authority of the official state church was represented by separatists, who refused to acknowledge the legitimacy of the territorial Lutheran church. In spite of severe persecutions in the sixteenth century, Anabaptism survived in rural Württemberg into the nineteenth century. During the eighteenth century, pietism gave rise to other separatist communities because the Württemberg state, unlike Prussia, failed to co-opt the movement.

In two investigations, in 1718 and 1725, authorities questioned separatists in communities southwest of Stuttgart. They discovered that the unity of throne and altar was precisely the reason for separatist resistance. Separatists held the Lutheran clergy in contempt, describing them as men who chat about God's Word for the sake of their salary. The pastors received their positions "by buttering up to patronage"; they were nothing but thieves and murderers. Their main function, according to a butcher, was to keep the people in fear. In defiance of their inquisitors, the separatists rejected official church sacraments: baptism was but magic; and Christ did not compel anyone to go to church.

At times, the refusal of pietists and Anabaptists to accept military duty won them the sympathy of the larger Lutheran population. Rejection of state coercion, not confessional differences, seemed to have been the cornerstone of popular moral judgment. Popular resistance occasionally involved the village community as a unit. In 1796, the villagers of Beutelsbach buried a live bull as a remedy for hoof and mouth disease. Scandalized by this blatant pagan sacrifice, the consistory ordered an investigation but failed to discover any ringleaders as the village closed ranks to outsiders.

Whereas Lutheran Württemberg and Catholic Bavaria represented large territorial states relatively successful in enforcing official religion and social control, the political fragmentation of Franconia thwarted the effort of the Counter-Reformation. Bergrheinfeld, a village on the Main some four kilometers from the imperial city of Schweinfurt, was a case in point. Resistance to the early modern state took the form of prolonged, if rather unspectacular, indifference that allowed the villagers to ward off the Counter-Reformation for 150 years.

In the mid-sixteenth century the confessional situation in this Franconian village was complicated by a fragmented feudal regime: the bishop, cathedral chapter, and the College of Haug in Würzburg held fiefs and tenants as well as the Bishop of Eichstätt,

whose rights were further enfeoffed to three Lutheran noble
families, the Thüningen, Schaumberg, and Grumbach. Secular
lordship was exercised primarily by the Bishop of Eichstätt until
1664, when the Julius Hospital (under the Bishop of Würzburg)
purchased these rights, while ecclesiastical authority had always
been exclusively in the hands of the Bishop of Würzburg.
Claiming the provisions of the Religious Peace of Augsburg of
1555, the three noble families, fiefholders of the Bishop of
Eichstätt, usurped the right of reformation, and by 1576, the
village was mostly Lutheran, and peasants attended services in
nearby Schweinfurt, owing to the lack of their own parish church.
The first Catholic Visitation (1576) discovered the presence of a
Lutheran schoolmaster. Repeated warnings to the village by the
Clerical Council in Würzburg in subsequent years were simply
ignored by the villagers, who stood behind the protection of their
Lutheran noble lords. A village ordinance of 1594, drawn up by
the three noblemen, required sermon attendance for all villagers,
and stipulated the selection of two church supervisors, and
communal control over the the church building and the church
bell.

In 1602, Bishop Julius of Würzburg attempted to introduce the
Counter-Reformation. Visitors found that the villagers possessed
the chalice and the cassock, that they controlled the church fund,
and that a schoolmaster still taught children Lutheran catechism.
A report in 1615 listed 113 male heads of households in
Bergrheinfeld: 24 were subjects of the Bishop of Würzburg, 4
stood under the cathedral chapter of Würzburg, 36 under the
Bishop of Eichstätt, 4 under the Teutonic Knights, 5 under three
collegiate churches, 16 under the knight Albrecht von Thüngen,
and 24 under the knight Schaumberg. Nominally, 73 households
belonged to Catholic lords, 40 to Protestants, but the report also
stated that only 14 householders were Catholic. In collaboration,
the governments of Würzburg and Eichstätt attempted to
recatholicize the village. A priest was appointed to say mass, the
schoolmaster was threatened with dismissal, and villagers were
admonished to confess and receive communion. Nonetheless, the
Bergrheinfelders stayed away from mass, sent their children out of
town to Lutheran sermons, observed the old calendar in spite of the
introduction of the Gregorian calender, and simply ignored the

mandates of their Catholic prince-bishops. Andreas Schwertlein, chaplain, complained in 1616 that his parishioners sang Lutheran hymns at mass, stood during the elevation of the host with hats on, and celebrated baptisms and weddings in neighboring Lutheran churches. In particular, the women and the young people were particularly recalcitrant. Warnings and citations were again ignored. Bishop Julius Echter von Mespelbrunn died in 1617, having achieved nothing by way of recatholicization in Bergrheinfeld.

For the chaplain, the footsoldier of the ecclesiastical state, this was indeed a lonely post. The new priest, Nithard Schmidt, complained in 1619/20 that the villagers, both Catholic and Lutheran, carried on their farmwork during feast days, mocked him during mass, threatened him with beatings, and threw stones at him. Schmidt quit his post in 1621. The new vicar, Johann Hesselbach, assessed in 1622 that 63 households were Catholic and 50 Lutheran. Hesselbach implored in vain for help from secular officials, recommending the use of heavy fines and imprisonment to the government for enforcing confessional conformity. In 1630, Bishop Johann Christoph von Wetterstetten (1616 – 36) of Eichstätt issued a new village ordinance for Bergrheinfeld, requiring Catholic service and sacraments. Whatever progress the Counter-Reformation had made was undone by the conquest of Franconia by Gustavus Adolphus of Sweden. For two years, 1632 to 1634, Bergrheinfeld and sixteen other villages were awarded by the Swedish army to the Lutheran Imperial city of Schweinfurt. Confessional allegiance, however, meant little in the face of devastations. In 1642, only twenty one households appeared in a tax list for the village, six widows and two orphans were named as householders.

The horrors of the Thirty Years' War seemed to have alleviated the rigors of confessional rigidity. In 1645, Endres Strenzel, subject of Eichstätt, wanted to marry Margaretha Rudolfin, daughter of the late headman of Würzburg in Bergrheinfeld. The Catholic priest refused to marry them because Strenzel was Lutheran. In his appeal to the cathedral chapter of Würzburg, Strenzel asked for intercession. He did not want to convert just to marry a Catholic woman, lest he be cursed by his coreligionists. In an uncharacteristically moderate letter, the General Vicar of

Eichstätt advised the Bergrheinfeld priest not to refuse marriage, but be accommodating "in these hard times" and to work toward converting Strenzel after the marriage.

The moderation of the Catholic officials was probably responsible for a greater success in recatholicization. In 1638, the first Catholic schoolmaster was appointed. In the 1650s and 1660s, more Bergrheinfelders were buried in the Catholic cemetery. When a Lutheran woman lay dying in 1656, the Catholic officials allowed a Lutheran preacher to visit her and administer communion. Encouraged by the new religious climate, the Lutherans in the village wrote a petition to Bishop Johann Philipp von Schönborn in 1657, citing the Peace Treaty of Westphalia, and asking the bishop to stop his bailiff in Werneck from harassing Bergrheinfelders who attended Lutheran services in nearby towns. At this time, the village had 44 Lutheran households with 106 adults and 55 children, and 31 Catholic households with 92 adults and 42 children. The bishop, however, rejected the villagers' claim to the Peace Treaty, renewed interdict of attendance of outside Lutheran services, and threatened fines. After 1664, when secular and ecclesiastical jurisdiction were united by the government in Würzburg, more effective means of control could be exercised. Most Lutherans emigrated, the older ones remained and died out, and a few converted. The records of deaths in the parish showed the unmistakable decline of Lutheranism. By 1681, only ten Lutherans remained in Bergrheinfeld. In 1705, Lutheranism died out with the 93-year old Rosina Köhler. After 150 years, the Counter-Reformation finally triumphed in this Franconian village.

8
Confessionalism and the people

Did princes and magistrates create "well ordered police states" based on the principle of confessionalism and social discipline? Or did the people of early modern Central Europe resist and contest incessantly the authority of the state and official religion? The many local studies have given us a complicated picture. Confessionalism progressed most unevenly, sometimes even retrogressively, measured by the yardstick of official proclamations and mandates. Nonetheless, the ecclesiastical and official apparatus of the early modern state did penetrate the countryside, slowly but surely. Various strategies were open to the people in dealing with the imposition of social and confessional discipline: resistance, indifference, acquiescence, collaboration, and active support. It would be misleading to describe confessionalization only as a historical process generated by the bureaucratic and intellectual elites and imposed on the rest of society. Equally significant was the active support given to confessionalization by various social groups whose interests and goals coincided with those of the confessional territorial states. Thus lawyers, professors, schoolteachers, the clergy, city magistrates, merchants, guild masters, students, village elders, rich peasants, petty functionaries, rural artisans all actively participated at different times in the creation of confessional society.

Four themes will be examined in this dialectic between confessionalism and the people. The first theme centers on the consolidation of an ethos of patriarchal family, the second discusses the importance of popular religion in defining confessionalism with

specific references to magic, the third theme concerns the relationship between confessionalization and psychohistory, and the last
theme relates to social groups excluded from the process of
confessionalization.

Patriarchy and the family

The Reformation intensified developments in late medieval society
to strengthen the bonds of the patriarchal family. Luther praised
marriage as a noble vocation. The theme of the evangelical family,
with idealized parents nurturing their children in God-fearing
piety, was echoed in the writings of all reformers following in
Luther's footsteps. Patriarchy represented a social model that
extended across the broad spectrum of the Reformation, and later
to the social ethos of the Counter-Reformation. The patriarchal
family was just as important in the theology of many radicals.
Bernhard Rothmann, reformer in Münster who became the leading
theologian of the Anabaptist millenarian kingdom, proclaimed
that Christ was to husbands what husbands were to wives. For the
Münster Anabaptists, the hierarchy of gender subordination
formed the foundation of salvation, and the ultimate development
of patriarchy was in the short-lived social experiment of polygamy.
In the major Protestant confessions, patriarchal authority in the
family was, on the one hand, buttressed by the status of the male
householder in the community, and, on the other hand, served as
the social fabric upholding the confessional state. While Luther
and the evangelicals exhorted spouses to be affectionate and pious,
and husbands to be mild and just, there was no question where
authority resided in the Protestant household. *"Hausväterliteratur"*
became a standard genre in Protestant literature and found
imitations among Catholic writers as well.

Patriarchy, however, was not born into a vacuum. In the
century before the Reformation, forces were at work to impose
stricter gender and familial roles. In comparison to the High
Middle Ages, city women increasingly lost out to males in the
urban guild economy. Sexual mores turned more conservative,
culminating in the great fear of the spread of syphilis at the end of
the fifteenth century. City fathers suppressed prostitution, closed
down bath houses, and punished sexual deviancy. Sentences for

infanticide, adultery, and homosexuality became more severe during the course of the sixteenth century. While very few women were executed for infanticide prior to 1500, the criminalization of infanticide in the sixteenth century reflected a greater magisterial anxiety to uphold sexual and familial stability. The *Carolina*, the imperial law code promulgated by Charles V in 1532, stipulated examination of infanticide cases by physicians and midwives. In the second half of the sixteenth century, beheading and drowning were standard sentences for infanticide. Nuremberg figures showed the rising rate of infanticide prosecutions: 4 women were executed for infanticide between 1500 and 1550; the next 50 years saw 20 executions; magistrates passed 21 death sentences in the first half of the seventeenth century, and 18 more for the second half. This severe sexual regime persisted until the end of the Old Reich, when imprisonment replaced execution as appropriate punishment for infanticides.

To enforce family morality, princes and magistrates resorted both to secular sanctions and to church discipline. In Lutheran Lippe, the count condemned an adulterer to death in 1579 but commuted his sentence to public penance on three consecutive Sundays in his parish church. In Catholic Münster, a furrier was fined in 1592 for adultery, sentenced to public penance in church for a relapse in 1596, and executed with the sword for a third offense in 1601. City fathers in Münster also sentenced prostitutes to be whipped, and homosexuals to die by the sword, a common punishment in the empire.

In punishing infanticide, sodomy, prostitution, and adultery, Christian magistrates were attempting to reinforce their vision of a Christian patriarchal family. Marital reforms came in the wake of the Reformation and Counter-Reformation. The Protestants took over marital jurisdiction from the Catholic Church courts, either by creating separate marriage courts (*Ehegericht*), presided over by secular magistrates (in Basel for example), by adjudicating marital disputes in consistory courts (for instance in Oldenburg), or by settling cases in presbyterial or higher meetings in Calvinist communities. While they granted divorces in cases of abandonment, adultery, and impotence, Protestant leaders tried to discourage the breakup of families, even in cases of spousal abuse. Church discipline could also work for the rights of women, when philandering husbands paid for their sins. In 1559, the presbyters of Emden condemned the surgeon Johann van Hulst to public penance, and ordered him to make restitution to his betrayed wife and to his maid, whom he had got pregnant. Three years later, when Hulst applied for a recommendation from the presbytery in preparation for moving to Antwerp, the elders and preachers first investigated whether he had paid child support on schedule to the young mother.

Although marriage was no longer a sacrament in Protestant areas, it assumed a far greater function as the cornerstone of state and society. It assured greater control for male householders over family members and the transmission of property. In rural Hohenlohe, the Lutheran Church strengthened the hands of parents in controlling their children. Young people had to obtain parental approval before the pastors would marry them. Withholding parental consent represented an effective means of conserving the familial estate against over fragmentation due to inheritance. Whereas canon law recognized the legitimacy of mutual marriage vows between young adults, the Protestant view of marriage shifted the focus of consent away from the potential partners to the householders and community.

The new Protestant view of marriage was consonant with the interests of the state. Princes and magistrates needed stable householders, self-sufficient taxpayers, and obedient subjects. Householders, whether artisans or peasants, all *Standespersonen* (members of social estates), represented members of fixed social levels who had a particular place in the socioreligious *ordines*. They embodied the forces of order and discipline, and formed a bulwark for the state against vagabonds, sectarians, robbers, and the unpropertied; all potential rebels against the sociopolitical order. State support for this patriarchal regime was especially important after the experience of the Peasant War of 1524 – 5. In 1525 propertied householders provided the leadership and much of the rank-and-file of the peasant armies. In Upper Austria, householders formed the solid ranks of peasant rebels against the Counter-Reformation state until the 1620s. Gradually, peasant householders were integrated into the official bureaucracy: by supporting their rights of inheritance and property ownership, the Habsburg policy of *Bauernschutz* (protection of peasants) strengthened the hands of male householders against farm laborers, minor relatives, and cottagers. In turn, the propertied peasants were won over to the Counter-Reformation, leaving the realm of religious and political protest to the more marginal groups in rural society. By the 1630s, as Hermann Rebel has shown, rural rebellion in Upper Austria had transformed itself from resistance by Lutheran peasant householders against the Counter-Reformation state to millenarian movements supported by marginal social groups – cottagers, laborers, and disenfranchised younger children of householders.

Did family life become more affectionate after the Reformation? Was Protestant marriage more companionable, more affectionate? The evidence is ambiguous. True, Luther, Bullinger, and other early reformers praised the virtues and joys of family life; and Protestant literature painted pictures of idealized Christian households. But indications of a repressive patriarchy also abound in this prescriptive literature. Following St Augustine, who saw human nature, even that of infants, as depraved and sinful, Protestant theology prescribed a strong patriarchy to correct the sins of the flesh. In 1539, Andreas Osiander, evangelical reformer in Nuremberg, composed a catechism based on this pessimistic Augustinian theology, and provoked a bitter attack by the Catholic Johann Eck for corrupting the innocence of children.

The Calvinist Church shared this negative view of human nature. Calvinist theologians, housefathers themselves, composed treatises to demonstrate the need for familial discipline. In a 1618 theological dissertation at Zürich in 1618, *Disquisition on the Spiritual Condition of Infants,* Jakob Lindinner stated that babies had a natural propensity toward evil. Hence, he argued, the will of children must be broken and tamed early, in order to turn their nature from sin to virtue. The agent of this godly work was the father. The mother's role was limited to childbearing, for her womanly nature represented potential corruption in raising children, as another Calvinist divine, Samuel Hochholtzer, admonished. In *On Disciplining Children, How the Disobedient, Evil, and Corrupted Youth of These Anxious Last Days can be Bettered* (1591), Hochholtzer condemned women as mothers:

> how they [women] love to accept strange, false beliefs, and go about with benedictions and witches' handwork. When they are not firm in faith and the Devil comes to tempt them . . . they

follow him and go about with supernatural fantasies. Daily experience also teaches us that many of them hide in the serious error that they could cure their children and others with blessings and devilish things, such as the many stories about herbs, which they first empowered with supernatural blessings.[1]

The clergy advised mothers to wean their infants early to break their will. Children should be clean, hardened, and not be kept too warm. Parents must exercise constant supervision to prevent masturbation. To counter the pernicious influence of mothers, the pastors suggested, fathers must be distant and stern, so that their children would grow up both loving and fearing them.

Among the lower classes, however, the Protestant bourgeois idea of patriarchal family took shallow root. For one thing, families of lower classes in cities and villages included working spouses; for another, parents seldom had time to enforce discipline. In peasant families of the Zürich canton, children worked at a very young age. Beatings and abuse were common, but so was love. Children called parents by familiar *"du"* terms, and not in the formal address *"Sie"* advocated by the clergy.

The imposition of patriarchy became a mark of social stratification between the godly, orderly burgher families and the unruly, childlike subjects. In burgher households, the father was to represent godly authority, just as schoolmasters, pastors, officials, and magistrates reinforced their authority from the patriarchal image of God. The image of paternity suffused the self-image of the ruling elite. Lutheran and Calvinist princes called themselves fathers to their people. Even magistrates of self-governing urban communes arrogated to themselves the image of benevolent, authoritarian father figures supervising the citizens, who assumed, in official eyes, the status of children. In her analysis of political iconography in the imperial city of Regensburg, Kristin Zapalac argues for the displacement of a late medieval mode of political discourse – centered on the dialectical interpenetrations of divine and earthly justice, presided over by God the Father – by a Lutheran humanist one, in which the language of paternal good government helped to define the relationships between city council and citizen. In the last three decades of the sixteenth century, city council decrees adopted the language of paternal self-invocation, imitating the political discourse of the territorial princes.

Evidence from both Protestant and Catholic areas indicate that the idea of marriage promulgated by the official churches had limited success in early modern Germany. Abstinence from premarital sex and church ceremonies officiated by the clergy represented an imposition on traditional Germanic marriage customs. In rural areas, most young couples "got married" by exchanging vows, usually with the consent of their kinsfolk, and "sealed" their promise by sleeping together. The exchange of gifts – the "morning gift" (*Morgengabe*) for the woman and dowries for the men – lubricated the conjugal network linking families and neighborhoods.

Until the early seventeenth century, this customary marriage, called *"truwen"* in East Friesland, was tacitly accepted by the Calvinist community. Preachers and elders began to condemn premarital sex to combat popular custom. In 1621, Calvinist communities in the Lower Rhine adopted a resolution to admonish couples living outside marriage. After the mid-seventeenth century, the presbyters in Emden also denounced traditional nuptials that had been tolerated by their predecessors. Before 1600, not a single case of *coitus anticipatus* came before the Emden presbytery. Between 1645 and 1649, they comprised 6.7 per cent of all sexual offenses investigated by the presbyters; in the 1740s, they reached 70 per cent. Parallel to the Calvinist condemnation of premarital sex was a campaign against single mothers and harsher stigmatization of bastardy in the late seventeenth and eighteenth century. How are these trends to be interpreted? One social consequence was greater repression of female sexuality and a widening gap between bourgeois families and the lower classes. The suppression of premarital sex and illegitimacy represented a logical extension of the establishment of patriarchy in early modern Germany. Another way of understanding this development is to see it in terms of the limited influence of the official Calvinist church on popular sexual and marital behavior.

A study of premarital sexuality and illegitimacy in rural Bavaria confirms the transconfessional nature of popular resistance to official views of marriage. In the Bavarian village of Unterfinning (about fifty families), there were very few illegitimate births between 1671 and 1770, in spite of the fact that premarital sex was the norm among young people. The notion of legitimacy in sexual/marital matters, dictated by the Council of Trent and enforced by repeated princely edicts, was fundamentally alien to village morality. As in East Friesland, young men and women normally engaged in sexual intercourse as a prelude to a more formal marriage alliance. Sexual and economic exchanges were linked. In exchange for her virginity, the woman gained the promise of economic support in the form of a marriage vow, enforcible in court should the man renege on his word. Marriage gifts from the man symbolized counter-gifts for the woman's sexual favors. Although premarital sex was widely practiced as part of a process of formalizing a marital–sexual alliance, promiscuity was not tolerated. Magistrates and clerics were powerless in repressing this custom. They depended on informants from the village for denunciations. The village community functioned as an autonomous moral body to "filter out" cases and reported only those who had stepped outside accepted norms.

Widespread popular resistance to official views of marriage does not imply that confession played no role in shaping the structure of marriage. By the late seventeenth and eighteenth centuries, particularly in confessionalized urban communities, confessional allegiance did have a bearing on marriage structures. Peter Zschunke has analyzed the church records of Oppenheim, a winegrowing town in the Rhineland, to establish correlations between confession and marital structure.

As a provincial town in the Palatinate, Oppenheim's religious history reflected the larger vicissitudes of confessional fortunes in the territory. In 1698, the three major confessions were all represented in the population (Calvinist 46.5 per cent, Lutheran 32.5 per cent, and Catholic 21.0 per cent). Although the ages at first marriages were similar for all three confessions between 1650 and 1794 (26.5 – 27.7 for men, and 23.5 – 23.7 for women), the fertility rate and household size varied according to confession. Protestant families had fewer children on the average, ranging from 5 to 9 births (average 6.8 births), while Catholic families often had over 10 births (average 8.3 children). In addition to the practice of birth control, widespread after the mid-seventeenth century, family planning seemed to have been more characteristic of Protestant households, especially among Calvinists. By the eighteenth century, Protestant midwives were trained as medical practitioners, while Catholic midwives adhered to more traditional magical lore, resulting in lower infant mortality rates for Protestant births and a slightly higher death rate for childbearing Catholic women (10 per cent for Protestants versus 12 per cent for Catholics). Household size and wealth also correlated differently: for Calvinist households, rising income was correlated with a decrease in the number of children; for Lutherans, rising income matched a slight increase in children; for Catholics, the number of children increased significantly with rising household income. Catholic mothers also tended to have higher fertility rates because they stopped bearing children later than Protestant women. Prenuptial conceptions ranged from highest for Catholics (3 per cent), to Lutherans (2.4 per cent), and lowest for Calvinist (0.9 per cent), reflecting the more rigorous sexual regime of the Calvanist church.

Magic

Plowing through the field of popular religion to sow the seeds of social discipline, the confessional state encountered the bedrock of magic. Practiced by the simple folk in towns and villages, magic had little in common with the erudite magical discourses of the intellectuals. The central function of popular magic was healing. Benedictions, medicaments, talismans, amulets, conjurations, and herbal medicine constituted a culture of health for communities immune from the arcane tortures of university medicine. The major Protestant confessions tried, without success, to stamp out these "superstitions and magic." By tapping the resources of popular magic, one major confession, Tridentine Catholicism, created moments of synthesis between official and popular religiosity, the revival of pilgrimages in the seventeenth century being the best example. Finally, popular magic and confessionalism interacted in defining the witch hunts that haunted the Empire during the centuries of confessionalization.

The success of the Counter-Reformation must be attributed in large part to the role Catholicism continued to play in meeting the needs of the people for magical healing. In seventeenth-century Strasbourg, long a bastion of Lutheranism, the few Catholic religious tolerated in the city's convents still administered to the layfolk who came to them for healing. In 1607, the magistrates accused the nuns of St Margaret and St Madeleine of magical healing. The sisters had given out small envelopes (*briefflin*) and consecrated candles to lower fevers. One artisan received a small envelope sewn with silk and was told to wear it, say many "Our Fathers" and "Hail Marys," then throw the envelope–amulet into water to cure his fever. Likewise, Jesuits in Münster practiced healing for the laity. They advised one frightened peasant to sprinkle holy water to drive the poltergeist from his house and impressed others with their many rites of exorcism that "cured" the possessed. Ridiculed by Calvinists, Catholic healing and "magic" alarmed Lutherans, who were hard pressed to explain that the age of miracles was in the past and that Catholic "wonders" represented nothing but "papist tricks." In any event, the profundity of popular magical beliefs transcended confessional divides. Until the mid-seventeenth century, Lutheran Germany reported many cases of spiritual possession; and exorcism, of course, remained a part of the Lutheran baptismal rite. Thus epidemics and healing assumed confessional character. Boasting of their success in practicing religious healing, the Jesuits in Münster described the plague as "the flagellation of God" to lead the people back to the true Church. Faith and health were one, claimed the Augsburg Jesuits. An entry in a plague year in the *History of the College* was not without *Schadenfreude*: "In this time of the plague nobody from the college or from the gymnasium has died. Among the citizens four hundred have died, including many Lutherans."

Reports of the many church visitations in the Palatinate, whose princes alternated between Lutheranism and Calvinism, demonstrated the persistence of popular magic despite three generations of reform between 1555 and 1618. Naturally, confessionalization made uneven progress: along the banks of the Rhine and its tributaries, folk magic seemed to have been suppressed, at least according to official records. But in more remote areas, in the mountains of Hunsrück for example, state religion made very little headway. Shepherds, midwives, blacksmiths, and peasants embodied the repertoire of traditional healing practices and beliefs. For every village that proudly presented children who could recite the catechism and a dozen psalms, there were others where most inhabitants knew nothing about the fundamental doctrines of

Christianity. Above all, magical healing, in the form of conjurations and blessings, could not be uprooted. The rural folk relied on magic for curing themselves and their animals. Even village notables were a part of this culture. In 1608, an innkeeper from Allenbach, otherwise a pillar of the Calvinist Church, consulted a fortuneteller to locate his missing horse. Clearly, accommodation with official religion and ingenious adaptation characterized the reaction of the people to confessionalization. From visitation reports and testaments, a picture emerges to cast light on this popular religion.

To Protestant clerics, the devil represented more the forces of irrationality and lies rather than the late medieval vision of evil power: defeated by the Reformation, Satan's power was limited. In popular imagination, however, the devil had a real existence. Occasionally, he could even appear benevolent. Peasants attributed a rich harvest to his help; some did not hesitate to invoke his power in times of need. Interestingly, the concept of "hell," frequently used in sermons, seemed to have a weak existence in popular religion.

Suppressing blasphemy was another goal of the Palatine confessional state. Between 1555 and 1590, officials imprisoned blasphemers; in exceptional cases, they exiled the ungodly. Thereafter, offenders paid fines. The campaign to purify popular language, however, enjoyed little success. Swearing by the name of God, by his power, or by the sacraments had been a part of popular discourse for centuries. To the rural folk, their speech reflected their world, in which lightning, thunder, and the forces of nature were simply, and unconsciously, invoked; for clerics and officials, the Decalogue commanded the purification of speech. The campaign met with incomprehension and ridicule. In 1608, the bailiff of Herrstein and the pastor called upon parents to stop their children from swearing and were met with derisive laughter.

Labeled "impious," "atheist," and "ungodly" in official records, those who stayed away from church services were often quite numerous. For some, it was a matter of genuine indifference to religion; for others, they found official religion incomprehensible and irrelevant; a small minority actively questioned official doctrines. These skeptics (at least fifteen cases showed up in the visitations) denied the resurrection and eternal life, and called

Christianity an invention, but believed God was benevolent, and that hell and the devil did not exist.

Calvinism proved in the long run to be an abstract, intellectual religion of the elite. Reformed religion in the Palatinate encountered this obstacle: a logocentric, individualistic, reflective religion was imposed by the state on the people, who were accustomed to collective piety and the presence of the holy in things and places. Most households in 1620 still did not have a bible; many refused to give up rosaries and crucifixes (often of considerable monetary value); villagers still considered churches and cemeteries hallowed ground, in spite of Calvinist notions of desacralization. The Calvinist reform scored lasting successes only among the upper strata in the cities and the village notables. For the vast majority of the populace, confessionalization represented a veneer that preserved traditional practices and beliefs.

With its revived claim to religious healing, the Counter-Reformation tapped into a vast popular appetite for the holy and channeled the magical toward ecclesiastically sanctioned practices. In Catholic Germany, the revival of pilgrimage bore testimony to this fruitful synthesis between confessionalization and popular magic. Pilgrimages in Germany reached widespread popularity in the two generations before the Reformation. A host of shrines – dedicated to Christ, Mary, the bleeding host, and to saints – dotted the landscape; some functioned as local points of holiness, others attracted pilgrims from far and wide. The Church dedicated to the Virgin Mary in Regensburg, built on the ground of the synagogue razed in 1519, flourished as a new shrine, promising miracles to numerous pilgrims. The cult enjoyed a brief but phenomenal success between 1520 and 1525. Thereafter, it died a quiet death, long before the city officially adopted the Reformation in 1542.

Many shrines did not survive the Reformation. Of the great bleeding host shrines of the fifteenth century, only two flourished again with the Counter-Reformation: Weingarten in Bavaria and Walldürn in the eastern Odenwald. An analysis of the Walldürn cult shows that it owed its revival to clerical promotion and to an urban culture. Although oral legends traced the Walldürn cult back to 1330, when a priest supposedly spilled consecrated wine causing the host to bleed, the earliest written record of the cult stemmed from 1589. It came from the pen of Jodocus Hoffmann, the local priest, and the tract, *On the Origins and Progress of the Pilgrimage at Walldürn*, helped to revive the cult that had died with the Reformation. At the time, Walldürn was a very poor parish. Hoffman promoted the cult in large part to bring wealth to his community. Sponsored by the Archbishop of Mainz, Walldürn began attracting pilgrims. By 1596, some 9,000 – 10,000 came every year. Miracles reported in Walldürn served as material for the Counter-Reformation press, and printing in turn helped to promote the cult. In 1598, Valentin Leucht included the story of the Walldürn Miracle in his collection of medieval miracles. In 1628, the Würzburg Jesuit Johann Strein, born in Walldürn, published another treatise on the cult. In the devotional literature of Baroque Germany, Walldürn featured as a standard theme, such as in the writings of the Mainzer Capuchin Martin von Cochem (1634 – 1712).

Walldürn flourished at the beginning of the Thirty Years' War. In 1614, more than 100 foreign priests visited the shrine; in 1620 20,000 to 30,000 pilgrims came; in 1622 construction began on the Holy Blood Altar to house the miraculous altar cloth; in 1628, the Capuchins settled in the town. Walldürn town grew in proportion to the popularity of the cult. Except for three years under Swedish occupation, the cult persisted through the hard times of the war. The second half of the century witnessed even greater growth of the cult. At the end of the century, between 40,000 and 60,000 pilgrims visited Walldürn annually. In 1728, on the occasion of the consecration of the new church, 116,000 people received communion. By the mid-eighteenth century, Walldürn was a religious industry, with fifty priests hearing confessions almost round the clock, and reading up to 7,000 masses per year.

Without the popular need for miracles, Walldürn could not have achieved its great success. The cult filled a deep yearning for magical healing. From the beginning, the official cult merged with popular religion to create a powerful locus of sanctity. The eucharistic cult expressed itself in parallel rituals of field peram-bulations, crucifix processions, and Corpus Christi displays, all intended to ward off storms and bring about good harvests. A brisk industry sprang up in the shadow of the pilgrimage church.

Visitors bought up numerous sacramental and devotional objects: handkerchiefs in the shape of the blood cloth, blood pictures, medals, and all kinds of memorabilia. The silk handkerchiefs came in bulk from Frankfurt, purchased on credit; payments were made at the next Frankfurt Fair. At the end of the seventeenth century, a company in St Gallen also delivered handkerchiefs to meet the additional demand. Blood pictures were printed in Würzburg; later, Frankfurt presses turned out these pilgrimage mementos in far greater numbers. In 1670, the Archbishop of Mainz gave permission to hold a "holy blood market" in front of the pilgrimage church, for the sale of official cultic objects. For Walldürners themselves, the economic boom of the town itself testified to the nature of the miracle. Theirs was a story of material success based on the power of faith.

For the thousands of pilgrims who flocked to Walldürn, the journey promised hope and health. Individuals signed names with their own blood and promised offerings. In their imagination, holy blood could prevent death, ward off bad weather, protect travelers, help cure children, and heal cattle. The faithful implored the power of the holy blood in three ways: by beseeching its power in direct prayer, by touching the holy object in a pilgrimage, or by resorting to the blood handkerchief, which had touched the holy blood shrine in Walldürn.

In addition to capturing the imagination of the rural folk, Walldürn also thrived in the urban milieu of the Counter-Reformation. In 1584, the Jesuit Marian sodality in Würzburg first went on a procession to Walldürn. After 1600, Jesuits in Würzburg and Aschaffenburg promoted the eucharistic and holy blood cult in Walldürn among their Marian sodalities in defense of the real presence of Christ against the Calvinists. The Counter-Reformation linked rural pilgrimage to urban eucharistic devotion. Around 1635, pilgrims to Walldürn came from a triangular area between Würzburg, Aschaffenburg, and Neckarsulm. In the eighteenth century, the cult spread geographically to Hesse, Alsace, and the Rhineland. Walldürn also helped to revive several minor shrines in Franconia devoted to the bleeding host, which had met their demise during the Reformation: Iphofen (sponsored by Bishop Julius of Würzburg), Burgwindheim, and Vierzehnheiligen, site of a famous horse pilgrimage.

In Catholic Germany south of the Main, holy blood shrines played an insignificant role in pilgrimage, compared to the enormous popularity of shrines devoted to Mary and the saints. The centers of the Marian cult in South Germany were Altötting, a traditional site honoring the "Black Madonna," and Mariahilf in the city of Passau, promoted by the cathedral deacon Marquard von Schwendi in the 1620s, with the depiction of Mary holding the infant Jesus as the iconographic and pietistic focus. After the Thirty Years' War, the revival of pilgrimage surpassed even its popularity on the eve of the Reformation. At Mariahilf, the number of communicants increased steadily after the foundation of the shrine, rising from around ten thousand communicants to a hundred and thirty thousand during the first half of the eighteenth century (see Figure 1). Shrines multiplied rapidly in the Catholic lands of the south, feeding off and nourishing the immense popular appetite for the sacred. In the Bishopric of Passau, there were 56 pilgrimage sites before the Reformation; thereafter, 132 new shrines sprang up. Table 8.1 analyzes the function of the shrines.

Table 8.1 Pilgrimage shrines in the Bishopric of Passau

	Trinity-Christ	*Mary*	*Saints*
Pre-Reformation	7	19	30
Post-Reformation	15	80	37
Total	22	99	67

Source: calculations based on Franz Mader, *Wallfahrten im Bistum Passau* (Munich, 1984).

The remarkable popularity of the Marian cult reflected the successful synthesis of state and popular religion in Catholic Germany. The cult of Mariahilf attracted devotees from all social classes. In the 1630 Passau Mariahilf confraternity, artisans, day laborers, and children were represented alongside academics, clerics, magistrates, merchants, and innkeepers (see Figure 8.2).

For the simple folk, the most common iconographic representation of the Virgin was Mary as mother, caressing the infant Jesus. Pilgrims beseeched good health, prosperity, familial harmony, and abundant harvests of Mary. The "miracle book" at Mariahilf lists over a thousand miracles reported between 1630 and 1744.

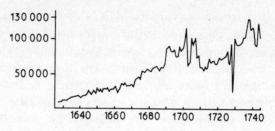

Figure 8.1 Communicants Mariahilf 1627-1745

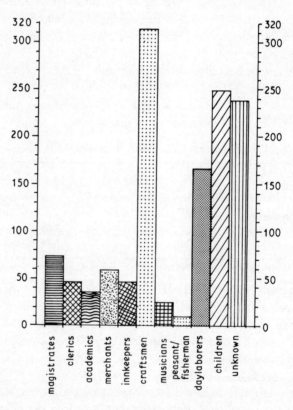

Figure 8.2 Social composition of the Mariahilf confraternity in Passau 1630.

Source: Walter Hartinger, *Mariahilf ob Passau* (Passau, 1985)

The list of wonders resembles a catalogue of human misery and misfortunes, reflecting the multiple implorations of the faithful. Miracle healings comprised the overwhelming number of reported wonders. Every ailment, every part of the human anatomy was involved. Here is a selected list of the numerous healings: heavy illness (284 cases), saved from drowning (124), blindness or bad eyesight (113), complications of pregnancy (100), fever (97), feet and leg troubles (77), shriveled limbs (49), troubles with arms and hands (28), bodily ruptures (41); miracles were reported over the plague (36), burns (12), ulcers (15), recovery of hearing (24) and speech (12); some were saved from fire (33), from falling (34), traffic accidents (51), and accidental choking (41); the Virgin cured mental illness (29), healed headaches (32), and saved the suicidally depressed (25), and those endangered by war (21). Still others attributed escape from prison, recovery of lost money, success in legal strife, avoidance of plagues of insects, lightning, and heavy frost to the Virgin. Four miracles each were also reported on healing of horses and cattle.

In Mary's tender embrace of the baby Jesus, the simple folk saw the hope of loving intercession in the struggle for salvation and survival. The shrine at Mariahilf functioned primarily as a healing cult, different in form but not substance from the recourse to magic in the daily life of the common people. For the ruling elites, the Wittelsbachs and Habsburgs, who fervently promoted the Marian cult as state rituals, the dominant representation was a glorious Virgin, the Regina Coeli, as depicted in the Black Madonna of Altötting, donning a majestic crown and regal robes. The two images of Mary coexisted in Baroque Germany, indicating one area where official and popular religiosity intersected.

Witchcraft

More women and men died as witches in Germany during the confessional centuries than in any other country of Europe. Lutherans, Calvinists, and Catholics all hounded and burnt magicians and witches. Two waves of persecutions, 1586 – 91 and 1626 – 31, claimed thousands of lives, while sporadic witch hunts and executions lasted until the early eighteenth century. The witch-craze was most ferocious in several episcopal principalities:

Würzburg, Bamberg, Eichstätt, Trier, and the Duchy of Westphalia (under the Archbishop of Cologne), and to a lesser extent in
Paderborn, Augsburg, Freising, and Cologne. Protestant lands,
however, were not free of witch hunts, with the southwest leading
in the number of executions. The major difference between
Protestant and Catholic territories, aside from the severity of
persecutions, consisted in the rigid ideology of the witches'
Sabbath, as formulated in the *Hammer of Witches* (*Malleus Malef-
icarum*, 1487), prevalent among the Counter-Reformation ecclesiastical states.

It would be misleading, however, to assume any necessary
correlation between confessional allegiance and the witchcraze.
True, the leading prosecutors were Catholic clerics and jurists,
schooled in the German College in Rome or by Jesuits, but as
Bernhard Duhr showed almost ninety years ago and as Wolfgang
Behringer has argued recently, an articulate, rigorous, and
vociferous opposition to the witchcraze existed in the Society of
Jesus, in the Catholic universities, and even at the Bavarian Privy
Council, the highest organ of government in the leading Counter-
Reformation state. Moreover, the rate of executions in Bavaria and
Austria was relatively low, compared to Franconia or Westphalia.
It appeared that well-consolidated, centralized territorial states,
whether Protestant or Catholic, conducted far fewer witch trials
than the politically fragmented territories. Moreover, some Cath-
olic lands – the abbey of Kempten, the Swabian Imperial Cloisters,
and the Bishopric of Regensburg – did not execute any witches.

I do not intend here to summarize the various theories of the
witchcraze, but merely to emphasize a theme in recent witchcraft
research that points to the conjuncture of subsistence crises and
state repression. The pressure for the trial and execution of witches
did not come from princes, clerics, and jurists alone, but often
swelled from communal demands to find and punish culprits for
harm done to persons, animals, and crops. The two great waves of
witch hunts corresponded to the worst agrarian crises of the early
modern period, namely the years 1585 – 94 and 1624 – 9. Famine
and epidemics heightened village tensions: the common folk
clamored for revenge against those who had worked harmful
magic. Two examples from the early seventeenth century indicate
this popular pressure for witch hunts: 1612 in Bergedorf in

Lutheran Schleswig and 1618 in Geseke in the Catholic Duchy of Westphalia.

In 1612, Joachim Witte from the village of Kirchwerder (in Bergedorf district) accused Peter Lüttke, the local village headman (*Landvogt*, an elected office), of defamation; the latter had called him a "magician, rogue, and thief." In the hearing conducted by the local bailiff, appointed jointly by the cities of Lübeck and Hamburg, the contest turned against the plaintiff Witte when other witnessess also accused him of witchcraft. Put under judicial torture, Witte confessed to practicing blood magic to harm cattle; he also named three women as fellow witches. When the case was referred to the city fathers of Lübeck, they dismissed this as a personal conflict in the village and instructed the bailiff to adhere strictly to the imperial law code (the *Carolina*), namely, that confessions obtained under torture from a suspect cannot implicate others in witchcraft. In the meantime, Witte had died in jail. The villagers refused him Christian burial, contrary to Lübeck orders, and on the strength of his posthumous infamy as a black magician, insisted on the arrest of the three named women. The local authorities shared the values of the community. The women were arrested and tortured, but refused to confess to the charges of witchcraft. When pressured by Lübeck to release them, the community appealed to the magistrates of Hamburg, their other lords, against the Lübeckers. At the heart of this conflict between city and village were two views of justice: for the city fathers, legality and jurisprudence were involved in what was otherwise a manifestation of popular superstition; for the villagers, justice consisted of the communal moral imperative to punish the witches responsible for the death and illness of their cattle. Eventually, the Lübeck magistrates ordered the release of the women. They further instructed local village authorities to guarantee their safety and fine the village council a heavy sum for disobedience.

In the second example popular pressure triumphed over magisterial prudence. In 1618, the reputed witch Alheit Dockes, a vagabond, was arrested by the town council of Geseke in Westphalia. Under torture, she named another ten people (nine women and one man) as witches. The town council and the city judge, appointed by Archbishop Ferdinand of Cologne, hesitated to act because the accused belonged to the town's elite. When the news leaked, a crowd gathered in front of the town hall, shouted down the magistrates, accused them of protecting the rich, and demanded the immediate arrest of all named witches. No lawyers were to represent the accused, clamored the crowd; the agitators threatened to storm the houses of lawyers, kill them, and burn their books. Faced by violent unrest, the magistrates gave in and arrested the accused. Dockes was executed, as were two of the women, but relatives of the accused pleaded with powerful patrons to secure the release of the rest after the trial had dragged on for a year. The Geseke trial represented an example of popular pressure for witch hunts that proceeded against the will of the magistrates and established judicial process.

Confessionalism and psychohistory

In his classic study on suicide, Emile Durkheim shows that suicide rates were higher in Protestant countries than in Catholic ones. The relationship between confessional culture and personality structure is a fascinating problem, but one rarely documented with precision. Commonplace ideas such as the asceticism of the Calvinist work ethic or the mysticism of German Lutheranism are meaningful only when placed within their historical contexts. One of the most fruitful approaches in the historical study of social psychology is the analysis of the social history and cultural representations of mental illness and suicide in the confessional age.

Madness occupied a middle ground between law, theology, and medicine. Prior to the rise of professional medical treatment for mental illness in the eighteenth century, the problem of madness, depression, and suicide was central to the understanding of salvation, free will, magic, and the struggle between God and Satan. While mental illness transcended culture and history, its symptoms, expressions, and treatment in early modern Central Europe reflected the specific cultural structure of confessional society. Madness, then, is as much a social phenomenon as an individual misfortune. Although much research is called for, the preliminary findings have presented an intriguing picture. Through the study of demonic possession, exorcism, melancholy,

witchcraft, and suicide, we can gain a deeper insight into the
psychological structures of a confessional society.

The most dramatic example of the long-term influence confessionalization exerted on society was provided by the changing
patterns of mental illness and suicide in the canton of Zürich.
With the triumph of Calvinism in the city and later in the
territory of Zürich, and with the inculcation of Calvinist values
among the rural elites, two developments began to complement
one another: incidents of violent assaults continued to decline
between 1500 and 1798, while the suicide rate shot up dramat-
ically (see Figure 8.3).

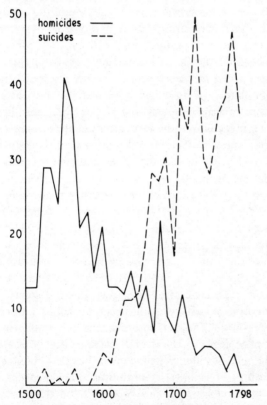

Figure 8.3 Homicides and suicides in Zürich Canton, 1500-1798

Source: Markus Schär, *Seelennöte der Untertanen. Selbsmord, Melancholie und
Religion im Alten Zürick, 1500-1800* (Zürich, 1985)

While the number of assaults ranged between 12 and 40 a year before the 1650s, the trend declined steadily to under 10 cases per year, with only an upsurge in the 1690s. Suicide rates tell a different story: for the entire sixteenth century, only 7 cases were recorded; the rate climbed steeply in the seventeenth century, reaching 11 cases in the 1630s, 18 in the 1660s, 27 in the 1680s, and averaging 30 to 40 cases per decade in the early eighteenth century, reaching a high of 49 cases in the 1730s. Altogether 511 men and women killed themselves between 1500 and 1800 in Zürich territory.

Comparing the two time series (assaults and suicides), the crucial link seems to be the mid-seventeenth century. It was precisely in the 1650s that the official religion of the city of Zürich began to establish itself firmly in the countryside: home visitations became a duty for rural pastors after 1658; only the sons of Zürich citizens, not rural dwellers, could study theology; rural pastors, urban folks learned in theology, were beginning to be feared and respected as "lords" in the villages; the extension of the city-state into the country also integrated the village elite more firmly into the moral regime through the institutions of the Calvinist Church.

With its stress on individual conscience, culpability, and discipline, and with its regime of endless self-examination and ascetic self-abnegation, Calvinism succeeded, over the generations in transforming outward emotional expression to inner severity. One of the key themes in Calvinist sermons after the Reformation was the need to control sudden outbursts of anger: violence was unbecoming of a Christian and subversive of the social order. The imposition of the Calvinist moral regime in the countryside, to the extent it succeeded (a theme I will return to), resulted in the redirection of social conflict to inner psychological space.

A comparison of village conflicts in Catholic, Lutheran, and Calvinist areas highlights this internalization of conflict in Zürich. In a study of violence in the district of Starnberg in early modern Bavaria, Bernhard Müller Wirthmann argues that "honor" defined all relationships in village communities. The concept implied credit, social status, and personal worth; it functioned as the hub of a network of social links for the individual. Thus, any insult to one's honor was countered by violence, whether in the form of fights, murders, or lawsuits, or, in the wider context, by accusations of witchcraft as well. A comparison of late sixteenth and early eighteenth-century cases of violent assault in Starnberg does not show declining rates but, rather, the shift from individual complaints to officially initiated prosecutions. Similarly, in Lutheran Württemberg, village conflicts took the forms of murder and accusations of witchcraft, as David Sabean has documented.

If witchcraft accusations represented a form of social conflict, and if executions served as a catharsis of violence, as many historians have argued, the Calvinist regime in Zürich blocked this outlet after the mid-seventeenth century. The height of the witch hunt had passed in Zürich by 1630: between 1571 and 1598, 79 witches were tried and 37 burnt; comparable figures were 43/19 for 1600 – 30; 27/6 for 1631 – 60; and for the last forty years of the eighteenth century, no executions resulted from the 16 trials of witchcraft. Naturally, the decline in witch hunts and theological condemnations of "anger" did not by themselves explain the sharp rise in suicides. But considering the Calvinist emphasis on the internalization of guilt, the harsh regime of childrearing, and the absence of rituals to regulate emotions, the result was a religious mentality and culture that intensified psychological stress. Depression, or melancholy, as contemporaries called it, became increasingly a "common" illness in the late seventeenth century, and afflicted more than scholars and geniuses. In the eighteenth century, several women in Zürich committed suicide out of guilt, convinced of the reality of sexual intercourse with the devil, imagined in their melancholic hallucinations. In a different confessional context, these sexual fantasies could have invited trials and executions as witches.

Of the 511 suicides committed between 1500 and 1800, preachers conducted 252 post-mortem inquests to determine the conduct of the deceased for consideration of a Christian burial. Only in 33 cases did the preachers condemn the dead for previous immoral behavior, while they praised 219 men and women as honorable, God-fearing, bible-reading, diligent, and quiet Christians in life. At least 61 (14 per cent) of the suicides came from families of the village elite, who held state and church offices, and constituted the backbone of the Calvinist regime in rural society.

How did the Calvinist regime intensify the desperation of these pious men and women? What relationship can one establish between confessional culture and psychohistory? The city fathers and preachers of Zürich themselves faced a crisis of consciousness in the 1680s, when cases of suicide rose sharply. By the turn of the century, theologians recognized the relationship between religious intensity and melancholy. The Church no longer condemned all those who had taken their lives as despondent sinners, nor denied them burials and the chance of salvation. The state took in the mentally ill in hospitals and allowed Christian burials for suicides, against the resistance of many village communities. The living sinner, however, stood alone before an omnipotent God. Responsible for resisting the myriad temptations of the Devil, the sinner must answer for all his or her failings. In a severe religious culture devoid of external rituals and suspicious of emotional expressions, the conscience remained the only theater of conflict. The Superego, represented by the concentric patriarchal authority circles of God, the state, the church, and the family, functioned as a punishing psychic force. Moreover, the Calvinist church condemned all magical efforts to influence fate, denouncing any fatalistic beliefs that might allow the individual to bear his misfortunes. Hence, the Calvinist faithful could only ascribe misfortune and failure to themselves, and explain evil thoughts and feelings to their own sinful nature. Deprived of communal solidarity – in the form of rituals – the despondent doubted their faith in God, questioned his justice, and even dreamed of killing him. The village elites, the mainstay of the Calvinist regime, were further alienated from their community. Under enormous internal pressure to live up to an ethical standard, and maintain a moral regime that earned them only the resentment of their neighbors, the rural elites were especially susceptible to mental illness and suicide. The rise in suicides and mental illness in Old Regime Zürich represented a "closing" in society. Through its symbolic power, the religion of the city state became repressive. Just as the doctrine of election limited salvation to a few, so society and politics underwent similar closings: new immigrants were unable to obtain citizenship; guilds and corporations closed ranks to outsiders; and the state and church became bureaucracies. For those who wanted to share in the rewards of this confessional society, the pressure was unrelenting.

In the history of mental illness, the fundamental development between the mid-sixteenth and eighteenth centuries was the displacement of theological by medical discourse, a transformation that separated Protestant from Catholic Germany. Among the three major confessions in the sixteenth century, theological categories were the ruling mode of representation of pyschic phenomena, in particular mental illness and spirit possession. To be sure, melancholy had long been a recognized medical category, but intense confessional rivalry tended to substitute theological categories for medical ones. Learned discourse over witchcraft was a case in point. Early voices that attributed witchcraft fantasies to melancholic old women sounded a faint echo amid the louder chorus of theological and legal condemnations. The most forceful critic of witch hunts of the sixteenth century was Johann Weyer, a physician at the court of the Duke of Cleve. He was deeply influenced by Erasmus and Luther, and synthesized arguments from Roman Law on contract, and his own extensive readings in theology and medicine to argue for the impossibility of witchcraft. Arguing that the Devil's pact, the witches' Sabbath, and similar ideas were unfounded in law and scripture, Weyer concluded that voluntary witchcraft confessions resulted from the hallucinations of melancholy women. Madness, not apostasy, was the root of witchcraft. During his lifetime, Weyer's arguments were rejected by most intellectuals of all confessions. Although his arguments undermined the theological foundations of witchcraft, it was more than half a century before a medical defense became accepted in trials of witchcraft.

By the early seventeenth century, the balance of intellectual discourse began to shift. The medicalization of mental illness in Protestant Germany even began to infiltrate theological discourse. In 1626, Johannes Wirtz, later to be Professor of Theology at Zürich, presented a dissertation, *Theological–Philosophical Disputation, on Demonic Possession of Humans, and on the Ejection of Demons.* Wirtz distinguished between two types of possession: fraudulent or self-induced cases and authentic cases. In the former category, even though the sick, poisoned, or bewitched spoke in strange tongues and uttered blasphemies, as if Satan were in them, they could be cured by physicians. The truly possessed, however, were attacked by the Devil who housed himself in their bodies. Neither medicine nor magic could help them, only God's Word. Wirtz's distinction between fraudulent and true possessions reflected the increasing skepticism in official Protestantism, which, by the early seventeenth century, had already experienced the height of demonic possession. In fact, Lutheran north Germany had about twice as many cases of demonic possession as south Germany. Exorcism, of course, remained part of the Lutheran baptismal rite, as in Catholicism; and rites of exorcism of the demonically possessed in Lutheran Germany took the form of fasting, hymn singing, and praying.

The general decline in cases of exorcism during the seventeenth century reflected a change in official Protestant doctrine. In Catholic Germany, it seemed that the medicalization of mental illness made slower progress. While the height of possession and witch hunts had passed for Protestant Germany by 1600, many instances of mental illness continued to be represented and treated as theological phenomena in Catholic Germany. Priests, particularly Jesuits, "cured" the depressed by religious methods: hearing confessions, giving spiritual counseling, and exorcising demons in elaborate and public rites. Thus, during the seventeenth century, while Protestant Germany incarcerated the mad, hospitalized the mentally ill, diagnosed the depressed, and exonerated those who had killed themselves, Catholic Germany held on to "church magic" and rituals as remedies for psychic disorders.

Marginal groups

Not everyone was included in the formation of confessional groups. But the outsiders – Jews, Anabaptists, freethinkers, and spiritualists – were nonetheless affected by the confessionalization of early modern Central Europe.

The Jewish communities in the empire long predated the Reformation. Like the rest of society, German Jews were forced to respond to the confessionalization of the empire. For the sixteenth-century Jewish Prague chronicler, David Gans, confessional division in Christianity signified the imminent coming of the Messiah and the deliverance of his people. Disturbed by the antisemitic polemic of Luther, Gans was a wholehearted supporter of the imperial cause. For Jews who converted, confessionalism offered an array of opportunities. The most remarkable story concerned one Stephan Isaac, born a Jew in 1542 in the imperial city of Wetzlar, who converted successively to Lutheranism, Catholicism, and Calvinism. In 1546, Stephan received baptism together with his father, Johann Isaac, according to evangelical rites. When Johann and his family moved from Marburg to Louvain in 1547, they were baptized as Catholics. The young Stephan grew up as a fervent Catholic, attended university, entered the priesthood, and eventually became a canon at St Ursula's collegiate church in Cologne. In the early 1580s, when Calvinism made substantial inroads in the Rhineland, Stephan began to preach against popular superstitions, vehemently attacking magical healings associated with Marian worship. Censored by his superiors, Stephan left the Catholic church and converted to Calvinism.

Stephan's was the example of one individual. How did confessionalization affect the Jewish communities of the Holy Roman Empire? In the short run, as confessional tensions increased up to the 1620s, intrachristian conflicts often spilled over onto Jewish targets. I shall cite three examples.

The first Bishop of Würzburg to endorse the Council of Trent, Julius Echter von Mespelbrunn, also reversed the policy of toleration of Jews adopted by his predecessors. Citing usury and religious contamination, Bishop Julius revoked residence permits for Jews in his territory and tried to prevent their resettlement in neighboring lands under the protection of Lutheran imperial knights.

The second example comes from Dortmund. Early attempts to introduce the Lutheran Reformation in this Westphalian imperial city failed owing to the opposition of the Catholic magistrates. A younger generation of clergy and city fathers, however, adopted the Reformation in the 1570s; the tiny Catholic minority in the city was restricted to several religious houses and patrician families. In the next two decades, the few but powerful Catholic families attempted to roll back the Reformation. They appealed to Emperor Rudolf II to restore church buildings to the Catholic Church and sponsored an unsuccessful plan to bring in the Jesuits. During the years of bitter confessional disputes in the early 1590s, the citizens of Dortmund strengthened their Lutheran identity to ward off imperial Catholic intervention. In the process, they also turned against the tiny Jewish community in the city, which was then under imperial protection, and expelled the Jews in 1595.

A third example is the well known civic uprising in Frankfurt led by Vincent Fettmilch in 1614. Recent scholarship has shown that confessional tensions in the decades prior to the uprising intensified antisemitic feelings. The opposition party among the citizens, Lutheran in confession, resented the oligarchy in control of the city council. The toleration of substantial numbers of Catholics, Dutch and French Calvinists, and Jews was a bitter bone of contention. Although the target of the insurrectionary crowd in 1614 focused on the Jewish ghetto, the structural factors underlying the uprising included longstanding confessional conflicts and class differences.

After 1648, when confessional tensions in the empire decreased, the general climate of religious toleration also benefited the Jews. As a political priority, toleration began to replace confessional conformity. While Jews were still considered marginal, outside respectable Christian society, the presence of religious dissenters and sects, in addition to the three major confessional groups, ameliorated the stigma. Policies toward Jews were most liberal in territories where confessionalism was subordinate to the reason of state. Brandenburg–Prussia, a state that encouraged Calvinist immigration and pietist dissent within Lutheranism, also promulgated favorable mandates to increase Jewish settlement.

By definition German Jews automatically stood outside the process of confessionalization. There were others, however, who chose to exclude themselves from confessional societies. A tiny minority were those intellectual dissenters who continued to embody the radical and spiritualist movements of the early Reformation and subsequent "freethinkers." Followers of Erasmus, Schwenckfeld, Paracelsus, Weigel, and Socinus rejected the rigid doctrines, fixed rituals, and bitter polemics of the three major confessions. They opposed the "closings" and "consolidations" that affected thought and social life. Numerically miniscule, these intellectual dissenters nevertheless represented an alternative to confessionalized society.

One example was the Friesian jurist Aggaeus von Albada, a follower of Schwenckfeld, who criticized all sacraments as impediments to salvation. In 1571 he lost his position on the bench of the Speyer Imperial Chamber Court, as a result of Jesuit and Spanish objection. But his radical spiritualist convictions did not prevent him from being appointed to the chancery of the Würzburg bishop, Friedrich von Wirsberg. Anxious to retain the service of this talented jurist, the prince-bishop granted Aggaeus an exemption from attendance at mass. Even in the first three years of Bishop Julius's reign Aggaeus did not come under attack. In 1576, he resigned to avoid conformity to Catholism but left the bishopric in good grace.

Another dissenter, a century later in Lutheran Saxony, was Matthias Knutzen, a more humble and obscure historical figure than Aggaeus. In 1674, Knutzen appeared in the university town of Jena and distributed three pamphlets he had composed on natural religion. Educated in theology, Knutzen failed to find a pastorate because of his unorthodox ideas. In Jena, he described himself as the founder of a sect of *"conscientiarii."* He exposed the Bible as full of contradictions, and argued that reason and conscience must replace the holy scriptures as the basis of faith. There was neither God nor Devil; religion was but an instrument of rulers and the state. Exploding the myth of an afterlife, Knutzen pleaded with his readers to lead an upright, moral life on earth. In his vision of a naturalistic, individualistic religion, strongly influenced by the ideas of Spinoza and Bayle, there was no room for official religion and the clergy. Professors, students, and citizens at Jena read the pamphlets and discussed Knutzen's ideas until the duke ordered his immediate expulsion. Johann Musäus, professor of theology at Jena, composed two treatises condemning Knutzen's atheism and anarchy.

While some dissenters were intellectual loners, others formed separatist conventicles. In Lutheran Nuremberg, different groups of religious dissenters appeared in trial records of the first half of the seventeenth century. In 1616, several professors and students at the Academy of Altdorf, allegedly followers of Socinus and Anti-Trinitarians, were rooted out in a trial. Two years later, the city fathers discovered Schwenckfeldian tracts and tracked down a group of dissenters – in Lutheran discourse almost always labeled enthusiasts (*Schwärmer*) – who were pacifist, mystical, in favor of freedom of conscience, and against the Lutheran church hierarchy. In the 1620s, a clandestine community of separatists, influenced by Schwenckfeld, existed in Nuremberg. Its leader was a rich merchant, Nikolaus Pfaff; and the community had outside contacts, including one with the famous Frankfurt engraver Merian. Brought to the attention of the city council in 1638, twelve men and their households, all merchant or artisan, were implicated. Under interrogation, all affirmed their quietist, pacifist convictions, their mystical and chiliastic beliefs, and their rejection of the external church. Until a second interrogation in 1644, the magistrates refrained from drastic actions. During the second interrogation, the spiritualists denied any confessional allegiance. In 1648, the city fathers expelled several men, while allowing others to remain in Nuremberg.

Anbaptists constituted a more numerous group among the separatists. Their predecessors had been hunted down and executed by Catholic and Lutheran authorities in the 1520s and 1530s. After the debacle of the Münster uprising, most Anabaptists in the empire became pacifists. Numerically much smaller than in the heyday in the 1530s, Anabaptist communities were still found in most areas of Central Europe, especially in the imperial cities of South Germany, the German–Dutch borderland, and in Moravia. After 1648, when several rulers granted charters of toleration, Anabaptist communities grew up in the Rhineland and in the German Southwest. Many Anabaptists lived quietly among their neighbors, keeping their faiths to themselves. City governments usually tolerated these industrious pacifists. In Münster, the city fathers only cracked down on them in 1588 when the city was under pressure to demonstrate its Catholic orthodoxy. During the 1610s, in the territorial towns of western Münsterland, magistrates refused to obey an order from Archbishop Ferdinand of Cologne to expel these model citizens. Other Anabaptists created separate, autonomous communities in the eastern borderlands of the empire. The Moravians were protected by local noblemen until the Catholic triumph in 1621. Expeled from Moravia, they migrated to Hungary, Siebenbürgen, and the Ukraine. A community settled in Mannheim between 1655 and 1684, where Grimmelshausen came into contact with and wrote about them in *The Adventures of Simplicissimus*, his novel of the Thirty Years' War:

There was no anger, no jealousy, no greed, no envy, no enmity, no anxiety for worldly things, no courtly manners, no regrets! In sum, it was such a thoroughly lovely harmony, that it seemed that nothing else was aimed at, other than the increase of honor for humankind and the Kingdom of God.

(Chapter 19, book 5)

In 1683, Anabaptists (Mennonites) from Krefeld were the first German immigrants to land in North America. They arrived in larger numbers during the eighteenth century – Moravians, Hutterites, and Mennonites – to escape the confines of a confessionalized society and to settle in the uncluttered land of earthly paradise.

Conclusion

In our brief survey of confessionalism in the Holy Roman Empire between the sixteenth and eighteenth centuries, we have focused variously on many specific problems and themes. In this concluding section, I would like to take a broader view, to discuss some long-term structural changes in society brought about by confessionalization. The main themes reflect the current focus of research as well as areas that await future attention. The three themes are: the periodization of a confessionalized early modern Central Europe; confessionalization and the formation of elites; and the transformation of social norms.

Periodization

It is a commonplace in history texts that the Reformation slid inexorably toward the outbreak of religious warfare in 1618; and only after the horrors of three decades of slaughter did religious differences subside in political conflicts in the empire. Recent research argues for a more nuanced judgment.

First, the Religious Peace of Augsburg (1555) – dismissed by many historians as a compromise accepted by neither Protestants nor Catholics – in fact worked to preserve the peace in the empire for at least one generation. The confessional situation between 1555 and the 1580s was extraordinarily fluid. The tradition of Christian humanism, exemplified by Erasmus and an earlier generation of scholars, still exerted an important moderating influence. Toleration, mutual acceptance, and social peace expressed a religious consciousness that stressed a common Christian identity, personal piety, and practical charity. For several decades, Catholic priests took common wives, dispensed communion in both kinds to the laity, and adopted Lutheran hymns. Naturally, confessional consciousness had already hardened in some areas, such as in the imperial city of Strasbourg. But the general mood reflected a weariness of religious violence: the period from the 1550s to the 1580s stood in marked contrast to the religious fervor and armed struggles of the first three decades of the Reformation. Even in Münster, with its memory of Anabaptist millenarian revolution, Lutherans and Catholics coexisted peacefully until the 1580s. The majority of burghers called themselves "good Christians" rather than "Catholics" or "Evangelicals" in their wills. Religious peace secured economic prosperity. German burghers were particularly apprehensive of developments in the Netherlands and in France, where religious strife led to massacres and large scale civil war.

The second period, from the 1580s to the outbreak of the Thirty Years' War, experienced rapid confessionalization. Calvinism, a dynamic force, advanced rapidly in the empire and encountered a resurgent Catholicism. In Lutheran Germany, developments tended toward orthodoxy and uniformity, bridging differences between north and south, and culminating in the articulation of the Formula of Concord. The mood had changed. Humanism, ecumenism, and toleration yielded to confessional militancy, as Calvinists and Catholics geared up for confrontation, and as Lutherans were inflamed by eschatological prophecies. A new generation was also taking over, in the three confessional churches, in the bureaucracy, and in the various territorial ruling houses. This new generation of princes, officials, clerics, and theologians hardened confessional fronts, increased hostility, and plunged Central Europe into three decades of warfare in 1618.

The Thirty Years' War represented a turning point in the history of confessionalism. God's work was not furthered by arms: visions of a permanent Catholic triumph in 1629 and the subsequent Protestant victory under Gustavus Adolphus proved equally chimerical. Within both Catholic and Protestant camps, political realists and ideologues ("politiques" and "clericals" in contemporary parlance) fell out over the pursuit of the war. France's entry into the fray removed any religious pretense from the conduct of the war. In many cities, German burghers, Protestant and Catholic, opposed the imposition of confessional hegemony by armies of their coreligionists. Religious peace had actually "broken out" among the populace well before the signing of peace treaties in 1648.

The fourth period, 1648 to the end of the century, represented the confirmation of religious toleration and confessional plurality in the empire. The Peace of Westphalia rested upon the legal basis of the 1555 Peace of Augsburg, with Calvinism newly included in the imperial constitutional structure. To the end of the Old Reich, this legalization of confessional plurality diffused potential conflicts. Its character defined by multiconfessionality, the Empire became the arena for arbitration, and imperial institutions – the Diet and the Chamber Court – handled cases of religious dispute. Another development in this period was the aristocratization of the Catholic Church in the Empire and the concurrent trend of the conversion of the Protestant nobility.

The last period under consideration lasted from the end of the seventeenth century to the 1740s. Two developments characterized these decades: the rise of pietism in Lutheran Germany and the height of the Catholic Baroque. Except for the expulsion of Protestants from Salzburg, intraconfessional differences seemed to overshadow interconfessional conflicts. In Lutheran Germany, pietists and orthodox Lutherans competed for influence, especially in Prussia and Württemberg. In Catholic Germany, the popular and elite religions began to part ways, thus paving the way for the Catholic reception of the Enlightenment later in the eighteenth century and the "reform" of popular superstitions.

The formation of elites

Confessionalization worked in different ways to transform the social structure of early modern Central Europe. The formation of elites is a well researched topic. Three developments were common to the major confessions: the rise of a confessionalized official elite, the consolidation of rural elites, and the appearance of a bourgeois clerical elite. Other trends were more specific: for Catholic Germany, the relationship between the nobility and the Church represented a major distinctive feature, whereas the strengthening of the laity was common to all Protestant areas, and the creation of an entrepreneurial–financial elite was closely linked to Calvinist and Mennonite communities.

The history of confessionalization in Central Europe unfolded in the framework of the territorial state and imperial cities. Secular authorities such as princes, officials, and magistrates – usually played a more crucial role than the clergy in determining the course of confessionalization. In Catholic ecclesiastical states, it was the prince-bishop's secular power, not his spiritual dignity, that proved pivotal in rolling back the Reformation. Again, in the Calvinist Second Reformation, the initiative emanated from the court and the bureaucracy, and not from the clergy. Indeed, the sixteenth century experienced a convergence of two developments: the consolidation of the territorial state – with expanding bureaucracies filled by jurists, the standardization of law, and the growth of the princely court – coincided with the waves of religious reform that subsumed the Lutheran, Calvinist, and Counter-Reformation movements. Having become the head of their territorial churches, princes understood the imposition of confessional conformity both as an extension of their secular authority and as the implementation of God's work. To enforce confessional conformity, local and particular privileges had to be swept aside: estates, towns, cloisters, and the nobility resisted confessionalization behind the bulwark of corporate privileges. In Bavaria, the Protestant movement flourished until the 1550s when the duke suppressed a confessional noble opposition in the provincial estates. At the end of the sixteenth century in the bishopric of Münster the towns banded together under the leadership of the capital city, citing communal autonomy, to resist their prince-bishop, Ferdinand of Bavaria. In the early seventeenth century, the Lutheran burghers of Lemgo insisted on their communal rights in order to block the Calvinist reformation of their count, Simon VI of Lippe. These three examples represent some of the many conflicts between the consolidating territorial state and forces of traditional estate society. While different patterns of confessional confrontation were manifest in these conflicts, the official elite always embodied the vanguard of confessionalization. In Bavaria, the most ardent supporters of the Counter-Reformation (aside from the Jesuits) were university educated lawyers in government service. During the suppression of the Protestant noble party in the mid-sixteenth century, these learned ducal councillors advocated a repressive policy, while their Catholic noble colleagues remained neutral in the struggle between the duke and the Protestant nobility. Likewise, in the policy debates over the conduct of the witch hunts, academic councillors again represented the "hardliners" in opposition to the "moderates," their noble colleagues on the Ducal Council (*Hofrat*). In Catholic Münster and Protestant Lippe, the split ran between the official elite and the civic elite, two distinct social groups in the territorial states. Trained as lawyers, often hailing from "new families," professing loyalty to the prince and the "state," and not to their native city, the official elite formed a connubially endogenous group. Their counterparts – the civic elite, elected magistrates – usually belonged to prestigious, well established families, whose loyalty rested with their civic community and family. The two groups of official and civic elites maintained their separate identities well into the seventeenth century and the dynamics of confessionalization cannot be adequately understood without taking their rivalry into consideration.

Compared to our knowledge of urban and official elites, the relationship between confessionalization and rural elites is a topic that awaits more research. Initiated in urban centers, the process of state building and confessionalization reached out slowly to the countryside. In assessing the impact of confessionalization in rural areas, it is essential to consider the pattern of rural settlements. Unsurprisingly, centrally located market towns and villages were most open to confessionalization. Ideas and orders followed roads and rivers; clerics and officials enjoyed easier access to compactly settled villages in flatlands than to mountain hamlets. We should not underestimate, however, the degree of religious feeling in the countryside. Franziska Conrad has demonstrated the widespread reception of evangelical ideas in Alsatian villages in the early Reformation. The examples of Salzburg and Upper Austria further argue that peasant religion was not simply something imposed from above. The crucial questions, therefore, concern the social process of confessionalization within the village community: who supported the policies of the confessional state? Which social groups stood to gain from an alliance with external agents? Who were the sacristans, curators, jurors, deacons, and presbyters in the villages? Our fragmentary knowledge does not give us definitive answers to these questions. Nevertheless, local studies indicate a complex picture: in the Canton of Zürich, Calvinism enhanced the social status of the village notables; in rural Hohenlohe Lutheranism consolidated the authority of male householders; and in Salzburg and Upper Austria propertied rich peasants comprised the supporters of the Counter-Reformation. A more accurate and comprehensive picture will emerge when further local studies are undertaken.

At first glance, the social composition of the Protestant and Catholic clergies seems very different. The Lutheran and Calvinist clergies were recruited overwhelmingly from the middle range of burgher society: the most common family background included professor, schoolteacher, lawyer, official, merchant, and artisan; but by the end of the sixteenth century, the Protestant clergy had clearly established itself as a self-replenishing estate that endured into the nineteenth century. Compared to the late medieval Catholic clergy, the most distinctive feature of the Protestant clergy was its embourgeoisement. Integrated into civic society as constituted by marriages and households, the Protestant burgher pastor or preacher exemplified the values of the Protestant Reformation, itself shaped by the culture of the civic community. Under-represented in the Protestant clergy were sons from noble and peasant families. For families of middling background, the pastorate or preachership provided a potential ladder for upward social mobility. In provincial towns, the Protestant clergy belonged to the social elite, although in imperial cities, they were treated as employees and not social equals by the patrician ruling families. A few clerics attained prominent positions as Superintendents and court preachers; marriage alliances with official families testified to their successful integration into the world of the court and high government.

The embourgeoisement of the Protestant clergy has been pointed out by many scholars as a distinctive feature in comparison to the social character of the Baroque Catholic Church. To stress the aristocratic character of the German Catholic Church, however, is to see only one aspect of its social dynamics. I would argue that until the end of the seventeenth century, the Counter-Reformation offered a similar avenue of upward mobility for talented and ambitious burghers. We need to think of Catholic Germany as two formations: the Imperial Church (*Reichskirche*) comprising the bishoprics, chapters, and noble cloisters dominated by the nobility; and the religious orders, particularly the Jesuits, which were open to the lower social estates. Compared to the Spanish Jesuits, the aristocratic component in the German-speaking provinces was minimal. Among the most prominent German and Austrian Jesuits, not a single nobleman comes to mind. The ethos of the Society of Jesus was sharply different from noble values: the Society represented a meritocracy, where learning, talent, piety, and hard work provided the ingredients for a successful career. In spirit and social background closer to the Catholic official elites (many of whom they trained), Jesuits in the empire, like Protestant clerics, came mostly from the middling burgher ranks, although there might have been a heavier representation of Catholic patrician families. For at least the first century of confessionalization, the Society of Jesus set the tone for Catholic Germany: they opposed the aristocratization of the German College in Rome, helped secure appointments to the episcopal bureaucracy for clerics of burgher background, and served as confessors to the most powerful Catholic princes. Their pre-eminent position in Catholic Germany persisted until the end of the seventeenth century, when the trend toward aristocratization intensified in the Baroque Church. The resurgence of Benedictine cloisters, the creation of female orders for noble-women, and the hegemony of the nobility over the Imperial Church signified a fundamental transformation in the social character of the German Catholic Church.

The aristocratization of the Imperial Church is a central issue in the relationship between confessionalization and the nobility. In 1600, the nobility in the Empire was divided into three grades: the princes or powerful territorial lords, a middle group of counts and *Freiherren*, and the lower nobility or knights. With a few minor exceptions, the first two groups enjoyed the right of direct representation in the Imperial Constitution (*Reichsunmittelbarkeit*); of the knights, some enjoyed the same legal status as *Reichsritter*, while others were subject to territorial lords.

In the Protestant North, territorial princes were the major beneficiaries of the Reformation. Secularized church properties filled the coffers of princely treasuries and expanded the prince's power. Deprived of traditional resources to provide for family members (cathedral chapters for males and noble cloisters for females) the Protestant nobility became more dependent on the princely court for patronage and income. The presence of the Wetterau counts and the imperial knights in the Heidelberg court before 1563 represented a symbiosis of a Lutheran state and Lutheran nobility. When the Palatinate turned Calvinist, the nobility was adversely affected. The Wetterau counts, as we have seen, adopted the Second Reformation and initiated their own process of territorial consolidation. The withdrawal of Lutheran imperial knights from the Heidelberg court forced them into organizing a corporation to defend their political and confessional interests in the empire.

For the Catholic nobility, there was a real material interest in preventing the secularization of the bishoprics. Two local conflicts in the late sixteenth century that foreshadowed the Thirty Years' War both broke out over episcopal succession when the Catholic canons of the cathedral chapters of Cologne and Strasbourg were determined to preserve these ecclesiastical patrimonies for their lineages and fought two small wars to prevent secularization (Cologne, 1585; Strasbourg, 1592). Unmistakably, the material self-interest of the nobility was linked to Catholicism. Habsburg policy under Ferdinand II put even more pressure on the Protestant nobility: in the hereditary lands of the Habsburgs, only Catholic noblemen received positions and patronage. Protestant noble reaction to the withdrawal of Habsburg patronage was the underlying factor in the Bohemian rebellion, the first salvo of the Thirty Years' War. The war accelerated a trend that was already discernible around the turn of the century: Protestant noblemen converted in greater numbers to Catholicism, reflecting the attraction and pressure of the clientage system of the Habsburgs and the allure of the wealthy Imperial Church.

If Catholic Germany was assuming the character of an aristocratic society, Protestant Germany, particularly in the cities, established institutions for the consolidation of the *Bürgertum*. In Lutheran communities, the social and political elites staffed the many new parish organizations, serving on committees to supervise parish affairs, the disbursement of poor funds, the maintenance of church buildings, and in general to articulate and represent the sentiments of their parishioners to the city council. Whether elected or appointed, service in these posts usually prepared the officeholder for later magisterial office. In Hamburg, for example, all senators served in parish administration before attaining higher office. A similar interpenetration of ecclesiastical and political officeholding for the laity can be observed for Calvinist civic communities. In cities of the Rhineland, in Emden, and also in Dutch cities, service in the presbytery represented an intermediate stage in the public career of the political elites. Whereas the deacons came from the middling ranks of the Calvinist community, the presbyters were men of substance, often members of the city council. Membership in Calvinist Church leadership reinforced the elites' public standing and political authority.

When confessionalization strengthened the domination of the political elites, minority religious groups were often excluded from power. In northwest Germany, the rise of an entrepreneurial, capitalist economic elite in the early modern period coincided with the process of confessionalization. In the second half of the sixteenth century, Lutheran and Catholic civic elites established hegemony and excluded Calvinists and Mennonites from power. Heinz Schilling argues that political exclusion, not the Protestant work ethic, was responsible for the accumulation of wealth in the hands of a Calvinist and Mennonite economic elite. Marginalized and shut out of city halls in cities such as Frankfurt and Cologne, the economic elites readily adapted their operations to investing in the new rural industries. It comes as no surprise that a disproportionate number of industrialists and capitalists in early nineteenth-century Rhineland were Calvinists and Mennonites.

From the above discussion of elite formation, I hope that it is abundantly clear that confessionalization was much more than an abstract historiographical construct. Rather, different groups of social elites owed their status, identity, career, and power to confessionalization. Living men and women found their lives shaped and fashioned by confessional ideologies, and in turn, gave meaning and value to their own lives by furthering the goals of confessionalization. Confessionalization transformed the inner values of the elites of early modern Central Europe, and they, in turn, set the norms for the rest of society.

The transformation of social norms

The most fundamental transformation in early modern Central Europe was the desacralization of society. By this I do not mean merely the secularization of social life, but an antithetical development to the process of sacralization in late medieval Germany. In the late fourteenth and fifteenth centuries, the laity had remade religion in their own image. Pilgrims flocked to shrines for miraculous cures; the layfolk interpreted and used church sacraments for magical healing; Christians accused Jews of host desecrations and ritual murders, creating thereby their own martyrs, saints, and loci of sanctity; artists depicted the Holy Family living the life of the working people; and the common folk understood Jesus, Mary, and their family in the context of their own social existence. For the reform-minded clergy, this was an alarming picture. Decried as superstitions, these phenomena actually represented the attempt by the common people to sanctify their lives and society. The moments and localities of sanctity proliferated and threatened to get out of clerical control.

One central aim of the reformers was to bring popular piety under professional clerical control, for they claimed alone to know the difference between true religion and false superstitions. After the Reformation, the confessionalization of society thus implied competition by contending elite groups to control and restrict the expression of sanctity in social life. Moreover, the very fact of confessional competition itself hastened desacralization. This was most evident in the cities.

In the early Reformation, the ideology of the urban commune as a "sacral corporation" furnished a powerful theologicopolitical discourse to contending social groups struggling to define clashing visions of a reformed civic community. The consolidation of confessional identity might seem to have strengthened this corporate communal ideology in the short run in Lutheran imperial cities such as Strasbourg and Hamburg, but in the long run, confessionalization undermined any notion of sacral communalism. Catholics and Lutherans cohabited the urban space of many imperial cities, where their equality was legally guaranteed. Even in confessionally uniform cities, the presence of religious minorities was a fact dictated by the realities of demographic, social, and economic exchanges. Confessionalization even subverted the "sanctity" of ecclesiastical space, as Protestants and Catholics shared church buildings and married one another, or as cemeteries and churches were consecrated, desecrated, and reconsecrated during the Thirty Years' War.

Desacralization was replaced by commercialization in the restoration of sanctity by the Counter-Reformation. In the seventeenth century, a brisk trade sprang up between Bavaria and the Protestant north, with relics heading south in exchange for Catholic money and products. Or, to take Walldürn as an example, this great Counter-Reformation pilgrimage cult was part of a structure of commercial exchange that depended on the great Protestant metropolis of Frankfurt for bankers and printers. By creating different competing confessional groups and a fragmented Christian society, the process of confessionalization destroyed sacralization as a force of social integration. Instead, toleration was the only means of achieving social peace, and confessionalization eventually paved the way for the secularization of society, when the separation of church and state provided a new basis for social integration.

In early modern Central Europe the confessionalization of daily life replaced the sacralization of society. Translated into psychological terms, it meant the internalization of discipline, based on decorum and piety, and the suppression, or at least, the redirection, of violence and anger. While confessional variance can be observed, as in the relative austerity of a Calvinist persona or the emotional effusiveness of Baroque Catholicism, the larger transformation, however, represented a process subsuming Lutheran, Calvinist, and Catholic confessionalization. Described variously as "the civilizing process," or "social disciplining," the transformation of social norms expressed itself also in the spread of bourgeois values, epitomized by the emphasis on learning and self-quest, and by the simultaneous praise of family life and more rigid definition of its sexual boundaries.

For Germans of the Old Reich, confessional differences exerted sometimes a subtle, at other times a profound influence on life. From marriage, fertility, childrearing, household size, literacy, and life expectancy to culinary ideas, work habits, medical treatment, and rituals of death and burial, the confessional groups shared common characteristics yet maintained distinctive cultural differences. Most people knew their confessional allegiance. But confessional consciousness did not imply intolerance: for example the Oppenheimers of the seventeenth and eighteenth centuries went about their different ways peacefully, while attending Calvinist, Lutheran, Catholic, and Jewish services. Far from being unique, Oppenheim typified many communities in the Empire, where people from different confessions married one another, stood as godparents, did business, and managed government. The remarkable thing about the Holy Roman Empire in the early modern period was not its multiconfessionality and religious wars, but the stable and longlasting social peace achieved in a complicated constitutional framework that accommodated such social diversity.

Notes

1 Lutheran Germany

[1] This observation is made by Kristin E. D. Zapalac, "*In His Image and Likeness": Political Iconography and Religious Change in Regensburg, 1500–1600* (Ithaca, NY: forthcoming).

[2] Bernhard Klaus, "Soziale Herkunft und theologische Ausbildung lutherischer Pfarrer der reformatorischen Frühzeit," *Zeitschrift für Kirchengeschichte 80* (1969), 22–49.

[3] From Paul Drews, *Das Evangelische Geistliche in der deutschen Vergangenheit* (Jena, 1905), p. 70, cited in Bruce W. H. Tolley, "Pastors and Parishioners in Württemberg during the Late Reformation (1581–1621): A Study of Religious Life in the Parishes of Districts Tübingen and Tuttlingen," Ph.D diss., Stanford University, 1984, p. 19.

[4] Tolley, p. 41.

2 Calvinist Germany

[1] Karl Czok, "Der 'Calvinistensturm' 1592/93 in Leipzig–seine hintergründe und bildliche Darstellung," in *Jahrbuch zur Geschichte der Stadt Leipzig* (1977), 123 – 44.

3 Catholic Germany

[1] Cited in Peter Schmidt, *Das Collegium Germanicum in Rom und die Germaniker. Zur Funktion eines römischen Ausländerseminars (1552 – 1914)* (Tübingen, 1984), xvi.

4 The confessional state

[1] Cited in Franz Ortner, *Reformation, Katholische Reform und Gegenreformation im Erzstift Salzburg* (Salzburg, 1981), 185 – 6.

5 Cities and confessionalization

[1] On the typology of *Exulantenstädte* see Heinz Stoob, *Forschungen zum Städtewesen in Europa*, vol. 1 (Cologne, 1970).

6 Culture and confessionalism

[1] A. Martino, "Barockpoesie, Publikum und Verbürgerlichung der literarischen Intelligenz," in *Internationales Archiv für Sozialgeschichte der deutschen Literatur* 1 (1976), 110.
[2] I mean to convey by the term "acculturation" a positive sense of popular interaction with elite culture. Popular culture was not necessarily destroyed or impoverished through the policies of the early modern state. Such a view underestimates the flexibility and creative adaptability of popular culture and overestimates the coercive force of the state. For this argument, see Robert Muchembled, *Popular Culture and Elite Culture in France 1400 – 1750*, trans. Lydia Cochrane (Baton Rouge, LA, 1985).
[3] Dieter Breuer, "Besonderheiten der Zweisprachigkeit im Katholischen Oberdeutschland während des 17. Jahrhunderts," in J.-M. Valentin, ed., *Gegenreformation und Literatur*, 145.
[4] *Ibid.*, 149.
[5] Cited in Ernst Walter Zeeden, "Literarische und 'Unliterarische' Texte als Quellen zur Geschichte des Zeitalters der Gegenreformation," in J.-M. Valentin, ed., *Gegenreformation und Literatur*, 23.

7 The moral police

[1] Heinrich Kessel, "Reformation und Gegenreformation im Herzogtum Cleve 1517 bis 1609," *Düsseldorfer Jahrbuch* 1918/19.
[2] The following items are cited from Wolfgang Petri, ed., *Die reformierten Klevischen Synoden im 17. Jahrhundert. Bd. 1. 1610–1648* (Düsseldorf, 1973).

8 Confessionalism and the people

[1] Cited in Markus Schär, *Seelennöte der Untertanen. Selbstmord, Melancholie und Religion im Alten Zürich, 1500 – 1800* (Zürich, 1985), 189 – 90.

Further reading

Abbreviations for periodicals:

AKG	Archiv für Kulturgeschichte
ARG	Archiv für Reformationsgeschichte
BWKG	Blätter für Württembergische Kirchengeschichte
CEH	Central European History
HJ	Historisches Jahrbuch der Görres-Gesellschaft
HZ	Historische Zeitschrift
JGNKG	Jahrbuch der Gesellschaft für Niedersächsische Kirchengeschichte
JMH	Journal of Modern History
JWKG	Jahrbuch für Westfälische Kirchengeschichte
PP	Past and Present
RJKG	Rottenburger Jahrbuch für Kirchengeschichte
WDgb	Würzburger Diözesangeschichtsblätter
WZ	Westfälische Zeitschrift
ZBKG	Zeitschrift für Bayerische Kirchengeschichte
ZBL	Zeitschrift für Bayerische Landesgeschichte
ZHF	Zeitschrift für Historische Forschung
ZKG	Zeitschrift für Kirchengeschichte

Introduction

The concept of "social disciplining" is advanced by Gerhard Oestreich in "Strukturprobleme des europäischen Absolutismus," in his *Geist und Gestalt des frühmodernen Staates* (Berlin, 1969), 179 – 97; English translation, *Neostoicism and the Early Modern State*

(Cambridge, 1982). For the writings of Ernst Walter Zeeden, see: *Die Entstehung der Konfessionen. Grundlagen und Formen der Konfessionsbildung* (Munich, 1965); his collection of essays, *Konfessionsbildung* (Stuttgart, 1985); and E. W. Zeeden and H. Molitor, eds, *Die Visitation im Dienst der kirchlichen Reform* (Münster, 1977), an early collection of essays pointing to the significance of visitation records. The research of his students, Peter Thaddäus Lang and Paul Münch, evaluates, respectively, Catholic and Calvinist church records (for titles see chapter 7). For reflections on the problems of "confession formation" and reports on visitation records, see: Ernst Walter Zeeden and Peter Thaddäus Lang, eds, *Kirche und Visitation. Beiträge zur Erforschung des frühneuzeitlichen Visitationswesens in Europa* (Stuttgart, 1984). Six authors in this collection report on the extant visitation records in French, Italian, Polish, English, and German archives; Peter Lang and Paul Münch write respectively on German Catholic and German Calvinist records (131 – 90, 216 – 48). Peter Thaddäus Lang, "Die Ausformung der Konfessionen im 16. und 17. Jahrhundert: Geschichtspunkte und Forschungsmöglichkeiten," in Jean-Marie Valentin, ed., *Gegenreformation und Literatur. Beiträge zur interdisziplinären Erforschung der katholischen – Reformbewegung* (=Beiheft zum *Daphnis* 3) (Amsterdam, 1979), 13 – 29, is a description of the research of the "Visitation Project" at Tübingen University (now defunct). See also Peter Thaddäus Lang, "Konfessionsbildung als Forschungsgegenstand," *HJ* 100 (1980), 480 – 93; and his "Die Bedeutung der Kirchenvisitation für die Geschichte der Frühen Neuzeit. Ein Forschungsbericht," *RJKG* 3 (1984), 207 – 12. Three volumes of source inventories in the series on church visitations have been published: *Repertorium der Kirchenvisitationsakten aus dem 16. und 17. Jahrhundert in Archiven der Bundesrepublik Deutschland*; Vol. 1: C. Reinhardt and H. Schnabel-Schüle, eds, *Hesse* (Stuttgart, 1982); Vol. 2: P. T. Lang, ed., *Baden–Württemberg, Part I: The Catholic Southwest* (Stuttgart, 1984); Vol. 2: H. Schnabel-Schüle, ed., *Baden–Württemberg, Part II* (Stuttgart, 1986).

Wolfgang Reinhard's conceptual framework is outlined in: "Zwang zur Konfessionalisierung? Prolegomena zu einer Theorie des konfessionellen Zeitalters," in *ZHF* 10 (1983), 257 – 77; his views on the Counter-Reformation are developed in greater detail in, "Gegenreformation als Modernisierung? Prolegomena zu einer

Theorie des konfessionellen Zeitalters," *ARG* 68 (1977), 226 – 52; see also his "Konfession und Konfessionalisierung in Deutschland," in W. Reinhard, ed., *Bekenntnis und Geschichte* (Augsburg, 1981), 165 – 89.

The most systematic theoretical formulation of "confessionalization" by Heinz Schilling appears in two essays: "Die Konfessionalisierung im Reich. Religiöser und gesellschaftlicher Wandel in Deutschland zwischen 1555 und 1620," *HZ* 246 (1988), 1 – 45; and "Die 'Zweite Reformation' als Kategorie der Geschichtswissenschaft," in H. Schilling, ed., *Die reformierte Konfessionalisierung in Deutschland – Das Problem der "Zweiten Reformation"* (Gütersloh, 1986), 387 – 438. A more condensed version of Schilling's theoretical views in English is his "Between the Territorial State and Urban Liberty: Lutheranism and Calvinism in the County of Lippe," in R. Po-chia Hsia, ed., *The German People and the Reformation* (Ithaca, NY, 1988), 263 – 83. This article also summarizes the major arguments in Schilling's book, *Konfessionskonflikt und Staatsbildung: Eine Fallstudie über das Verhältnis von religiösem und sozialem Wandel in der Frühneuzeit am Beispiel der Graftschaft Lippe* (Gütersloh, 1981).

Several collections of essays by historians, literary historians, and folklorists open up new territory for the study of confessional culture, see: Wolfgang Brückner, ed., *Volkserzählung und Reformation. Ein Handbuch zur Tradierung und Funktion von Erzählstoffen und Erzählliteratur im Protestantismus* (1974); E. Blühm *et al.*, eds, *Hof, Staat und Gesellschaft der Literatur des 17. Jahrhunderts* (=*Daphnis* 11: i–ii, (1982)); Dieter Breuer, ed., *Frömmigkeit in der Frühen Neuzeit. Studien zur religiösen Literatur des 17. Jahrhunderts in Deutschland* (Amsterdam, 1984); Valentin, ed., *Gegenreformation und Literatur*; Wolfgang Brückner, Peter Blickle, Dieter Breuer, eds, *Literatur und Volk im 17. Jahrhundert. Probleme populärer Kultur in Deutschland* (=*Wolfenbütteler Arbeiten zur Barockforschung* 13) 2 vols. (Wolfenbüttel, 1985).

1 Lutheran Germany

For the most recent spectrum of scholarship on Lutheranism in Germany, see Hans-Christoph Rublack, ed., *Konfessionalisierung im*

Luthertum (Gütersloh, forthcoming); the collection includes papers and discussions from the symposium sponsored by the Verein für Reformationsgeschichte, September 7 – 10, 1988, Reinhausen. The Interim of 1548 represented a watershed in the formation of Lutheran confessional identity; for an analysis of the social dynamics of confessionalization in one imperial city see Erdmann Weyrauch, *Konfessionelle Krise und soziale Stabilität: Das Interim in Strassburg (1548 – 1552)* (Stuttgart, 1978). On the consequences of the Religious Peace of Augsburg for early modern Germany see Martin Heckel, *Staat und Kirche nach den Lehren der evangelischen Juristen Deutschlands in der ersten Hälfte des 17. Jahrhunderts* (Munich, 1968). Another landmark of confessionalization was the Reformation Centennial of 1617, for the various forms of Lutheran anti-Catholic propaganda see Ruth Kastner, *Geistlicher Rauffhandel. Form und Funktion der illustrierten Flugblätter zum Reformations-jubiläum 1617 in ihrem historischen und publizistischen Kontext* (Frankfurt, 1982); and Hans-Jürgen Schönstädt, *Antichrist, Weltheilsgeschehen und Gottes Werkzeug. Römische Kirche, Reformation und Luther im Spiegel des Reformationsjubilaeums 1617* (Wiesbaden, 1978).

Among the many studies of the social origins of the Lutheran clergy, I have found the following particularly helpful: the older classic by Paul Drews, *Das Evangelische Geistliche in der deutschen Vergangenheit* (Jena, 1905); Martin Brecht, "Herkunft und Ausbildung der protestantischen Geistlichen des Herzogtum Württembergs im 16. Jahrhunderts," *ZKG* 80 (1969), 163 – 75; Martin Hasselhorn, *Der altwürttembergische Pfarrstand im 18. Jahrhundert* (Stuttgart, 1958); Günther Franz, ed, *Beamtentum und Pfarrerstand 1400 – 1800* (Limburg/Lahn, 1972); K. E. Demandt, "Amt und Familie," *Hessisches Jahrbuch für Landesgeschichte* 2 (1952), 79 – 133; Bernhard Klaus, "Soziale Herkunft und theologische Ausbildung lutherischer Pfarrer der reformatorischen Frühzeit," *ZKG* 80 (1969), 22 – 49; Otto Haug, "Die evangelische Pfarrerschaft der Reichsstadt Schwäbisch Hall in Stadt und Land," *Württembergisch Franken* 58 (1974), 359 – 73; and Albert Gaier, "Die Pfarrer-Dynastie der Maier-Crusiani in Alt-Württemberg und Nordbaden, im Kraichgau und im Zaubergäu," *BWKG* 75 (1975), 85 – 117. Two works on the Lutheran clergy in English also provide important information: Susan Karant-Nunn,

Luther's Pastors: The Reformation in the Ernestine Countryside
(=*Transactions of the American Philosophical Society* 69) (Philadelphia,
PA, 1979), concentrates on the early and mid-16th century; Bruce
W. H. Tolley, "Pastors and Parishioners in Württemberg during
the Late Reformation (1581 – 1621): A Study of Religious Life in
the Parishes of Districts Tübingen and Tuttlingen" (Ph.D disserta-
tion, Stanford University, CA, 1984), contains interesting data for
the crucial period of the consolidation of Lutheran orthodoxy in
Württemberg. Three portraits of individual Lutheran pastors
render a picture of their cultural and social world: Gerald Strauss,
"The Mental World of a Saxon Pastor," in Peter N. Brooks, ed.,
Reformation Principle and Practice: Essays in Honour of A. G. Dickens
(London, 1980), 157 – 70, is a study based on the analysis of the
book inventory of a rural pastor in the mid-16th century. The
diary of Thomas Wirsing paints the daily life of a Lutheran pastor
in rural Franconia; see August Gabler, *Altfränkisches Dorf- und
Pfarrhausleben 1559–1601. Ein Kulturbild aus der Zeit vor dem 30-
jährigen Krieg. Dargestellt nach dem Tagebüchern des Pfarrherrn Thomas
Wirsing von Sinnborn* (Nuremberg, 1952). For the social thought of
a Lutheran preacher in Hamburg see Guillaume van Gemert,
"Johann Balthasar Schupp und der gemeine Mann. Das Leben der
unteren Schichten aus der Sicht des Seelsorgers und Volk-
serziehers," in Wolfgang Brückner, Peter Blickle, Dieter Breuer,
eds, *Literatur und Volk im 17. Jahrhundert. Probleme populärer Kultur
in Deutschland*, vol. 1 (Wiesbaden, 1985), 259–71. For the social
and political critique of the Lutheran clergy during the inflation of
the 1620s, see Barbara Bauer, "Lutheranische Obrigkeitskritik in
der Publizistik der Kipper- und Wipperzeit (1620 – 1623)," in
Wolfgang Brückner, Peter Blickle, Dieter Breuer, eds, *Literatur
und Volk im 17. Jahrhundert. Probleme populärer Kultur in Deutschland*, vol. 2 (Wiesbaden, 1985), 649 – 81.

For the structure and governance of the Lutheran Church, a
splendid series of publications makes available Protestant Church
Ordinances, see Emil Sehling, ed., *Die evangelischen
Kirchenordnungen des 16. Jahrhunderts* (Leipzig, 1901 – 13), continued by the Institut für evangelisches Kirchenrecht der evangelischen Kirche in Deutschland (Tübingen, 1955 –). An example
of the study of church discipline based on Church Ordinances is
Martin Brecht, *Kirchenordnung und Kirchenzucht in Württemberg vom*

16. bis zum 18. Jahrhundert (Stuttgart, 1967). See also Günther Franz, "Reformation in Hohenlohe – 400 Jahre Hohenlohische Kirchenordnung 1578 – 1978," *BWKG* 79 (1979), 5 – 27 and his *Die Kirchenleitung in Hohenlohe in den Jahrzehnten nach der Reformation. Visitation, Konsistorium, Kirchenzucht und die Festigung des landesherrlichen Kirchenregiments 1556 – 1586* (Stuttgart, 1971).

For general works on pietism, the older history by Albrecht Ritschl, *Geschichte des Pietismus in der lutherischen Kirche des 17. und 18. Jahrhunderts*, 3 vols. (Bonn, 1880 – 1886), still remains a standard reference work for its chronological structure and details, although Ritschl's equation of pietism with a secular expression of medieval monasticism has been repudiated. The best study of the origins of the movement is a biography of Spener; see Johannes Wallmann, *Philipp Jakob Spener und die Anfänge des Pietismus* (Tübingen, 1970). Two publications in English offer an introductory view; see F. Ernst Stoeffler, *The Rise of Evangelical Pietism* (Leiden, 1965) and his *German Pietism during the Eighteenth Century* (Leiden, 1973). A fascinating picture of pietism and of Protestant Church history in general is offered by one of its adherents, Gottfried Arnold, *Unparteyische Kirchen- und Ketzerhistorie von Anfang des Neuen Testaments bis auff das Jahr Christi 1688* (Frankfurt, 1700); part two of this monumental book describes the 16th century, parts three and four are devoted to the 17th century precedents of pietism. For studies on the relationship between pietism and Prussia, see under chapter 4.

2 Calvinist Germany

For a succinct account of the Second Reformation in Germany, see Henry J. Cohn, "The Territorial Princes in Germany's Second Reformation, 1559 – 1622," in Menna Prestwich, ed., *International Calvinism 1541 – 1715* (Oxford, 1985), 135 – 66. The use of the term "Second Reformation" to describe the Calvinist movement in Germany, however, has been challenged by several historians in a symposium held by the Verein für Reformationsgeschichte in Reinhausen (1985). For this debate and for the most recent research on German Calvinism, see the proceedings of the symposium, Heinz Schilling, ed., *Die reformierte Konfessionalisierung in Deutschland – Das Problem der "Zweiten Reformation"* (Gütersloh, 1986), 439 – 55.

On "cryptocalvinism" and the origins of German Calvinism, see Karl Czok, "'Der Calvinistensturm' 1592/93 in Leipzig – seine Hintergründe und bildliche Darstellung," *Jahrbuch zur Geschichte der Stadt Leipzig* (1977), 123 – 44; Thomas Klein, *Der Kampf um die zweite Reformation in Kursachsen 1581 – 1591* (Cologne, 1962); and Jürgen Moltmann, *Christoph Pezel (1539 – 1604) und der Calvinismus in Bremen* (Bremen, 1958), which is really much more about Pezel's theology than about Bremen.

On the consolidation of the Calvinist territorial state: for the Wetterau, see Georg Schmidt, "Die 'Zweite Reformation' im Gebiet des Wetterauer Grafenvereins. Die Einführung des reformierten Bekenntnisses im Spiegel der Modernisierung gräflicher Herrschaftssysteme," in Schilling, *Reformierte Konfessionalisierung*, 184 – 213. For Westphalia, see Harm Klueting, "Die reformierte Konfessions- und Kirchenbildung in den westfälischen Grafschaften des 16. und 17. Jahrhunderts," in Schilling, *Reformierte Konfessionalisierung*, 214 – 32. For the Palatinate, the definitive politicoconfessional history is by Volker Press, *Calvinismus und Territorialstaat. Regierung und Zentralbehörden der Kurpfalz 1559 – 1619* (Stuttgart, 1970), which contains a wealth of prosopographical material that sheds light on the role of confessionalization on the formation of political factions. This study of the state is matched by an equally comprehensive analysis of popular religion in the thesis by Bernard Vogler, *Vie religieuse en pays rhenan dans la seconde moitié du 16e siècle, 1556 – 1619*, 3 vols. (Lille, 1974). Vogler has also presented his research in two shorter works, a book on the Palatine clergy, *Le clergé protestant rhenan au siècle de la réforme, 1555 – 1619* (Paris, 1976) and an article, "Die Entstehung der protestantischen Volksfrömmigkeit in der rheinischen Pfalz zwischen 1555 und 1619," ARG 72 (1981), 158 – 95.

For Swiss influence on the Palatinate, see Kaspar von Greyerz, "Basels kirchliche und konfessionelle Beziehungen zum Oberrhein im späten 16. und frühen 17. Jahrhundert," in Martin Bircher, Walter Sparn, Erdmann Weyrauch, eds, *Schweizerisch-deutsche Beziehungen im konfessionellen Zeitalter. Beiträge zur Kulturgeschichte 1580 – 1650. (=Wolfenbütteler Arbeiten zur Barockforschung* 12) (Wiesbaden, 1984), 227 – 52.

On the peculiarities of German Calvinist Church structure see Paul Münch, *Zucht und Ordnung. Reformierte Kirchenverfassungen im*

16. und 17. Jahrhundert (*Nassau–Dillenburg, Kurpfalz, Hessen–Kassel*) (Stuttgart, 1978); and W. H. Neuser, "Die Einführung der presbyterial–synodalen Kirchenordnung in den Grafschaften Nassau-Dillenburg, Wittgenstein, Solms und Wied im Jahre 1586," *JWKG* 71 (1978), 47 – 58. For the composition and reception of the Heidelberg Catechism, see Walter Henss, *Der Heidelberger Katechismus im konfessionspolitischen Kräftespiel seiner Frühzeit. Historisch-bibliographische Einführung der ersten vollständigen deutschen Fassung, der sog. 3. Auflage von 1563 und der dazugehörigen lateinischen Fassung* (Zürich, 1983).

3 Catholic Germany

On Bavaria, the best survey of the Counter-Reformation is Max Spindler, ed., *Handbuch der Bayerischen Geschichte*, vol. 2 (Munich, 1966). For the bishoprics, see Joachim Köhler, *Das Ringen um die Tridentinische Erneuerung im Bistum Breslau vom Abschluss des Konzils bis zur Schlacht am Weissen Berg 1564 – 1620* (Cologne, 1973), a study based on the Vatican and Breslauer archives; August Franzen, *Der Wiederaufbau des kirchlichen Lebens im Erzbistum Köln unter Ferdinand von Bayern, Erzbischof von Köln 1612 – 1650* (Münster, 1941); a more recent study, Brigitte Garbe, "Reformmassnahmen und Formen der katholischen Erneuerung in der Erzdiözese Köln (1555 – 1648)," *Kölnischer Geschichtsverein Jahrbuch* 47 (1976), 136 – 77; H. E. Specker, "Die Reformtätigkeit des Würzburger Fürstbischof Julius Echter von Mespelbrunn (1573 – 1617)" *WDgb* 27 (1965), 29 – 125; Hansgeorg Molitor, *Kirchliche Reformversuche der Kurfürsten und Erzbischöfe von Trier im Zeitalter der Gegenreformation* (Wiesbaden, 1967); Manfred Becker-Huberti, *Die Tridentinische Reform im Bistum Münster unter Erzbischof Christoph Bernhard von Galen 1650 bis 1678* (Münster, 1978). For a specific case study of the effectiveness of the Counter-Reformation in Würzburg, see Peter Thaddäus Lang, "Die tridentinische Reform im Landkapitel Mergentheim bis zum Einfall der Schweden 1631," *RJKG* 1 (1982), 143 – 72. The major shortcoming of the scholarship on the Counter-Reformation is its exclusive emphasis on religious history from the top down, focusing mainly on prominent reforming Catholic bishops and institutions. An exception to this is Hans-Christoph Rublack, *Gescheiterte Reformation.*

Frühreformatorische und protestantische Bewegungen in süd- und west-deutschen geistlichen Residenzen (Stuttgart, 1978), an illuminating comparative study of the suppression of the Protestant movements in episcopal cities.

On the Catholic social order see R. Po-chia Hsia, *Society and Religion in Münster 1535 – 1618* (New Haven, CT, 1984); and R. J. W. Evans, *The Making of the Hapsburg Monarchy 1550 – 1700* (Oxford, 1979). More numerous are local studies documenting the survival of Protestant minorities in Catholic states; see for example, Walter Scherzer, "Die Augsburger Konfessionsverwandten des Hochstifts Würzburg nach dem Westfälischen Frieden," *ZBKG* 49 (1980), 20 – 43, and his "Die Protestanten in Würzburg," *ZBKG* 54 (1985), 97 – 117.

On the Catholic clergy, the definitive work on the German College is Peter Schmidt, *Das Collegium Germanicum in Rom und die Germaniker. Zur Funktion eines römischen Ausländerseminars (1552 – 1914)* (Tübingen, 1984). For the Jesuits, the exhaustive study by Bernhard Duhr, *Geschichte der Jesuiten in den Ländern deutscher Zunge* 4 vols. in 5 (Freiburg, 1907 – 28), will probably never be superceded.

Much more research needs to be undertaken on Baroque Catholicism. For now, see Manfred Finke, "Toleranz und 'Discrete' Frömmigkeit nach 1650. Pfalzgraf Christian August von Sulzbach und Ernst von Hessen-Rheinfels," in Dieter Breuer, ed., *Frömmigkeit in der frühen Neuzeit. Studien zur religiösen Literatur des 17. Jahrhunderts in Deutschland* (Amsterdam, 1984), 193 – 212; the older but still useful study by L. A. Veit and L. Lenhart, *Kirche und Volksfrömmigkeit im Zeitalter des Barock* (Freiburg, 1956); Friedhelm Jürgenmeister, "Die Eucharistie in der Barockfröm-migkeit am Mittelrhein," *Archiv für Mittelrheinische Kirchengeschichte* 23 (1971), 103 – 20; and Peter Hersche, "Die geistlichen Staaten im Gefüge des Alten Reiches," in G. Schmidt, ed., *Stände und Gesellschaft im Alten Reich* (Wiesbaden, 1989), a revisionist and positive evaluation of the ecclesiastical principalities in comparison to the larger absolutist states. Ernst W. Zeeden, "Ein landesherr-liches Toleranzedikt aus dem 17. Jahrhundert. Der Gnadenbrief Johann Philipps von Schönborn für die Stadt Kitzingen (1650)," *HJ* 103 (1983), 156 – 65, is a case study of the tolerant ecclesiastical policy of the Schönborn bishops. The expulsion of

Protestants from Salzburg is analyzed in a detailed study that describes the process of Reformation and Counter-Reformation from the 1520s to 1731, in Franz Ortner, *Reformation, Katholische Reform und Gegenreformation im Erzstift Salzburg* (Salzburg, 1981).

4 The confessional state

For a general reflection on the relationship between confessionalism and the early modern state, with Catholic, Calvinist, and Lutheran examples, see Dieter Breuer, "Absolutistische Staatsreform und neue Frömmigkeitsformen. Vorüberlegungen zu einer Frömmigkeitsgeschichte der frühen Neuzeit aus literarhistorischer Sicht," in Dieter Breuer, ed., *Frömmigkeit in der frühen Neuzeit. Studien zur religiösen Literatur des 17. Jahrhunderts in Deutschland* (Amsterdam, 1984), 5 – 25. For reflections on the Lutheran Reformation and the state, see Heinz Schilling, "The Reformation and the Rise of the Early Modern State," and Karlheinz Blaschke, "The Reformation and the Rise of the Territorial State," both in James D. Tracy, ed., *Luther and the Modern State in Germany* (Kirksville, 1986), 21 – 30, 61 – 76.

On *pietas Austriaca*, see Anna Coreth, *Pietas Austriaca. Österreichische Frömmigkeit im Barock* (Munich, 2nd rev. ed., 1982). For a detailed analysis of the formation of confessional ideology and court politics in Habsburg Vienna see Robert Bireley, *Religion and Politics in the Age of the Counterreformation: Emperor Ferdinand II, William Lamormaini, S. J., and the Formation of Imperial Policy* (Chapel Hill, NC, 1981). For Calvinist *raison d'état* in Brandenburg–Prussia see Otto Hintze, "Calvinism and Raison d'Etat in Early Seventeenth-Century Brandenburg," in Felix Gilbert, ed., *The Historical Essays of Otto Hintze* (New York, 1975), 88 – 154; Bodo Nischan, "Reformed Irenicism and the Leipzig Colloquy of 1631," *Central European History* 9, i (1976), 3 – 26; and his "Brandenburg's Reformed Räte and the Leipzig Manifesto of 1631," *Journal of Religious History* 9, i (1976), 365 – 80; Wolfgang Gericke, *Glaubenszeugnisse und Konfessionspolitik der brandenburgischen Herrscher bis zur Preussischen Union 1540 bis 1815* (Bielefeld, 1977), documents appended (101 – 245), include the politicoconfessional testament of various electors; Rudolf von Thadden, *Die Brandenburgisch–Pressischen Hofprediger im 17. und 18. Jahrhundert* (Berlin,

1959), is an analysis of the social and political history of Calvinist court preacherships in Brandenburg. On the relationship between the Prussian state and pietism, there are two excellent studies: Klaus Deppermann, *Der hallesche Pietismus und der preussische Staat unter Friedrich III (I)* (Göttingen, 1961); and Carl Hinrichs, *Preussentum und Pietismus. Der Pietismus in Brandenburg-Preussen als religiös-soziale Reformbewegung* (Göttingen, 1971). For peasant resistance in Salzburg, see Franz Ortner (cited in Chapter 3). For the Wetterau, Georg Schmidt is working on *Habilitationsschrift* on the Union of Wetterau Counts.

5 Cities and confessionalization

For general reflections on the urban reformation after 1555 see Kaspar von Greyerz, *The Late City Reformation in Germany: The Case of Colmar, 1522 – 1628* (Wiesbaden, 1980), which includes a comparative discussion of the model of a "late city reformation." Two general articles represent reflections by a church historian and a political historian: Martin Brecht, "Luthertum als politische und soziale Kraft in den Städten," and Volker Press, "Stadt und territoriale Konfessionsbildung," both in Franz Petri, ed., *Kirche und gesellschaftlicher Wandel in deutschen und niederländischen Städten der werdenden Neuzeit* (Cologne, 1980), 1 – 22, 251 – 96.

On the great Alsatian city of Strasbourg see the insightful synthesis by L. Jane Abray, *The People's Reformation: Magistrates, Clergy, and Commons in Strasbourg, 1500 – 1598* (Ithaca, NY, 1985) and Francois J. Fuchs, "Les catholiques strasbourgeois de 1529 à 1681," *Archives de l'église d'Alsace* 38 (1975), 141 – 69.

On Hamburg see Joachim Whaley, *Religious Toleration and Social Change in Hamburg 1529 – 1819* (Cambridge, 1985). On Cologne see Clemens von Looz-Corswarem, "Köln und Mülheim am Rhein im 18. Jahrhundert. Reichsstadt und Flecken als wirtschaftliche Rivalen," in Helmut Jäger, Franz Petri, Heinz Quinn, eds, *Civitatum Communitas. Studien zum europäischen Städtewesen*, Part II (Cologne, 1984), 543 – 64; and Wolfgang Herborn, "Die Protestanten in Schilderung und Urteil des Kölner Chronisten Hermann von Weinsberg (1518–1598)," in W. Ehbrecht, H. Schilling, eds, *Niederlande und Nordwestdeutschland. Studien zur Regional- und Stadtgeschichte Nordwestkontinentaleuropas im Mittelalter und in der Neuzeit. Franz Petri zum 80. Geburtstag* (Cologne, 1983), 136 – 53.

On bi-confessional imperial cities, Paul Warmbrunn, *Zwei Konfessionen in einer Stadt: Das Zusammenleben von Katholiken und Protestanten in den paritätischen Reichsstädten Augsburg, Biberach, Ravensburg, und Dinkelsbühl von 1548 bis 1648* (Wiesbaden, 1983), offers a solid and informative study that stresses typology; Peter [Thäddaus] Lang, *Die Ulmer Katholiken im Zeitalter der Glaubenskämpfe: Lebensbedingungen einer konfessionellen Minderheit* (Frankfurt, 1977), is an useful analysis of the sociopolitical position of the Catholic minority. Peter Zschunke, *Konfession und Alltag in Oppenheim: Beiträge zur Geschichte von Bevölkerung und Gesellschaft einer gemischtkonfessionellen Kleinstadt in der frühen Neuzeit* (Wiesbaden, 1984), represents a model for quantitative analysis in which social mobility, wealth stratification, and demographical characteristics are systematically compared for the Calvinist, Lutheran, and Catholic communities of the city. For a thorough reconstruction of confessional groupings and oligarchic networks in Augsburg, see Katarina Sieh-Burens, *Oligarchie, Konfession und Politik im 16. Jahrhundert. Zur sozialen Verflechtung der Augsburger Bürgermeister und Stadtpfleger 1518 – 1618* (Augsburg, 1986).

On mercantilism, toleration, and urban foundations for religious minorities, see Heinz Stoob, *Forschungen zum Städtewesen in Europa*, vol. 1 (Cologne, 1970) for a general urban typology. For case studies see Walter Grossmann, "Städtisches Wachstum und religiöse Toleranzpolitik am Beispiel Neuwied," *AKG* 62/63 (1980/81), 207 – 32. For Calvinist exile communities in Germany, and the impetus they gave to urban development, see Heinz Schilling, *Niederländische Exulanten im 16. Jahrhundert* (Gütersloh, 1972); the conclusions of the book are summarized in his "Innovation through Migration: The Settlements of Calvinistic Netherlanders in Sixteenth- and Seventeenth-Century Central and Western Europe," *Histoire sociale-Social History* 16, xxxi (1983), 7 – 33.

6 Culture and confessionalism

Baroque Catholicism

Most of the research on Baroque Catholic culture has been written by scholars of literature. For Catholic book censorship see Wolfgang Brückner, "Der kaiserliche Bücherkommissar Valentin

Leucht, Leben und literarisches Werk," *Archiv für Geschichte des Buchwesens* 3 (1960/61), 97 – 180; and Rotraut Becker, "Die Berichte des kaiserlichen und apostolischen Bücherkommissars Johann Ludwig von Hagen an die römische Kurie (1623 – 1649)," *Quellen und Forschungen aus italienischen Archiven und Bibliotheken* 51 (1971), 422 – 65. An important work on South German Catholic literature is Dieter Breuer, *Oberdeutsche Literatur 1565 – 1650. Deutsche Literaturgeschichte und Territorialgeschichte in frühabsolutistischer Zeit* (Munich, 1979), which argues for the significance of a bilingual Catholic culture and for understanding its origins and reception in the context of the confessional territorial state; see also his "Besonderheiten der Zweisprachigkeit im Katholischen Oberdeutschland während des 17. Jahrhunderts," in Jean-Marie Valentin, ed., *Gegenreformation und Literatur. Beiträge zur interdisziplinären Erforschung der katholischen Reformbewegung* (Amsterdam, 1979). On Catholic Baroque literature, see also Wolfgang Brückner, "Geistliche Erzählliteratur der Gegenreformation im Rheinland," *Rheinische Vierteljahrsblätter* 40 (1976), 150 – 69; Hans Pörnbacher, "Eigenheiten der Katholischen Barockliteratur dargestellt am Beispiel Bayerns," in Valentin, ed., *Gegenreformation und Literatur*, 71 – 92.

For the production of Catholic devotional literature and translations of Spanish authors, see the following publications by Guillaume van Gemert: "Übersetzung und Kompilation im Dienste der Katholischen Reformbewegung. Zum Literaturprogramm des Aegidius Albertinus," in Valentin, ed., *Gegenreformation und Literatur*, 123 – 42; *Die Werke des Aegidius Albertinus (1560 – 1620). Ein Beitrag zur Erforschung des deutschsprachigen Schrifttums der Katholischen Reformbewegung in Bayern um 1600 und seiner Quellen* (Amsterdam, 1977); "Teresa de Avila und Juan de la Cruz im deutschen Sprachgebiet. Zur Verbreitung ihrer Schriften im 17. und im 18. Jahrhundert," in Dieter Breuer, ed., *Frömmigkeit in der Frühen Neuzeit. Studien zur religiösen Literatur des 17. Jahrhunderts in Deutschland* (Amsterdam, 1984) 77 – 107; "Zum Verhältnis von Reformbestrebungen und Individualfrömmigkeit bei Tympius und Albertinus. Programmatische und intentionale Aspekte des geistlichen Gebrauchsschrifttums in den Katholischen Gebieten des deutschen Sprachraums um 1600," in Breuer, ed., *Frömmigkeit in der Frühen Neuzeit*, 108 – 26. With the

Counter-Reformation so heavily identified with Spanish culture, it was not surprising that German Protestant propaganda seized on the "black legend" as well; see Gerhart Hoffmeister, "Das spanische Post- und Waechterhoernlein. Zur Verbreitung der Leyenda Negra in Deutschland (1583 – 1619)," *AKG* 56 (1974), 350 – 71 and his "'Spannische Sturmglock' (1604) und 'Spanischer Curier' (1620). Zur Verbreitung der Leyenda Negra in Deutschland II," *AKG* 61 (1979), 353 – 68.

There is a vast bibliography on Jesuit theater, the following titles are among the most recent publications: Jean-Marie Valentin, "Gegenreformation und Literatur: Das Jesuitendrama im Dienste der religiösen und moralischen Erziehung," in *HJ* 100 (1980), 240 – 56; his survey is the standard work: *Le théâtre des jésuites dans les pays de langue allemande (1554 – 1680),* 3 vols (Bern, 1978); the most comprehensive study in German is Elida Maria Szarota, *Das Jesuitendrama im deutschen Sprachgebiet,* 2 vols. in 4 (Munich, 1979/80), which concentrates on South German Jesuit theater. For narrower studies focused on themes, playwrights, and periodization, see: Fidel Rädle, "Das Jesuitentheater in der Pflicht der Gegenreformation," in Jean-Marie Valentin, ed., *Gegenreformation und Literatur, Beiträge zur interdisziplinären Erforschung der katholischen Reformbewegung* (= Beiheft zum *Daphnis* 3) 167 – 99; Peter-Paul Lenhard, *Religiöse Weltanschauung und Didaktik im Jesuitendrama. Interpretationen zu den Schauspielen Jacob Bidermanns* (Frankfurt am Main, 1976); Elida Maria Szarota, "Versuch einer neuen Periodisierung des Jesuitendramas der oberdeutschen Ordensprovinz," *Daphnis* 3, ii (1974), 158 – 77; and Ruprecht Wimmer, *Jesuitentheater. Didaktik und Fest. Das Exemplum des ägyptischen Joseph auf den deutschen Bühnen der Gesellschaft Jesu* (Frankfurt, 1982).

On the Benedictine theater in Salzburg see Klaus Zelewitz, "Propaganda Fides Benedictina. Salzburger Ordenstheater im Hochbarock," in Valentin, ed., *Gegenreformation und Literatur,* 201 – 15. For catechism plays see two articles by Theo G. M. van Oorschot: "Katechismusunterricht und Kirchenlied der Jesuiten (1590 – 1640)," in Wolfgang Brückner, Peter Blickle, Dieter Breuer, eds, *Literatur und Volk im 17. Jahrhundert. Probleme populärer Kultur in Deutschland,* vol. 2, (Wiesbaden, 1985), 543 – 558; "Die Kölner Katechismusspiele. Eine literarische Sonderform aus der Zeit der Gegenreformation," in Valentin, ed., *Gegenreformation und Literatur*, 217 – 43. The best discussion of Catholic hymns as medium of confessional propagation is Dietz-Rüdiger Moser, *Verkündigung durch Volksgesang. Studien zur Liedpropaganda und -katechese der Gegenreformation* (Berlin, 1981); for the beloved hymns of the Jesuit Friedrich Spee see Theo G. M. van Oorschot, "Neue Frömmigkeit in den Kirchenliedern Friedrich Spees," in Dieter Breuer, ed., *Frömmigkeit in der Frühen Neuzeit. Studien zur religiösen Literatur des. 17 Jahrhunderts in Deutschland* (=*Chloe*, Beiheft zum *Daphnis* 2) 156 – 71. Architecture represented another achievement of the Catholic Baroque. For a beautifully illustrated art historical guide see Helga Wagner, *Bayerische Barock- und Rokokokirchen* (Munich, 1983); the social history of Catholic architecture, however, has yet to be written.

Luther and Lutheranism

The figure of Martin Luther occupied the central place in the confessional culture of Lutheran Germany. The following works discuss the Luther-heritage in larger socio-cultural perspectives, using iconographical, literary, and polemical sources: Ernst W. Zeeden, *Martin Luther und die Reformation im Urteil des deutschen Luthertums. Studien zum Selbstverständnis des lutherischen Protestantismus von Luthers Tod bis zum Beginn der Goethezeit*, 2 vols (Freiburg, 1950/52); Robert W. Scribner, "Incombustible Luther" *PP* 110 (1986), 38 – 68; Adalbert Eischenbroich, *"Der Eislebische Christliche Ritter* von Martin Rinckart. Reformationsgeschichte als lutherische Glaubenslehre im volkstümlichen Drama des 17. Jahrhunderts," in Brückner *et al.*, eds, *Literatur und Volk*, vol. 2, 559 – 78; Wolfgang Brückner, "Luther als Gestalt der Sage," in W. Brückner, ed., *Volkserzählung und Reformation*, 260 – 324.

For Lutheran hymns, see Inge Mager, "Das lutherische Lehrlied im 16. und 17. Jahrhundert," *JGNKG* 82 (1984), 77 – 95; Irmgard Scheitler, "Geistliches Lied und persönliche Erbauung im 17. Jahrhundert," in Breuer, ed., *Frömmigkeit in der Frühen Neuzeit*; and Ernst W. Zeeden, "Literarische und 'Unliterarische' Texte als Quellen zur Geschichte des Zeitalters der Gegenreformation," in Valentin, ed., *Gegenreformation und Literatur*, 21 – 49. On the relationship between the visual arts and Lutheranism, see: Kristin

E. D. Zapalac, *"In His Image and Likeness:" Political Iconography and Religious Change in Regensburg, 1500 – 1600* (Ithaca, NY, forthcoming); Robert W. Scribner, *For the Sake of Simple Folk. Popular Propaganda for the German Reformation* (Cambridge, 1981); and Hartmut Mai, "Kirchliche Bildkunst im sächsisch-thüringischen Raum als Ausdruck der lutherischen Reformation," *Sächsische Heimatblätter* 29 (1983), 244 – 50. On Protestant book ownership and literacy, including initial quantitative surveys, see Erdmann Weyrauch, "Die Illiteraten und ihre Literatur," in Brückner *et al.*, eds, *Literatur und Volk*, vol. 2, 465 – 74; the articles collected in Herbert G. Göpfert, Peter Vodosek, Erdmann Weyrauch, Reinahrd Wittmann, eds, *Beiträge zur Geschichte des Buchwesens im konfessionellen Zeitalter*, (Wiesbaden, 1985), represent the ongoing research of the seminar for the history of books and libraries in early modern Europe, sponsored by the Herzog August Bibliothek, Wolfenbüttel. Richard Gawthrop and Gerald Strauss, "Protestantism and Literacy in Early Modern Germany," *PP* 104 (1984), 31 – 55, argue that lay bible reading was uncharacteristic of the 16th century and blossomed as a result of the pietist movement. On Lutheran literature for young girls and women, see Cornelia Niekus-Moore, "Mädchenlektüre im 17. Jahrhundert," in *Literatur und Volk*, vol. 2, 489 – 97. On the significance of apocalypticism in Lutheran self-identity, see Robin Bruce Barnes, *Prophecy and Gnosis. Apocalypticism in the Wake of the Lutheran Reformation* (Stanford, 1988). Hartmut Lehmann, "Die Kometenflugschriften des 17. Jahrhunderts als historische Quelle," in Brückner *et al.*, eds, *Literatur und Volk*, vol. 2, 683 – 700, argues for different elite (scientific) and popular perceptions of comets.

Schools

The central thesis of Lutheran primary education as a failure is presented in Gerald Strauss, *Luther's House of Learning: Indoctrination of the Young in the German Reformation* (Baltimore, 1978); for Lutheran education for girls see Karl Heinz Bielefeld, "Ein Ordnung der Mädchenschule in Göttingen vom Jahre 1593," *Göttinger Jahrbuch* 26 (1978), 133 – 40. Chapters relevant for Catholic primary education in Bavaria can be found in Richard Steinmetz, *Erziehung und Konfession. Eine problemgeschichtliche Studie zur kulturhistorisch arbeitenden Volkskunde in Bayern. Spätmittelalter bis Aufklärung* (Frankfurt, 1976).

Universities

Publications on universities are more abundant. For Calvinist institutions: on the Academy of Herborn and its significance for Calvinist Germany see Gerhard Menk, *Die Hohe Schule Herborn in ihrer Frühzeit (1584 – 1660). Ein Beitrag zum Hochschulwesen des deutschen Kalvinismus im Zeitalter der Gegenreformation* (Wiesbaden, 1981); for the University of Heidelberg, see Notker Hammerstein, "Vom 'Dritten Genf' zur Jesuiten-Universität: Heidelberg in der frühen Neuzeit," and Volker Press, "Hof, Stadt und Territorium. Die Universität Heidelberg in der Kurpfalz 1386 – 1802," both in Ruprecht-Karls-Universität, Heidelberg, ed., *Die Geschichte der Universität Heidelberg* (Heidelberg, 1986), 34 – 68. For Lutheran universities see: Winfried Zeller, "Die Marburger Theologie Fakultät und ihre Theologen in Jahrhundert der Reformation," *Jahrbuch der hessischen Kirchengeschichtlichen Vereinigung* 28 (1977), 7 – 25; Martin Brecht, ed., *Theologen und Theologie an der Universität Tübingen* (Tübingen, 1977); Werner Mägefrau, "Die Universität Jena und das lutherische Erbe zwischen Reformation und Aufklärung," *Wissenschaftliche Zeitschrift der Friedrich-Schiller Universität Jena. Gesellschafts- und Sprachwissenschaftliche Reihe* 31, (1983), 163 – 202; Horst Reller, "Die Auswirkungen der Universität Helmstedt auf Pfarrer und Gemeinden in Niedersachsen," *JGNKG* 74 (1976), 35–52. For Catholic universities see Karl Hengst, *Jesuiten an Universitäten und Jesuitenuniversitäten. Zur Geschichte der Universitäten in der Oberdeutschen und Rheinischen Provinz der Gesellschaft Jesu im Zeitalter der konfessionellen Auseinandersetzung* (Paderborn, 1981).

7 The moral police

The classic formulation of the concept of "social disciplining" is stated in Gerhard Oestreich "Strukturprobleme des europäischen Absolutismus"; see also the rest of his two essay collections: *Geist und Gestalt des frühmodernen Staates* (Berlin, 1969) and *Strukturprobleme der frühen Neuzeit* (Berlin, 1980).

On Calvinist church discipline, there are many published documents; see, for example: Wolfgang Petri, ed., *Die reformierten Klevischen Synoden im 17. Jahrhundert, vol. 1, 1610 – 1648* (Düsseldorf, 1973) and *idem, vol. 2, 1649 – 1672* (Cologne, 1979); also his (ed.), *Sitzungsberichte der Convente der reformierten Klever Classis 1611 – 1670* (=*Schriftenreihe des Vereins für Rheinische Kirchengeschichte* 16) (1963); also his (ed.), *Generalsynodalbuch. 1. Teil, Die Akten der Generalsynoden von 1610 bis Die Zeit des Krieges 1611 – 1648* (=*Schriftenreihe des Vereins für Rheinische Kirchengeschichte* 16) (1963); also his (ed.), *Generalsynodalbuch. 1. Teil, Die Akten der Generalsynoden von 1610 bis 1755*, 2 parts (=*Schriftenreihe des Verein für Rheinische Kirchengeschichte* 29/34) (1966/70). The publications of Heinz Schilling, drawing upon extensive research on Calvinist church archives in Germany and the Netherlands, are providing a new picture of church discipline as social control. His most important findings on German Calvinism, based on a systematic quantitative exploration of the Calvinist church records in Emden, have appeared in two long articles: "Reformierte Kirchenzucht als Sozialdisziplinierung? Die Tätigkeit des Emder Presbyteriums in den Jahren 1557 – 1562," in Wilfried Ehbrecht, Heinz Schilling, eds, *Niederlande und Nordwestdeutschland. Studien zur Regional- und Stadtgeschichte Nordwestkontinentaleuropas im Mittelalter und in der Neuzeit* (Cologne, 1983), 261 – 327; and "Die Bedeutung der Kirchenzucht für die neuzeitliche Sozialdisziplinierung," in Georg Schmidt, ed., *Stände und Gesellschaft im Alten Reich* (Wiesbaden, 1989).

For examples of Catholic confessionalization, I have relied on: Richard Steinmetz, "Das Religionsverhör in der Herrschaft Aschau–Wildenwart im Jahre 1601," *ZBL* 38 (1975), 570 – 97; Theodor Penners, "Zur Konfessionsbildung im Fürstbistum Osnabrück. Die ländliche Bevölkerung im Wechsel der Reformationen des 17. Jahrhunderts," *JGNK* 72 (1974), 25 – 50; Franz Flaskamp, "Die grosse Osnabrücker Kirchenvisitation an der oberen Ems. Ein Beitrag zur Geschichte der Gegenreformation," *JGNK* 70 (1972), 51 – 105. Lucenius's visitation records have been published as Franz Flaskamp, ed., *Die Kirchenvisitation des Albert Lucenius im Archidiakonat Wiedenbrück*, (1952); and Ludwig Weiss, "Reformation und Gegenreformation in Bergrheinfeld," *WDgb* 43 (1981), 283 – 341.

206   *Social Discipline in the Reformation*

On popular resistance in Calvinist territories, see: Karl August Eckhardt, ed., *Eschweger Vernehmungsprotokolle von 1608 zur Reformation des Landgrafen Moritz* (Witzenhausen, 1968), published records of the inquest; and Paul Münch, "Kirchenzucht und Nachbarschaft. Zur sozialen Problematik des calvinistischen Seniorats um 1600," in Ernst Walter Zeeden and Peter Thaddäus Lang, eds, *Kirche und Visitation. Beiträge zur Erforschung des frühneuzeitlichen Visitationswesens in Europa* (Stuttgart, 1984), 216 – 48. On popular resistance in Lutheran Württemberg, see: David W. Sabean, *Power in the Blood. Popular Culture and Village Discourse in Early Modern Germany* (Cambridge, 1984), especially chapters 1, 5, and 6; the limits of the "police state" are documented in Robert W. Scribner, "Police and the Territorial State in Sixteenth-century Württemberg," in E. I. Kouri and Tom Scott, eds, *Politics and Society in Reformation Europe*, (London, 1987), 103 – 20. For examples of separatist resistance to the official territorial church, see Martin Scharfe, "The Distance between the Lower Classes and Official Religion: Examples from Eighteenth-Century Württemberg Protestantism," in Kaspar von Greyerz, ed., *Religion and Society in Early Modern Europe 1500 – 1800* (London, 1984), 157 – 74.

8 Confessionalism and the people

The arguments in Marc Raeff, The *Well-Ordered Police State: Social and Institutional Change through Law in the Germanies and Russia, 1600 – 1800* (New Haven, CT, 1983), based entirely on the study of statutes and decrees, tell us little about the actual impact of the imposition of social discipline. The most forceful argument for the independence of a folk tradition in culture and politics is made in Peter Blickle, *Der deutsche Untertan. Ein Widerspruch?* (Munich, 1981). On patriarchy and the family, Steven E. Ozment has emphasized the positive effect the Reformation had for women; see his *When Fathers Ruled: Family Life in Reformation Europe* (Cambridge, MA, 1983) and *Magdalena and Balthasar: An Intimate Portrait of Life in Sixteenth-Century Europe Revealed in the Letters of a Nuremberg Husband and Wife* (New York, 1986). On the patriarchal figure in political and theological discourse, see: Otto Brunner, "Das 'ganze Haus' und die alteuropäische 'Oekonomik,'" in his

Neue Wege der Verfassungs- und Sozialgeschichte (1968), 103 – 27; Paul Münch, "Die 'Obrigkeit im Vaterstand' – Zur Definition und Kritik des 'Landesvaters' während der frühen Neuzeit," in Elger Blühm, Jörn Garber, Klaus Garber, eds, *Hof, Staat und Gesellschaft der Literatur des 17. Jahrhunderts* (=*Daphnis* 11, i–ii, 1982), 15 – 40; and Julius Hoffmann, *Die "Hausväterliteratur" und die "Predigten über den christlichen Hausstand"* (Weinheim, 1959); and Kristin Zapalac on Regensburg (see Chapter 6).

For the social impact of the patriarchal regime and resistance, the literature does not quite cover the extensive field; on infanticide see Alfons Felber, *Unzucht und Kindsmord in der Rechtsprechung der freien Reichsstadt Nördlingen vom 15. bis 19. Jahrhundert* (Bonn, 1961); on the suppression of prostitution see Lyndal Roper, "Discipline and Respectability: Prostitution and the Reformation in Augsburg," *History Workshop* 19 (Spring 1985); on the closure of the workplace for German women in the 16th century see Merry Wiesner, *Working Women in Renaissance Germany* (New Brunswick, NY, 1986); on patriarchy, polygamy, and religious radicalism see R. Po-chia Hsia, "Münster and the Anabaptists," in R. Po-chia Hsia, ed., *The German People and the Reformation* (Ithaca, NY, 1988), 51 – 59. On the concurrent use of church and secular discipline to enforce sexual discipline see Dietrich Kluge, "Die 'Kirchenbusse' als staatliches Zuchtmittel im 15. – 18. Jahrhundert," *JWKG* 70 (1977), 51 – 62.

On the impact confessionalization had on marriage and youth control see Thomas M. Safley, "Civic Morality and the Domestic Economy," in Hsia, ed., *The German People*, 173 – 90, and his study of marital courts, *Let No Man Put Asunder: The Control of Marriage in the German Southwest: A Comparative Study, 1550 – 1600* (Kirksville, MO, 1984); Thomas Robisheaux, "Peasants and Pastors: Rural youth Control and the Reformation in Hohenlohe, 1540 – 1680," *Social History* 6 (1981), 281 – 300; and Rainer Beck, "Illegitimität und voreheliche Sexualität auf dem Land Unterfinning 1671 – 1770," in Richard van Dülmen, ed., *Kultur der Einfachen Leute. Bayerisches Volksleben vom 16. bis zum 19. Jahrhundert* (Munich, 1983), 112 – 50. For the convergence of interests between patriarchal householders and the Habsburg state see Herman Rebel, *Peasant Classes: The Bureaucratization of property and Family Relations under Early Habsburg Absolutism, 1511 – 1636*

(Princeton, NJ, 1983). For Oppenheim see Peter Zschunke (Chapter 5).

Magic

On the persistence of magical beliefs and practices in Palatine folk religion see Bernard Vogler, "Die Entstehung der protestantischen Volksfrömmigkeit in der rheinischen Pfalz zwischen 1555 und 1619," *ARG* 72 (1981), 158 – 95. For Lutheran Germany see Sabean, *Power in the Blood*. More numerous are studies on Catholic folk religion, especially in Bavaria see Hermann Hörger, *Kirche, Dorfreligion und bäuerliche Gesellschaft. Strukturanalysen zur gesellschaftsgebundenen Religiosität ländlicher Unterschichten des 17. bis 19. Jahrhunderts, aufgezeigt an bayerischen Beispielen*, 2 Parts (Munich, 1978/83), a comparative study of four village communities; a precis of this work is available in English: Hermann Hörger, "Organisational Forms of Popular Piety in Rural Old Bavaria (Sixteenth to Nineteenth Centuries)," in Kaspar von Greyerz, ed., *Religion and Society in Early Modern Europe 1500 – 1800* (London, 1984), 212 – 22.

On the social history of pilgrimage in Baroque Germany, the pioneering work by the folklorist Wolfgang Brückner is indispensable: *Die Verehrung des Heiligen Blutes in Walldürn. Volkskundlich–soziologische Untersuchung zum Strukturwandel barocken Wallfahrtens* (Aschaffenburg, 1958). For a comprehensive survey of all pilgrimage shrines in the diocese of Passau see Franz Mader, *Wallfahrten im Bistum Passau* (Munich, 1984); for a folkloristic and social history of the Mariahilf cult in Passau see Walter Hartinger, *Mariahilf ob Passau. Volkskundliche Untersuchung der Passauer Wallfahrt und der Mariahilf-Verehrung im deutschsprachigen Raum* (Passau, 1985). Helmut Lausser, "Die Wallfahrten des Landkreises Dillingen," *ZBL* 40 (1977), 75 – 119, advances the simplistic argument that the revival of pilgrimages represented an attempt of ideological control of the people by the Counter-Reformation state.

For readings on witchcraft, I have included only those studies directly relevant to my arguments here. H.-C. Erik Midelfort has found that confessional allegiance played a part, though not a determining role, in the witchcraze in Southwest Germany; see his *Witchhunting in Southwest Germany 1562 – 1684: The Social and*

Intellectual Foundations (Stanford, 1972). A recent monograph on Bavarian witch hunts brilliantly reconstructs the policy debates and the relationship between the agrarian cycle and witch hunts; see Wolfgang Behringer, *Hexenverfolgung im Bayern. Volksmagie, Glaubenseifer und Staatsräson in der Frühen Neuzeit* (Munich, 1987). Michael Kunze, *Die Strasse ins Feuer* (Munich, 1982) [English translation, *The Highroad to the Stake* (Chicago, 1987)], argues from the Pappenheimer trial that the witch hunt represented the repression of disorder and popular culture by the Counter-Reformation state. For local case studies see Rainer Decker, "Die Hexenverfolgungen im Hochstift Paderborn," *WZ* 128 (1978), 315 – 56, for the argument that the Counter-Reformation territorial state created the witchcraze. The example of Geseke is taken from Rainer Decker, "Die Hexenverfolgungen im Herzogtum Westfalen," *WZ* 132/3 (1982/3), 339 – 86, which contains more archival information than Gerhard Schormann, *Hexenprozesse in Nordwestdeutschland* (Hildesheim, 1977), a more quantitative and schematic approach. The case study of Bergdorf is by Dagmar Unverhau, "Aufruhr und Rebellion im Amt Bergedorf wegen eines Zauberers und dreier Zauberinnen im Jahre 1612," *Zeitschrift des Vereins für Hamburgische Geschichte* 68 (1982), 1 – 22.

On the social history of confessionalism, medicine, psychiatry, and mental illness, the research of H.-C. Erik Midelfort breaks new ground; see his "Protestant Monastery? A Reformation Hospital in Hesse," in Peter N. Brooks, ed., *Reformation Principle and Practice; Essays in Honour of A. G. Dickens* (London, 1980), 73 – 93; and his "Johann Weyer and the Transformation of the Insanity Defense," in Hsia, ed., *The German People*, 234 – 61. An insightful monograph that integrates sociological and psychoanalytical theories in the social and theological study of suicide is Markus Schär, *Seelennöte der Untertanen. Selbstmord, Melancholie und Religion im Alten Zürich, 1500 – 1800* (Zürich, 1985).

Marginal groups

For a general reflection on the relationship between confessionalization and Jews in the empire see R. Po-chia Hsia, "Die Juden im Alten Reich: Bemerkungen zu einer Forschungsaufgabe," in Georg Schmidt, ed., *Stände und Gesellschaft im Alten Reich* (Wiesbaden,

1989). The autobiography of Stephan Isaac, *Wahre und einfältige historia Stephani Isaaci* . . ., first published in 1586, is edited and republished by Wilhelm Rotscheidt in *Quellen und Darstellungen aus der Geschichte des Reformationsjahrhunderts*, vol. 14 (Leipzig, 1910), 1 – 75. For the expulsion of Jews from Dortmund, see: R. Po-chia Hsia, "Printing, Censorship, and Antisemitism in Reformation Germany," in Sherrin Marshall, Philip Bebb, eds, *The Process of Change in Early Modern Europe: Festschrift for Miriam Usher Chrisman* (Athens, OH, 1988). On the Fettmilch uprising see Matthias Meyn, *Die Reichsstadt Frankfurt vor dem Bürgeraufstand von 1612 bis 1614: Struktur und Krise* (Frankfurt am Main, 1980); Christopher R. Friedrichs, "Politics or Pogrom? The Fettmilch Uprising in German and Jewish History," *CEH* 19 (1986), 186 – 228; see also his "Urban Conflicts and the Imperial Constitution in Seventeenth Century Germany," *JMH*, 58, Supplement (December 1986), S98 – 123. On the better treatment of Jews after 1618 see Jonathan I. Israel, "Central European Jewry during the Thirty Years' War," *CEH* 16 (1983), 3 – 30, the arguments of which are elaborated in his larger survey, *European Jewry in the Age of Mercantilism 1550 – 1750* (Oxford, 1985).

On Aggaeus von Albada see Heinz Schilling, "Die Konfessionalisierung im Reich. Religiöser und gesellschaftlicher Wandel in Deutschland zwischen 1555 und 1620," *HZ* 246 (1988), 1 – 45. For the case of Matthias Knutzen, see: Werner Mägdefrau, "Die Universität Jena und das lutherische Erbe zwischen Reformation und Aufklärung," *Wissenschaftliche Zeitschrift der Friedrich-Schiller Universität Jena. Gesellschafts- und Sprachwissenschaftliche Reihe* 32 i/ii (1983). For Anabaptists, Claus-Peter Clasen, *Anabaptism: A Social History, 1525 – 1618* (Ithaca, NY, 1972), provides the basic statistical material. For nonconformists in Nuremberg see Richard van Dülmen, "Schwärmer und Separatisten in Nürnberg (1618 – 1648)," *AKG* 55 (1973), 107 – 37. Rolf Wilhelm Brednich, "Hutterische Liedtraditionen des 17. Jahrhunderts," in Wolfgang Brückner, Peter Blickle, Dieter Breuer, eds, *Literatur und Volk im 17. Jahrhundert, Probleme populärer Kultur in Deutschland* (= *Wolfenbütteler Arbeiten zur Barockforschung* 13), vol. 2, 589 – 600, stresses the importance of music and oral communication in Hutterite culture.

Conclusion

For periodization, I have found Heinz Schilling's arguments persuasive for the period 1555 – 1648, see his "Die Konfessionalisierung im Reich. Religiöser und gesellschaftlicher Wandel in Deutschland zwischen 1555 und 1620" *HZ* 246 (1988), 1 – 45. On confessionalization and elite formation among the nobility, see the following richly informative and suggestive articles by Volker Press: "Der Niederösterreichische Adel um 1600 zwischen Landhaus und Hof – Eine Fallstudie. Adel im Reich um 1600," in Grete Klingenstein and Heinrich Lutz, eds, *Spezialforschung und "Gesamtgeschichte". Beispiele und Methodenfragen zur Geschichte der frühen Neuzeit* (Munich, 1982), 15 – 47; "Adel, Reich und Reformation," in W. J. Mommsen, ed., *Stadtbürgertum und Adel in der Reformation* (Stuttgart, 1979), 330 – 83; "Stadt und territoriale Konfessionsbildung," in F. Petri, ed., *Kirche und gesellschaftlicher Wandel in deutschen und niederländischen Städten der werdenden Neuzeit* (Cologne, 1980), 251 – 96. For Protestant elites in northwest Germany, see Heinz Schilling, "Wandlungs- und Differenzierungsprozesse innerhalb der bürgerlichen Oberschichten West- und Nordwestdeutschlands im 16. und 17. Jahrhundert," in M. Biskup and K. Zernack, eds, *Schichtung und Entwicklung der Gesellschaft in Polen und Deutschland im 16. und 17. Jahrhundert*, (=*Vierteljahrshefte für Sozial- und Wirtschaftsgeschichte*, Beiheft 74) (Wiesbaden, 1983), 121 – 73; a slightly modified version of the same argument is presented in his "Vergleichende Betrachtungen zur Geschichte der bürgerlichen Eliten in Nordwestdeutschland und in den Niederlanden," in H. Diederiks, H. Schilling, eds, *Bürgerliche Eliten in den Niederlanden und in Nordwestdeutschland. Studien zur Sozialgeschichte des europäischen Bürgertums im Mittelalter und in der Neuzeit* (Cologne, 1985), 1 – 32. Franziska Conrad's study of the Reformation in rural Alsace takes a first step in filling a large gap in scholarship, see her *Reformation in der Bäuerlichen Gesellschaft: Zur Rezeption reformatorischer Theologie im Elsass* (Wiesbaden, 1984).

For the integration of the Protestant clergy in Protestant courts, the comparative study of Luise Schorn-Schütte, "Prediger an protestantischen Höfen der Frühneuzeit. Zur politischen und sozialen Stellung einer neuen bürgerlichen Führungsgruppe in der höfischen Gesellschaft des 17. Jahrhunderts, dargestellt am

Beispiel von Hessen–Kassel, Hessen–Darmstadt und Braun-
schweig–Wolfenbüttel," in H. Diederiks, H. Schilling, eds,
Bürgerliche Eliten, 275 – 336, represents a preview of her
Habilitationsschrift.

The argument for the sacralization of late medieval society is
presented in R. Po-chia Hsia, "Die Sakralisierung der Gesellschaft.
Blutfrömmigkeit und Verehrung der Heiligen Familie vor der
Reformation," in Peter Blickle, ed., *Kommunalisierung und Christianisierung in Mitteleuropa. Voraussetzungen und Folgen der Reformation, 1400 – 1600 (=Beiheft der ZHF)* (1989); in the same volume
see also Heinrich R. Schmidt, "Die Christianisierung des
Sozialverhaltens als permanente Reformation. Aus der Praxis refor-
mierter Sittengerichte in der Schweiz während der frühen Neuzeit," for arguments that support the thesis of the transformation
of social norms. The classic thesis of "imperial cities as sacral
corporations" was formulated by Bernd Moeller in 1962; for an
English translation, see *Imperial Cities and the Reformation*, trans.
M. U. Edwards and H.-C. Erik Midelfort (Philadelphia, PA,
1972). For multiconfessionality in German cities, see Étienne
François, "De l'uniformité à la tolérance: confession et société
urbaine en Allemagne, 1650 – 1800," *Annales: E. S. C.* 37
(1982), 783 – 800.

Index

Aachen 26
Abraham a Sancta Clara 51, 102
Adolf XIV, Count of Holstein–Schaumburg 88
Agricola, Johann 111
Albada, Aggaeus von 170, 171
Albrecht V, Duke of Bavaria 91, 115
Alsted, Johann 120
Althusius, Johann 120
Altona 77–9, 88
Altötting 55, 157, 159
Amsterdam 77
Anabaptists 1, 6, 9, 64, 81, 124, 128, 130, 139, 144, 168, 172, 175; *see also* Hutterites, Mennonites, Moravian Brethren
Andreae, Jakob 117
Andreae, Johann Valentin 21, 23, 117
Antichrist 13, 29, 76, 108, 110, 112
Antwerp 92
Arminianism 127–8
Arndt, Johann 23, 94, 117
Arnold, Count of Bentheim–Tecklenburg 33
Arnold, Gottfried 24, 62
Aschaffenburg 156
Aschau–Wildenwart 130–1
Aufklärung 77, 95, 116, 176
Augsburg 11, 13, 48, 74, 82–4, 96, 114, 152, 160
August, Elector of Saxony 30
Aurifaber, Johann 104
Avancini, Nikolaus 54

Bamberg 39, 42, 160
baroque 4, 7, 40, 50–1, 54, 56–7, 70, 90–1, 93, 95, 98–9, 102, 104, 159, 176, 184
Basel 145
Bavaria 7, 39–42, 51, 69, 91, 99, 103, 114, 116, 129–30, 139, 164, 177–8, 184
Beauvais, Vincent de 102
Behringer, Wolfgang 160
Bergrheinfeld 139, 141–2
Berlin 36, 58–61, 63, 99
Biberach 74, 82, 84
Bidermann, Jakob 100
Binsfeld, Peter 47
Bisterfeld, Johann Heinrich 121
blood, cult of 154–7, 161, 183
Bohemia 48, 120, 181
Böhme, Jakob 23
Book of Concord 12, 22, 28, 30–1, 35
books 90–1; Catholic 91–4, 102; censorship 90–1, 117–18, 125; Lutheran 111–12; ownership 99, 110–11; printing 80, 90–4, 103–4, 111
Brandenburg–Prussia 12, 24, 25, 35–7, 53, 58, 60–1, 81, 170
Bredenbach, Tilmann van 90, 102
Bremen 30, 128
Brenz, Johannes 19
Brunswick 12, 110–11
Bucer, Martin 10
Bullinger, Heinrich 33, 147

calendars 106–7
Calixt, Georg 117–18
Calvin, John 105
Calvinist 26–8, 31–4; church discipline 124–9, 137–8, 149, 164–6; church

Social Discipline in the Reformation

ordinances 32, 34–5; church organization 2–3, 37–8, 71, 123–7, 164; clergy 33–4, 36, 38, 58–9, 121, 128, 164, 179; "crypto-" 12, 28, 30; minorities 78–9, 81–2, 86–8, 124; political theory 38, 121; social order 36, 58–60, 72, 122, 154, 165–6, 182; state church 35–7, 58–61, 71–2, 123, 126, 136–8

Canisius, Peter 48, 99, 115

Capuchins 41, 65, 67, 69, 155

Carolina, the (1532) 145

Carpzov, Johann Benedikt 21

Catholic: architecture 51; bishoprics 39, 42–4, 46–8, 50–1, 63–70, 131–5, 140, 160, 177; church ordinances 43; church organization 2–3, 41, 43; clergy 14–15, 40–3, 45–8, 64–70, 74–5, 80, 83, 90, 102, 115, 132, 152, 155, 169, 175, 179–80; imperial ideology 53–7; literature 51, 103–4; minorities 74–5, 77–8, 82–3, 88, 169; social order 44–5, 69, 99, 102, 104

Catholic League 13, 41, 83

Charles V, Emperor 10, 55, 73, 82–3, 96, 145

Christian, Elector of Saxony 30–2

Christian IV, King of Denmark 86

Christian August of Sulzbach 44

Christoph, Duke of Württemberg 20

Christoph Bernhard von Galen, Bishop of Münster 48

Christoph Wilhelm of Brandenburg 44

Clement VII, Pope 96

Clement IX, Pope 77

Cleve 126–9

Cochem, Martin von 102, 155

Cochläus, Johann 106

Collegium Germanicum 42, 45–8, 180

Cologne 33, 39, 47–8, 74, 80–2, 90–4, 100, 103, 132, 160, 181–2

Comenius, Amos 121

confraternities 98, 156, 158

Conrad, Franziska 178

Conring, Hermann 117

Constance 11, 103

Contzen, Adam 97, 100

conversions 35–6, 40–1, 44–5, 57, 65, 71, 95, 98, 128, 134, 142, 176, 181

Council of Trent 42–4, 150, 169

Craco, Georg, Dr 30–1

Cranach, Lucas, the Elder 109

Cranach, Lucas, the Younger 109

Delrio, Martin 92

demonic possessions 167–8

Dietrich von Fürstenberg, Bishop of Paderborn 33

Dillingen 103, 118

Dinkelsbühl 74, 82–3

Dohna, Abraham von 58

Dohna, Count Alexander von 57

Dohna, Fabian von 58

Donauwörth 82

Dortmund 169

Douai 92

Duhr, Bernhard 160

Duisburg 126–8

Durkeim, Emile 162

Eber, Paul 106

Eck, Johann 147

Edict of Restitution (1629) 13, 83

Eichstätt 42, 160

Eisleben 105

Eleonora Magdalena of Palatinate–Neuburg, Empress 56

elites 16, 129, 136, 138, 143, 154, 163, 165, 176–9, 183

Emden 26, 123–4, 146, 149, 182

Emmerich 127–8

Erasmus, Desiderius 167, 170, 174

Erastus, Thomas 33

Erfurt 109

Ernst, Archbishop of Cologne 33, 43

Ernst, Count of Holstein–Schaumburg 88

eschatology 13, 29, 111–13, 172, 175

eucharist 54–5, 131, 133, 135–6, 138, 183; bleeding 154–5; *see also* Walldürn

Faber, Peter 48

family: peasant 148; Protestant ideals 106, 109, 111, 123, 129, 144, 147; size 151

Ferdinand, Archbishop of Cologne 162, 172

Ferdinand II, Emperor 22, 41, 54–6, 85, 93, 118, 121, 181

Ferdinand III, Emperor 54–5, 98

Ferdinand Maria, Duke of Bavaria 56, 115, 177

Fettmilch, Vincent 170

Firmian, Leopold Anton, Archbishop of Salzburg 51, 69

Flaccius, Matthias 104, 112, 117

Formula of Concord 60, 62, 74, 76, 117–18, 175

Franciscans 54, 64, 101

Franck, Sebastian 23
Francke, Hermann 24, 62, 63
Frankenthal 87
Frankfurt-am-Main 6, 13, 26, 87–8, 90,
  103, 156, 170, 182, 184
Frankfurt Book Fair 90–1, 103
Freising 160
Friedrich, Landgrave of Hesse–Darmstadt
  44
Friedrich I, King of Prussia (Friedrich III,
  Elector of Brandenburg) 24, 26, 34, 60,
  62–3
Friedrich III, Elector of Brandenburg *see*
  Friedrich I, King of Prussia
Friedrich IV, Count Palatine 86
Friedrich V, Count Palatine 12, 34, 37,
  41, 44, 57
Friedrich August, Elector of Saxony 44
Friedrich von Wied 85–6
Friedrich von Wirsberg, Bishop of
  Würzburg 171
Friedrich Wilhelm, Elector of Brandenburg
  37, 57, 59, 60, 128
Fugger 83

Gebhard Truchsess, Archbishop of Cologne
  33
gender 8, 111, 144
Georg Wilhelm, Elector of Brandenburg
  58, 128
Gerhard, Johann 21, 23
Gerhardt, Paul 13, 109
Glückstadt 77, 79, 86
Göttingen 99, 114
Graz 103
guilds 76, 78–9, 166
Gustavus Adolphus 175

Habsburg 53–6, 58, 77, 159, 181
Halle 61–2
Hamburg 21, 74–9, 88, 161, 182–3
Hanau 86
Heidelberg 33–4, 37, 81
Heidelberg Catechism 29, 34
Heilbronn 12
Henry of Navarre 44, 58
Hesse 10, 12, 35–6, 38
Hesse–Kassel 135–6
Hochholtzer, Samuel 147
Hoffaeus, Paul 49
Hohenzollern 57–9, 61
Holy Family, the 101, 183

Huguenots 61, 78; *see also* Calvinist
  minorities
humanism 29, 31, 174–5
Hunnius, Nicolaus 113
Hus, John 11
Hutterites 86, 173
hymns *see* music

iconoclasm 36
Imperial Chamber Court 81, 171, 176
imperial cities 73–4, 80, 82–4, 177, 179,
  183–4
Imperial Diets 70, 81, 106, 176
Imperial Knights 43, 180–1
infanticide 145
Ingolstadt 48, 118
Innsbruck 48
Interim 10–11, 29, 73–4, 82, 112
Isny 73

Jakob III, Archbishop of Trier 42
Jan of Nepomuk 56
Jena 171
Jesuit 7, 33, 40–2, 45–50, 64, 69–70,
  74–8, 80, 83, 88, 91–2, 94, 100–2,
  105, 118, 128, 130–1, 152, 155–6,
  160, 168–9, 171, 178, 180; colleges 84,
  95–6, 99, 115, 120; in universities
  119–20
Jews 6, 9, 21, 24, 43, 50, 74, 76–7, 136,
  168–70, 183; Portuguese 76–7, 79, 86,
  88
Johann VI, Count of Nassau 32, 71–2, 120
Johann VII, Archbishop of Trier 42
Johann Ernst, Count of Thun, Archbishop
  of Salzburg 68
Johann Friedrich, Duke of Württemberg
  85, 118
Johann Georg, Duke of Saxony 13
Johann Philipp, Archbishop of Mainz 50
Johann Sigismund, Elector of Brandenburg
  35–6, 57–8
Johann Wilhelm, Count Palatine 82
Juan de la Cruz 93–4
Julius, Duke of Brunswick–Wolfenbüttel
  118
Julius Echter von Mespelbrunn, Bishop of
  Würzburg 43, 140–1, 169, 171
jurists 5, 14, 22, 29, 31, 33, 45, 143,
  160, 162, 170, 178

Karl Ludwig, Count Palatine 86
Kempten 73, 160
Kitzingen 110–11

Königsberg 59, 61, 63
Konrad, Count of Solms–Braunfels 71

Lamormaini, Guillaume 54–5, 85
Lecler, Joseph 84
Leipzig 31, 116
Leopold I, Emperor 56
Leucht, Valentin 90, 102, 155
Lipsius, Justus 2, 44, 54
literacy 110–11
Louis, Count of Nassau 32
Louvain 92
Lübeck 161
Lucerne 103
Ludwig, Count of Sayn–Wittgenstein 71
Luther, Martin 7, 10, 12–14, 23, 76, 99, 104–7, 111–12, 116, 144, 167–8
Lutheran: church ordinances 19–20, 108; church organization 2–3, 38, 79; clergy 14–19, 21–3, 45, 59, 61–3, 74, 76–9, 83, 105–6, 111–13, 117–19, 139, 179; minorities 51–2, 63–70, 80–1, 133–4; social order 63, 79, 106, 143–9, 181–2; state church 18–22, 118, 139; theological divisions 11–12, 22–5, 28–31, 61–3, 76, 78, 105, 117–18

madness 162–3, 167–8
magic 8, 20, 92, 137, 144, 151–5, 161, 162, 169, 183
Mainz 39, 47, 90, 92, 156
Mannheim 86
Marbach, Johann 30
Marburg 35
marriage 125, 127–8, 132, 143–51; common law 149–50; courts 145; fertility rates in 150–1; interconfessional 75, 83, 127, 133, 141–2, 185; Protestant ideals 146
Matthäus Lang, Archbishop of Salzburg 64
Maurice, Prince of Orange 58
Max Gandolf, Archbishop of Salzburg 67, 99
Maximilian I, Duke of Bavaria 41, 55, 92, 97, 100, 103, 115
Melanchthon, Philip 11, 29–30, 106, 116
Mennonites 79, 86–8, 173, 177, 182
Mentzer, Balthasar 118–19
mercantilism 6, 79–80, 84–8
Metz 26
Molsheim 120
Moravian Brethren 86, 172, 173
Moritz, Duke of Saxony 11, 117
Moritz, Landgrave of Hesse–Kassel 35, 135

Morone, Giovanni, Cardinal 46
Mühlheim 81–2
Munich 41, 55, 97–9, 103, 115, 130
Münster 1, 33, 39, 43–4, 48–9, 92–3, 107, 120, 144–5, 152, 172, 175, 177–8
Müntzer, Thomas 105
Musculus, Andreas 111
music 90, 109; hymns, Catholic, 41, 100–2; hymns, Lutheran 13–14, 100, 107–9, 141, 175

Nassau–Dillenburg 32, 38, 135–6
Neidhart von Thungen, Bishop of Bamberg 42
neo-stoicism 2, 58
Neu-Hanau 87–8
Neuwied 85–6
Nicolai, Philipp 23
nobility 180; Calvinist 57–8, 70–2, 120–1; Catholic 46–7, 98, 102–7, 177, 180–1; Lutheran 58, 60, 63, 181
Nuremberg 13–14, 67, 91, 145, 147, 171–2

Oldenburg 15, 145
Olevian, Kaspar 34, 120
Opitz, Martin 33
Oppenheim 6, 150, 185
Osiander, Andreas 147
Osiander, Lucas 23, 117–18
Osanbrück 7, 39, 93, 120, 129, 131, 132, 134

Paderborn 92, 120, 160
painting 109–10
Palatinate, the 33, 36–8, 41, 181
Pankraz von Freiberg, Lord of Hohenaschau 130
Paracelsus 23, 170
Passau 39, 157–8
patriarchy 8, 111, 123, 143–51, 166; see also family
Peace of Augsburg (1555) 73, 82, 104, 140, 174, 176
Peace of Westphalia (1648) 44, 60, 86, 132, 142, 176
peasant religion 64–5, 67–8, 131–42, 146–7, 152–9, 178–9, 183
Peasants' War (1524–6) 1, 64, 105, 146
Pezel, Christian 30
Philip, Landgrave of Hesse 12, 118
Philipp Ludwig II, Count of Hanau–Münzenberg 86–7

pietism 22–5, 61–3, 78–9, 139, 176
pilgrimages 8, 40, 51, 56, 151, 154–9, 183, 184
Piscator, Johann 120
Pontanus, Jacob 96
Prague 56, 168
prophecy 112–13
Protestant Union 12
Prussia 57, 63, 85, 139, 176

Quakers 63, 86

Rader, Matthäus 40
Ravensburg 74, 82–4
Rebel, Hermann 147
Reformation bicentennial 77
Reformation centennial 12–14, 76, 105
Regensburg 11, 64–5, 67, 69, 148, 154, 160
Rinckart, Martin 105
Rococco 4
Roman Law 5, 167
Rothmann, Bernhard 144
Rudolf II, Emperor 169

Sabean, David 165
St Gallen 156
saints 56, 90, 92–5, 98, 101–2, 106, 131, 154, 157
Salzburg 39, 51–3, 61, 63–7, 69–70, 99, 176, 178–9
Saxony 10, 12, 14, 22, 30–1, 58, 63, 100, 118
Schaitberger, Josef 67
Scherer, Georg 49
Schilling, Heinz 3, 124, 129, 182
Schmalkaldic League 10
Schmidt, Heinrich 128
school teachers 15, 19, 93, 96, 105–6, 111, 114–16, 128, 131, 140, 142–3
schools: Calvinist 72, 120–1; Catholic 84, 95–6, 99, 114–16; girls 111, 114–15; Latin 16–17, 105, 115, 121, 127; Lutheran 113–14
Schwäbisch Hall 16
Schwenckfeld, Caspar 23, 170, 172
Schütz, Heinrich 109
Scribner, Robert 107, 110, 138
Scultetus, Abraham 34, 36, 58
Seckendorff, Veit Ludwig von 22
sexuality 7, 20, 123, 125, 127–9, 144–5, 149–50, 165
Silesia 47
Silesius, Angelus 94

Sittikus, Markus, Archbishop of Salzburg 65
Socinians 86, 128, 171
Socinus, Faustus 170
Spain 92–4
Spangenberg, Cyriacus 104, 108
Spee, Friedrich 100–1
Spener, Philipp Jakob 24, 61–2, 78
Stengel, Georg 96
Stoob, Heinz 85
Strasbourg 10, 13, 74–6, 79, 82, 111, 152, 175, 181, 183
Strauss, Gerald 113
Sturm, Johann 29
Stuttgart 20
suicide 162–6
Szarota, Elida Maria 95

Teresa de Avila 93–4
theater 90, 94, 99, 104; Benedictine 99; Jesuit 54, 94–100, 105; Lutheran 13, 104–6
Thirty Years' War 11, 13, 24, 40, 44, 50, 55, 75, 83, 85, 95, 98, 113, 115, 132, 133, 141, 155, 157, 172, 175, 181, 184
Thuringia 22
Timpius (Timpe), Matthäus 93
toleration, religious 50–2, 59–61, 76, 79–81, 83–4, 88, 130–1, 134, 170, 175, 184
Trier 26, 39, 42, 47, 160
Tübingen 17

Ulm 13, 82
universities 7, 15, 116–21
University of Dillingen 120
University of Frankfurt-an-der-Oder 36, 58
University of Giessen 118
University of Heidelberg 120
University of Helmstedt 118
University of Herborn 120–1
University of Jena 29, 117
University of Marburg 118–20
University of Tübingen 29, 117
University of Wittenberg 13, 29, 61, 116, 119
University of Würzburg 63
Ursinus, Zacharias 29, 33
Ursulines 41

Valentin, Jean-Marie 95
Veit II, Bishop of Würzburg 42
Vienna 48, 55, 69, 94, 98–9, 103

Virgin 55–6, 66, 95, 98, 102, 132, 154, 157–9
visitations, church 2–3, 7, 19, 41, 43, 65–6, 89, 123, 128, 130, 132–3, 137, 140, 152–3, 164

Walldürn 154–5, 184
Wallenstein (Albrecht von Waldstein) 56, 84–5, 97
Weigel, Valentin 23, 117, 170
Weingarten 154
Weinsberg, Hermann von 80
Welser 83
Wesel 26, 126–8
Westphalia 11, 32, 160
Wetterau 32, 70–2
Weyer, Dietrich, Dr 34
Weyer, Johann 34, 167
Weyrauch, Erdmann 74, 110
Wied, Friedrich von 85–6
Wilhelm V, Duke of Bavaria 41, 55, 93, 97, 130

William of Orange 32
witch hunts 8, 66, 100, 151, 159–62, 165, 167, 178
Wolf Dietrich von Raitenau, Archbishop of Salzburg 64–5
Wolfgang Wilhelm, Duke of Jülich 41, 44
women 144–5, 149–51; education 114–15; Protestant views 111, 144, 147–8
Worms 48
Württemberg 12, 14–20, 25, 67, 117, 123, 135, 138–9, 165, 176
Würzburg 39, 42, 94, 103, 135, 140, 142, 156, 160, 171

Xanten 127, 129

Zapalac, Kristin 110, 148
Zepper, Wilhelm 26, 137
Zschunke, Peter 150
Zürich 147–8, 163–7, 179
Zwingli, Huldrych 105